D1318047

Women and the Public Sphere

Contemporary Politics

Series editors

David Held (general editor)
David Beetham
Bob Jessop
John Keane
Anne Sassoon

Already published

Contradictions of the Welfare State
Claus Offe
Edited by John Keane

Women and the Public Sphere
A critique of sociology and politics
Edited by Janet Siltanen and Michelle Stanworth

In preparation

The Economic and Social Context of British Politics
David Coates

On Freedom and Power
Vaclav Havel et al.

Class and State in Britain and America
Joel Krieger

The Rule of Law and the British Constitution
Norman Lewis and Ian Harden

The Myth of the Plan
Peter Rutland

Women and the Public Sphere

A critique of sociology and politics

Edited by Janet Siltanen and
Michelle Stanworth

Hutchinson

London Sydney Melbourne Auckland Johannesburg

Hutchinson & Co. (Publishers) Ltd

An imprint of the Hutchinson Publishing Group

17–21 Conway Street, London W1P 6JD

Hutchinson Group (Australia) Pty Ltd
30–32 Cremorne Street, Richmond South, Victoria 3121
PO Box 151, Broadway, New South Wales 2007

Hutchinson Group (NZ) Ltd
32–34 View Road, PO Box 40–086, Glenfield, Auckland 10

Hutchinson Group (SA) (Pty) Ltd
PO Box 337, Bergvlei 2012, South Africa

First published 1984

© Janet Siltanen and Michelle Stanworth 1984

The paperback edition of this book is sold subject to the
condition that it shall not, by way of trade or otherwise, be
lent, resold, hired out or otherwise circulated in any form of
binding or cover other than that in which it is published and
without a similar condition including this condition being
imposed on the subsequent purchaser

Set in Linotron Times by Rowland Phototypesetting Ltd,
Bury St Edmunds, Suffolk
Printed and bound in Great Britain by Anchor Brendon
Ltd, Tiptree, Essex

British Library Cataloguing in Publication Data
Siltanen, Janet
  Women and the public sphere.
  1. Women in politics
  I. Title   II Stanworth, M.D.
  306'.2   HQ1236

ISBN 0 09 153450 X cased
     0 09 153451 8 paper

Contents

305.4
W 8428
1984

Tables

Acknowledgements

The editors and publishers would like to thank the copyright holders below for their kind permission to reproduce the following material:

Roslyn L. Feldberg, Evelyn Nakano Glenn and the Society for the Study of Social Problems for 'Male and female: job versus gender models in the sociology of work'.

Ian Watt and Routledge & Kegan Paul for 'Industrial radicalism and the domestic division of labour' (original title, 'Linkages between industrial radicalism and the domestic role among working women').

Pauline Hunt and Macmillan, London and Basingstoke, for 'Workers side by side: women and the trade union movement' (from the chapter 'Workers side by side').

Kate Purcell and Croom Helm Ltd Publishers for 'Militancy and acquiescence among women workers'.

Richard Brown, The British Sociological Association and Longman for 'Women as employees: social consciousness and collective action' (original title, 'Women as employees: some comments on research in industrial sociology').

Hew Beynon, Robert Blackburn and Cambridge University Press for 'Unions: the men's affair?' (original title, 'The development of unionism at Brompton – "the men's affair"').

Michèle Barrett and *New Socialist* for 'Unity is strength? feminism and the labour movement'.

Susan Bourque, Jean Grossholtz and Geron-X, Inc. Publishers for 'Politics an unnatural practice: political science looks at female participation'.

Murray Goot and Elizabeth Reid for 'Women: if not apolitical then conservative'.

Jill Hills and Routledge & Kegan Paul for 'Women and voting in Britain' (from the chapter, 'Britain').

Stan Taylor and Routledge & Kegan Paul for 'The party identifications of women: Parkin put to the test' (original title, 'Parkin's theory of working class conservatism: two hypotheses investigated').

Goldie Shabad, Kristi Andersen, *Public Opinion Quarterly* and The Trustees of Columbia University Press for 'Candidate evaluations by men and women'.

M. Kent Jennings, Barbara Farah and Cambridge University Press for 'Gender, levels of political thinking and political action' (original title, 'Ideology, gender and political action').

Donna S. Sanzone and George Allen & Unwin for 'Women in positions of political leadership in Britain, France and West Germany' (original title, 'Women in politics: a study of political leadership in the United Kingdom, France and the Federal Republic of Germany').

Hilary Wainwright and Alyson Publications Ltd for 'Beyond leadership'.

A modified version of 'The politics of private woman and public man' appears in *Theory and Society* (forthcoming).

Ivor Crewe for the British Election Study Data used in Table 13.

Preface

Women and the Public Sphere represents our attempt to retrieve, out of a mass of incomplete and sometimes contradictory data in political science, political sociology and industrial sociology, a clearer understanding of the political capacities of women and men. Our survey of the literature concerning electoral and work-based politics highlights in both areas a conception of politics, and of sophisticated political activity, that devalues the political experience of women and privileges that of men. It took us a year and a half of collaborative work to identify the problems that contribute to this misconception, and to specify ways in which they might be overcome.

This book is offered as a way of sharing the problem and the beginnings of its solution with others – as a step towards overcoming the deficiencies of forms of political analysis developed without sensitivity to gender. We believe that the volume has significant things to say in three areas: about the disciplines of political science, political sociology and industrial sociology – and about underlying male-stream terms of reference that transcend disciplinary boundaries; about the process by which heavily distorted accounts of reality are overturned, a process involving empirical critique, the proffering of alternative interpretations and evidence, and the emergence of new terms of reference; about notions of the political and their relation to the public and private spheres within which women and men live their lives. Thus, the book is intended as much for students of politics and sociology as for those involved in women's studies and the analysis of gender.

Women and the Public Sphere is not a reader in the conventional sense. It is an argument – an argument against traditions of political analysis which fail to consider seriously women's capacity for political thought and action, and an argument for the reconstruction of political analysis in ways that take into account the importance of gender. As we say in the introduction, whether this argument is convincing depends upon the reader approaching the volume not as a series of discrete essays but as a continuous account. The general introduction sets out the features of women's political profile that are common to the analysis of electoral and work-based politics. The extracts reprinted in Parts One and Two, on work-based and electoral politics respectively, combine to provide an extensive and varied critique of this profile. The extracts are written from different political perspectives, at different points in time. They span critique and reconstruction, pin-pointing problems within the traditional literature, as well as challenging its conceptual framework. The introductions to each part place these extracts within an overall account of the process by which distorted characterizations of women's political capacity have been challenged. In Part Three, we pull these critical strands together and present a thematic summary of their implications for the analysis of gender and politics, as well as examining further the nature of the political and its connection to public and private spheres of life.

In developing our views on the public and private, the political and the personal, and their relationship to gender, we have benefited greatly from the thoughtful and generous comments of Michèle Barrett, Sarah Conibear, Elizabeth Garnsey, Anthony Giddens, John Keane, Meg Stacey, Sandy Stewart and Albert Wheale, and most of all from the help of our editor and friend, David Held.

Janet Siltanen
Michelle Stanworth
Cambridge, 1982

General introduction

All social scientists acknowledge a connection between work and politics. For some, the connection is confined to the relationship between electoral behaviour and position in an occupational hierarchy, with 'paid work' and 'politics' treated as distinct spheres. Others insist upon the political nature of the labour contract itself, and regard the workplace and the collective struggles that arise there as *the* arena for meaningful political involvement. Whatever the disagreements as to the pre-eminence of electoral politics versus work-based politics, there is in political science, political sociology and industrial sociology a remarkable coincidence of assumptions about the political capacity of women.

Accounts of women's relation to electoral and to work-based politics have four features in common.[1]* First, women are held to participate in politics less frequently, less forcefully, and less readily than men.[2] Within political science, such observations cover voting rates, expressions of interest in political affairs, and involvement in 'more intense forms' of political activity. In a similar vein, within work-based politics women are thought to be less eagerly inclined towards trade union membership and activism, less likely to take part in routine forms of worker resistance at the point of production, and less likely to initiate militant action to support their demands. Women are, on these accounts, on the periphery of political engagement.

Second, where women's participation is acknowledged, it is commonly held to be less sophisticated, and in many cases less authentically *political*, than the involvements of men.[3] In the area of electoral politics, the political nature of women's activity is called into question on several grounds. The alleged tendency for women to make political choices on the basis of candidates' personal qualities, rather than by reference to issues, is one such ground and,

---

* Superior figures refer to the Notes and references on pages 209–42.

in some cases, this is treated as evidence of the extent to which women 'personalize' politics, denying its political content. The alleged tendency for women to echo mindlessly the political preferences of their husbands further undermines their political credibility. Unsophisticated levels of political understanding are alleged to underlie women's political choices, and their supposedly lower levels of 'conceptualization' give rise to the occasional inference that, in effect, women do not know what they are talking about. Add to the foregoing, comments concerning women's restricted area of political competence (local rather than national) and their tendency towards deferential voting (where an automatic reaction to high status figures replaces a sober assessment of political ends and means) and the picture of women's comparatively irrational and unsophisticated involvement in the electoral process is complete.

It should be noted that the alleged marginality of women is to some extent less explicit in the literature on work-based politics. Many analyses of electoral politics treat 'sex' as a 'variable' much like 'religion' or 'educational level'. In industrial sociology, by contrast, the leaning towards qualitative accounts produces numerous detailed discussions of work-based politics in which sex is seldom specifically addressed, and in which 'workers' are taken by omission to be male. It is not surprising, therefore, that in industrial sociology the devaluation of women's political participation follows a different route. Experiences in wage work provide the vital spark for class consciousness and political awareness: women, however, are held to regard their employment as secondary to domestic commitments, or to be located in occupations which by virtue of their 'femininity' do not carry the seeds of radical consciousness. In short, women workers are treated as women first and workers second. The upshot is that women's workplace struggles are sometimes considered to be more short-sighted in their aims and objectives than those of men, to reflect a more rudimentary understanding of the realities of class struggle, and to be motivated by 'extra-political' factors – with a concern for bettering the lives of their children and fulfilling domestic obligations, rather than a broader commitment to the betterment of workers as a whole.

Third, the attention women give to the political is often seen to be underpinned by concerns and objectives which are distinctive to their sex.[4] Where women exercise the vote as frequently as men, where the attitudinal profiles of the sexes turn out to be similar, where girls display a stronger sense of 'citizen duty' and 'political efficacy' than boys, the explanation offered by some political analysts is that the impetus to vote, the issue underlying the attitudes, and the showing of political commitment and confidence reflect – for women and girls – a moral rather than a political engagement. In its most extreme form the greater enthusiasm of men and boys for war is designated political, and taken as an index of political awareness, while the comparatively strong objections of girls and women to war are designated 'moral': thus the different positions of women and men on the subject of war are read as evidence of the superior politicization of men.

The parallel case in industrial sociology is the contrast sometimes made between women's attention to the 'social' dimensions of wage work, and men's to economic and political issues. Men are characterized as career-oriented, alert to the importance of promotion and prospects, concerned with the central issues of wages and security of employment. Women, by contrast, are said to concern themselves with working conditions rather than wages, with sociable work companions rather than career advancement, and with flexible hours that accommodate domestic commitments rather than security of employment. This contrast is extended to the politics of the workplace, where women are regarded as less prepared than men to engage forcefully over wages, security and prospects, but more responsive to 'humanistic' issues – to the aura of friendliness in the workplace, to health and safety arrangements, to demands for a shorter working day. In work-based politics, as in electoral politics, men are characterized as hard-headed bargainers who understand central issues and the strategies for pursuing them, while women go for softer options.

Fourth, and finally, women are often presented as more conservative than men.[5] Despite evidence to the contrary, one writer after another has claimed recourse to the 'tried-and-true' in asserting the electoral conservatism of the female sex. In work-based politics, the 'humanistic' concerns to which women are allegedly attached have been argued to represent a less radical orientation to workplace struggle than the objectives of men. Few writers on industrial politics are prepared to assert that women are in general less militant or more acquiescent than men; but the overwhelming failure to discuss the 40 per cent of the labour force who are female in analyses of work-based politics often gives that impression by omission – the fist that is raised in defiance of management is a male fist, and the examples of confrontational politics are taken from men.

In both electoral politics and work-based politics, the characterization of women's political life as marginal, shallow or conservative is a product of male-stream analysis – that is, it derives from traditions of thought which are, in both their theoretical and empirical dimensions, rooted in masculine experience. In this volume, we bring together a variety of contributions which challenge the male-stream portrait of women's relation to politics, and which show it to be profoundly mistaken.

Since the publication in the early 1970s of seminal critiques of the male-stream literature by, for example, Bourque and Grossholtz,[6] Goot and Reid[7] and Brown,[8] comments about women in political science, political sociology and industrial sociology have become more circumspect in tone. Such reticence, however, does not mark the overcoming of the very deficiencies in political analysis that gave rise to distorted profiles of women in the first place – the deficiencies, that is, of a political science and sociology developed without sensitivity to gender. The intention of this volume is not merely to exorcise sexist clichés, but to interrogate the assumptions and the explanatory frameworks underlying male-stream accounts, so as to lay the foundations for a clearer understanding of the political capacities of both women and men.

We should emphasize that in this volume readers will not find extensive discussions of why women are excluded from political elites, of recent developments in the politics of the women's movement, or of current changes that have highlighted a 'gender factor' in elections. Although the general argument of the text is related to these topics, our direct concern is to contribute to changing the conception of politics, and of political involvement, so that women's political capacity is no longer obscured, and men's no longer privileged. This involves acknowledging the existence of the political whenever and wherever elements of social life are (or become recognized as) contingent – as susceptible to change or transformation. The emphasis on the potential for change directs attention to conditions structuring social life and the power relations involved in obstructing or promoting social transformation. Politics is, then, an activity which may take individual or collective forms, centred around the struggle over power. Power is the capacity to shape or form social and political relations, i.e., the capacity to perpetuate a given order or to transform it. Power is structured by asymmetrical access to resources and the ability to mobilize them. Political struggles are, therefore, both constituted by and the result of the organization of relations of 'public' and 'private' life. Our conception of politics affirms the claim of the women's movement that the object of political struggles inevitably includes the means as well as the ends of struggle itself.

Whether our argument for a particular reconstruction of political analysis is sustained depends upon the reader approaching the volume not as a series of discrete essays but as a coherent account. The extracts on work-based politics in Part One and electoral politics in Part Two span attempts at the critical examination and rethinking of political analysis. The introductions to Parts One and Two indicate how each extract contributes to the overall argument. But the lessons to be learned from these extracts are not fully revealed until the final article. In Part Three, 'Women and the public sphere: conclusions', we provide a thematic summary of critical points raised in Parts One and Two, and elaborate their implications for the analysis of gender and politics. We point first to the ways in which gender differences in political experience have been exaggerated, and to the recovery through feminist analysis of an unacknowledged political dimension underlying distinctive elements of women's experience. Second, we take issue with some of the feminist responses to male-stream arguments, and explore the conceptual terrain on which skirmishes between feminist and male-stream writers have taken place. Accounts of the relation of gender to electoral and work-based politics are founded, we argue, on the analytical separation of the public world of politics and employment from the private sphere of family and interpersonal relations. Such a separation is embedded in the notion of 'private woman' and 'public man'. While feminist writers have challenged the apolitical characterization of 'private' women, many have to a large extent accepted the explanatory framework which seals women's experience in the private, and men's in the public. In the process, we highlight the need for a more rigorous analysis of exaggerated claims concerning men's political activity and political consciousness, and we argue for a more adequate understanding of politics – an understanding which would recognize that the relationship between public and private is itself a political issue.

Part One

Women and work-based politics

1 Introduction

In this section, we have compiled a series of articles that further the debates concerning the relation of gender to the politics of waged labour. Is the importance women attribute to work overshadowed by the family? How does 'women's work' feature in industrial conflicts? Do women, like men, endeavour to exert control by collective action? Are they union minded? What conflicts exist between men and women within work-based politics? The essays discuss these questions, bringing to the fore three important issues in the analysis of work-based politics: the relationship between paid work and the family; the importance of job characteristics in determining workplace militancy; and gender divisions within work struggles and the labour movement.

Paid work and family life

Feldberg and Glenn's critique of male-stream assumptions in the sociology of work involves a direct challenge to those who would assess women's relation to work-based politics via an analysis of their position within the family. They demonstrate, by reference to two classic studies in industrial sociology, how analyses of male and female workers employ different explanatory models. In a nutshell, the 'job model' connects men's work attitudes and behaviour to their conditions and relations of employment. The 'gender model', invoked only for women, treats work attitudes and behaviour as a consequence of family experiences. Thus, Feldberg and Glenn identify an underlying framework in the sociology of work which systematically highlights one aspect of women's relation to paid work, while de-emphasizing the effects of the employment situation itself. In the next two articles, dealing directly with women and work-based politics, the gender model emerges with a new twist. Watt and Hunt explore the ways in which women's perspectives in industrial politics are shaped by their family life.

Watt demonstrates a firm commitment to trade unionism and collective action among his sample of women factory workers and, like Taylor in Part Two, rejects the view that employment experience is less salient for women than for men. But to Watt, women's industrial militancy is underpinned by their commitment to the family. He argues that women are militant at work precisely because they take their responsibility as mothers seriously.

According to Hunt, the isolation of full-time houseworkers is an obstacle to class consciousness, yet women who have been full-time houseworkers bring to industrial politics a less jaded expectation of work. Although the latter condition may be temporary, it indicates women's potential for widening the issues of industrial struggle to include, for example, greater attention to working conditions. Thus, denying the usual claims that full-time houseworkers exert a drag on working-class struggles, Hunt proposes such women may offer, when they enter paid work, a perspective more radical than the one informing much of workplace politics.

Job characteristics and workplace militancy

Purcell and Brown highlight the importance of the differential location of women and men *within* waged work for explanations of workplace militancy. Men and women do different jobs, in different industries, under different forms of supervision and control. All these factors affect the degree and quality of collective organization and may give rise to a variety of forms of opposition, from strikes and sabotage to high rates of turnover.

Purcell pursues the question of the difference in women's and men's employment and its political effects. She isolates the conditions which make the industries and jobs where women are concentrated notoriously difficult to organize. The context of work, rather than the gender composition of the workforce, is stressed as the factor determining the frequency and type of militant action. Purcell also ventures a defence of full-time housewives who oppose strike action by their menfolk; and while her argument is clearly controversial, it does point to the need to examine more closely the effects of sex-differentiated family responsibilities on working-class solidarity.

Brown also questions the characterization of women workers as deferential to management and disinclined to collective action. His review of women as employees in industrial sociology studies up to the early 1970s, supports the proposition that in so far as women refrain from practices to regulate output, from joining trade unions or taking strike action, the explanation lies in the traditions of particular occupations and industries, rather than in specifically feminine orientations. Brown mentions, in passing, the part played by the unresponsive and sometimes hostile attitude of some male trade unionists in discouraging women from collective organization. This raises the crucial question of how job protection strategies employed by male workers help sustain the weak bargaining position of women workers. In addition, it focuses attention on conflict arising from gender divisions within work.

Gender divisions, work-based politics and the labour movement

The politics of waged work extends beyond the confrontations of workers with those who own and manage the work process. Our excerpt from Beynon and Blackburn's study illustrates the conflict operating between women and men in the workplace. Their analysis of trade union commitment among women workers at the Gourmet factory in Brompton is one of the few studies to offer a direct and extensive comparison of male and female workers. The most striking of their findings is the high proportion of women workers who have a positive commitment to unionism but who are not union members. In fact, many of the women are ex-members of the union and express strong opposition to the way the union conducts its affairs. Further tensions between the female and male members of the union are displayed in the circumstances surrounding a strike that took place during the authors' study. Striking night-shift workers and shop stewards, all of whom were men, took great care to win the support of temporary student workers, and even framed demands to unite their interests. However, the men on the night shift refused to discuss the strike with the women day workers and rejected offers of support from the day shift. The union was indeed the men's affair.

Women's relation to workplace politics, then, is not simply a matter of union mindedness or workplace militancy. The conflict as to what it means in practical terms for women to have an equal place alongside men in workplace politics is in progress. Our last selection, from Barrett, considers the pressure being brought to bear on trade unions, and the labour movement generally, to address and represent the lives of women as well as men. Barrett indicates how fundamental a reworking of labour movement structures, policies and practices is entailed by a commitment to end male privileges that have been gained at the working woman's expense.

2 Male and female: job versus gender models in the sociology of work*

Roslyn Feldberg and Evelyn Nakano Glenn

Work has long been viewed as a central aspect of people's lives. It determines their daily activities, the rhythm of their days, the people they meet and the relationships they form. In addition, work largely defines a person's class and status in the social structure. While issues of work are framed as universal ones, the actual study of work has proceeded along sex-differentiated lines.

These sex-differentiated lines lead to three problems which characterize the sociological literature on work. First, women are rarely included in research. Studies of work concentrate on white males, particularly those in managerial, blue-collar and professional occupations.[1] Second, when women are studied, the analysis is shaped by sex-biased interpretations. Third, the entire analysis of work is distorted because certain factors are defined as appropriate either in the study of women's work, or in the study of men's work, but not in both.

Recently, the sociology of work has been criticized for its treatment of employed women. The critics argue that women have been excluded from the study of work, and that, when they are studied, the analyses have been distorted by sexist assumptions.[2] While these writers have documented many specific instances of sexist interpretations, they have not identified the underlying paradigm that gives rise to sex-differentiated approaches to men's and women's employment.

In this paper, we attempt to spell out the paradigm. First, we describe two principal models that have been used in the sociological analysis of work.[3] The first, the *job model*, has been applied principally to men; the second, the *gender model*, has been applied principally to women. We are concerned to specify the assumptions underlying these sex-segregated models. Next, we examine the connections between these models and the interpretations offered

* The full text of this article can be found in *Social Problems*, **26** no. 5 (June 1979), pp. 524–38.

in two important case studies. We argue that a spelling out of the basic assumptions and an understanding of the way they connect to biased interpretation are the most promising aids in developing a more valid framework for the sociological study of work.

Finally, we argue that this more valid framework must integrate those factors which have been defined as applicable only to employed women and those which have been defined as applicable only to employed men. We reach this position from our analysis of the problems in the dominant paradigm and our own experience. From personal experience, everyone knows that men and women have personal lives and that they work (whether paid, unpaid or both), and that experiences in each area have a continuous and closely linked impact on feelings and behaviour related to work. We believe that a valid analysis of work must be able to account for this range of experience.

Sex-segregated models

Separate models for men's and women's relationship to employment are a logical outcome of the sexual division of labour characteristic of the middle period of industrial capitalism. Although the separation of male and female spheres had long been part of the prescriptive literature in the United States and Britain, as well as elsewhere, the expansion of industry in the late nineteenth and early twentieth centuries made the realization of the ideal possible for middle- and upper-class women. The dichotomy became men = breadwinners and workers, women = wives. It was assumed that all male–female differences flowed from that dichotomy. Rather than trying to determine the extent to which this dichotomy applied to particular groups of men and women in specific historical periods, sociologists tended to incorporate it into their basic assumptions and concepts. Thus, even when women were employed, their employment was seen as atypical or as secondary to their 'real' roles. The result is the creation of two sociologies of work: the job model for men and gender model for women.[4]

Assumptions of the models

The sociology of work is essentially the study of how work connects individuals to the social structure. The models used in this field are, therefore, concerned with the nature of these links and their

Table 1 *Assumptions of the job model and the gender model*

Assumptions	Job model	Gender model
Basic social relationships determined by:	Work	Family
Family structure is:	Male-headed, nuclear	Male-headed, nuclear
Connection to family is:	As economic provider/worker	As wife/mother
Social position determined by:	Work	Family
Socio-political behaviour and attitudes derived from:	Occupational socialization, class/status of occupation, social relations of work	Gender role socialization, family roles, activities and relationships of household work
Central life interest is in:[5]	Employment and/or earnings	Family

consequences. The most common topic for investigation is workers' response to work. However, the assumptions underlying the explanations encompass not only the work setting, but also the basic connections of individuals to the larger social structure. These assumptions are different for men and women.

For men, it is assumed that economic activities provide the basis for social relationships within the family and in the society generally. For women, it is assumed that family care-taking activities determine social relationships. These different spheres of activity are, in turn, assumed to be combined in a nuclear family through the sexual division of labour – that is, man as economic provider and woman as wife and mother. Furthermore, male–female differences in relation to the family are expected to lead to differences in the nature of men's and women's connections to other parts of the social structure. For example, social class is assumed to be determined by economic position (i.e., relation to means of production, occupation) for the male, and by position in the family (i.e., wife, daughter) for the female. Similarly, the work attitudes and behaviour of men are seen as consequences of occupational experiences (for example, conditions of employment or occupational socialization), while the responses of women are viewed as outcomes of family experiences (for example, household burden, feminine socialization). The major assumptions are set out in Table 1.

Two further points require emphasis. First, these differences in assumptions are themselves connected. They are complementary aspects of a single conception of social structure: what is held to be true for males is, by definition, held not to be true for females and vice versa. Second, each model assumes homogeneity among members of each sex. Variations in the situations of members of each sex are ignored, and no allowance is made for class and ethnic differences or for changes over time.

Two studies in the sociology of work

In this section, we will analyse distortions arising from the use of the job/gender models in two major studies. These studies share the rare characteristics of studying men and women in similar job settings, thus making possible a comparison of the conceptual frameworks developed to explain men's versus women's work attitudes and behaviour. The authors of the two studies show differing degrees of awareness that they are using job and gender models.

The first study by Blauner, *Alienation and Freedom*,[6] compares men and women in somewhat different jobs within the textile industry. It illustrates the explicit use of a job model for men and a gender model for women. The job model is used to explain variations between groups of men; the gender model, applied only to the women, is used to explain differences between men and women. Beynon and Blackburn's study of English factory workers, *Perceptions of Work*,[7] incorporates both job and gender variables. They recognize that differences in domestic situations *and* in job conditions affect the work concerns of both men and women. Nevertheless, they tend to emphasize job factors for men and gender factors for women. Where women's behaviour departs from sex stereotypes, they either de-emphasize the behaviour or discount its significance. Detailed specification of the use of job and gender models in these studies is required because the differences are subtle, and because the authors tend to shift between models at various points in their analyses.

Blauner's Alienation and Freedom

Blauner's classic study of the relationship between the type of technology which characterizes an industry and the degree of worker alienation rests on the job model. Generally, he finds that in mechanized industries, where jobs are less skilled and more subdivided, workers experience more alienation. When automated technology is used to create more integrated jobs, worker alienation is reduced, although it remains higher than in craft industry.

Blauner uses that model for industries which employ almost exclusively male workers. In studying the textile industry, the only one with large numbers of women, Blauner switches to the gender model to analyse the women's responses to employment. By doing so, he obscures the relationship between the conditions of employment and the degree of alienation.

Initially, Blauner emphasizes the traditions of the southern textile town, which stress community ties. Next, he examines the conditions of work in men's and women's jobs in the industry. Women are observed to be 'especially unfree': performing 'most of the unrewarding jobs', and working under the most objectively alienating conditions. Then, he compares men's and women's perceptions of their work. More women than men complain about their job conditions: 42 per cent of women, compared with 24 per cent of men, say they have to work too fast; 49 per cent of women, compared with 29 per cent of men, say they are 'too tired' at the end of the day; and 49 per cent of women, compared with 27 per cent of men, complained of 'too much pressure' at work.[8]

To be consistent with his overall emphasis on job conditions, Blauner should attribute the differences between women's and men's perceptions to differences in their working conditions. Instead, he shifts, without warning or justification, to a gender model to interpret the women's responses. He notes, 'Since women have, on average, less physical stamina than men, and working women often double as housewives and mothers, it is to be expected that they would be more fatigued by their work.'[9]

This interpretation has two problems. First, by attributing complaints about work to female biology and family responsibilities, he obscures the previously argued link between working conditions and workers' responses. Second, he ignores data which show that women's work conditions are more demanding because they do more machine-paced work which requires constant movement and is more closely supervised.

Blauner is either unaware of his shift to a gender model, or takes it for granted as appropriate for employed women. He provides no evidence in support of the model. Thus, we do not know what proportion of the women are mothers and housewives, what family responsibilities the wives and mothers have, nor whether the most tired women are, in fact, wives and mothers. At the same time, again without apparent awareness of his inconsistency, Blauner maintains the job model for analysing men. He does not even mention differences in tiredness among men, or raise the possibility that any such differences could arise from variations in their levels of family responsibility.

If job conditions are poor, what are the workers' subjective responses to them? Blauner's analysis finds relatively little dissatisfaction and low levels of aspiration. This departure from the findings for other industries is attributed to low levels of education and the lack of alternative jobs; that is, to features of the southern textile town. But again, Blauner offers a separate gender-based analysis of women, who have even worse jobs, yet express no greater dissatisfaction than men. He says, 'Work does not have the central importance and meaning in their lives that it does for men, since their most important roles are those of wives and mother.'[10] Not only does Blauner revert to a gender model, he also fails to consider that women's poorer prospects for advancement may depress their aspirations below those of the men. Here again, assumptions about the meaning of women's roles are substituted for the author's own evidence.

Blauner next turns to a discussion of the impacts of working conditions on the sense of self. He finds that 59 per cent of men versus 41 per cent of women would choose a different occupation if they were starting over. To Blauner, this suggests that men feel degraded by this work, while women do not. His interpretation is worth quoting at length:

The submissiveness required of male textile workers must be damaging to the maintenance of a sure sense of masculinity; the low wages and status *undoubtedly* threaten the sense of worth and success in life. Despite the greater physical discomforts of her job, textile employment for the female worker is not as damaging to her sense of identity, since *successful work is not part of the traditional female role*.[11] (Emphasis added)

The last two examples are interesting for several reasons. First, they show the author's tendency to use men's responses as 'normal', while women's responses are seen as variants. Second, they show that Blauner treats the unpaid work of women as 'nonwork', implicitly defining women as 'nonworkers'. As a result, he is led to conclude that women are little affected by the *paid* work they do. Third, they show how reliance on separate job and gender models guides the analysis into stereotypical moulds. In the second example, it is assumed that men's masculinity is measured by the paycheque. In the rural South, where low wages are endemic, they may not impugn masculinity. Men may establish their masculinity by other criteria – for example, having many children, or being good woodsmen, hunters, farmers or musicians. Similarly, southern women's greater submissiveness to male authority on the job may have nothing to do with the degree of centrality of work roles. It may be due to their socialization in patriarchal families, thus their submissiveness may be part of an established tradition.

Beynon and Blackburn's Perceptions of Work

Beynon and Blackburn's book represents a conscious attempt to overcome the false separation between the conditions of working and non-working life. They criticize analyses that focus exclusively on either the technology and organization of work, or the 'orientations' which workers bring to work from their position in the social structure. They argue that the combination of these factors is necessary to explain workers' responses. By implication, one cannot focus only on family situations for women or only on work conditions for men.

The research setting offered an unusual opportunity for comparisons between men and women. Four groups of workers were studied: day men who operated the basic production machinery or assisted the assembly-line workers; full-time women who worked primarily on an assembly line wrapping and packaging the product; part-time women who did similar jobs in separate units, but also moved around to fill in for full-time women where extra help was needed; and night men, who did both the production and packaging, including jobs considered 'women's work' on the day shift. Each of the four groups represented a particular gender and marital status combination. The day men were mostly single, as were the full-time women. The part-time women and the night men were mostly married with children. With these four groups the authors had an opportunity to examine the interrelated influence of conditions of work and family situations.

For the most part, up to the conclusions at least, Beynon and Blackburn succeed in avoiding many of the problems found in other studies. Unfortunately, the assumptions underlying the job and gender models are so pervasive that unless one is constantly aware of their influence, they tend to creep back into the analysis, even when one starts with the intention of rejecting them. Beynon and Blackburn's study does not completely escape this tendency. Thus, at specific points in this book, they drift back into a job–gender dichotomy.

This happens in three ways. First, they focus on behaviour and attitudes which fit gender stereotypes and de-emphasize those that don't. For example, they don't attach much significance to the fact that the full-time women are the most critical of the company and are most likely to press their grievances. Instead, they focus most of their attention on the part-time women who are the least critical of the company, and who, therefore, fit the stereotype of the uninvolved worker.

Second, they overlook job factors that could explain women's responses, preferring to fall back on explanations based on 'women's characteristics'. In one chapter, they point out that the company accords special treatment – including leniency about working hours, leaves of absences and the like – to the part-time women so they can carry out their domestic responsibilities. Yet, they fail to suggest that it is the company's paternalistic policies towards them, rather than the women's commitment to family responsibilities *per se*, that explains these women's lack of criticalness towards the firm. Again, they fall back on a gender stereotype.

With regard to the women's attitudes towards the union, Beynon and Blackburn overlook the influence of union policies and structure which they earlier admitted ignore women and their concerns. Instead, they view women's critical stance towards the union as a reflection of a 'different style of trade unionism'. (Perhaps, a product of feminine psychology?)

Finally, Beynon and Blackburn, at times, explain similar behaviour of men and women differently. In separate parts of the book, they point out that the day men and both groups of women express a concern with social aspects of the job. The men's focus on sociability is explained by the alienating job conditions and lack of opportunities for mobility which turn the men's interests away from intrinsic job concerns.[12] The women's interest in social aspects is interpreted as a product of low commitment to work resulting from their primary commitment to family roles. This interpretation ignores the fact that job conditions and mobility are even worse for the women and that, therefore, their orientation can be explained in the same terms as the men's.

Moving away from the details of specific points of analysis, we find a more general pattern emerging: the authors devote substantial attention to describing and analysing differences between the men and women, but pass lightly over differences within each sex – that is, between the day and night men and between the part-time and full-time women. As a corollary, little attention is paid to the similarities between the full-time women and the day or night men.

Throughout the various areas of response the data presented indicate that the part-time women differ most from the other three groups. The full-time women's responses differ from those of the part-time women at least as much as they do from the two groups of men. In many areas – such as the meaning of work or sources of satisfaction – the full-time women's responses fall between those of the day men and the night men. Sometimes they are more similar to the day men, sometimes they are more similiar to the night men. Thus, the question should not be why women differ from men, but why part-time women differ from the other three groups. Moreover, the answer should be sought not only in these women's family commitments, but also, in possible differences in their experiences in the workplace. Thus, we might ask, is the experience of doing part-time work, irrespective of family situation, sufficiently distinct that it leads to a divergent pattern of responses? Since there are no part-time men, this possibility cannot be tested. However, Beynon and Blackburn do not even mention it. Presumably, they are comfortable using gender assumptions to 'account for' the results.

While assumptions from the job and gender models pop up throughout the book, it is in the conclusions that they emerge as the dominant framework. The contrast between specific analyses in the text and the summary statements in the concluding chapter illustrates this shift in framework. In Chapter 4, the women's specific dissatisfactions with their work are described graphically. One woman said that it is 'terrible just thinking about coming to work in the mornings. It's not hard work, but it seems to wear you out . . . .'.[13] Another said, 'You can't imagine how boring it is. It really can get you down. The girls are O.K. – they're great. It's just the job. The job is terrible.' Yet, in the concluding chapter the conditions that are complained about are minimized as a cause of major dissatisfaction. 'Many of them found the work boring and tedious. However, they did not have high expectations of the intrinsic job, so that was not a major cause of dissatisfaction. Where they did expect some satisfaction was in social relationships, and it was here that they were critical of the firm.'[14]

This interpretation seems strangely distant from the data. Knowing that they have little hope of finding more interesting jobs, the full-time women concentrate on deriving satisfaction from their social relationships. One suspects that were men to respond similarly, their dissatisfaction would be fully acknowledged. Their emphasis on social rewards would be recognized as a tactic for coping with powerlessness. Furthermore, their social ties might be seen as potentially useful in establishing solidarity and group control in the work situation.

Discussion and conclusions

The review of the two studies demonstrates the different ways in which the job and gender models inform analyses of men's and women's responses to work. In some cases (for example, Blauner) the models are explicitly incorporated into the analysis; in others (for example, Beynon and Blackburn) the models are never explicitly elaborated, but some of the assumptions of the models slip in as 'taken for granted'. Some analyses rely exclusively on job or gender variables to explain the behaviour of one or the other sex, as does Blauner's treatment of women textile workers. Other analyses include a variety of other factors, such as labour market structure, as does Beynon and Blackburn's examination of women factory operatives.

Despite these differences in the mode of incorporation, the studies demonstrate similar distortions. First, data which do not fit the models are overlooked and ignored. Second, the significance of data which violate the models' assumptions is discounted or de-emphasized in the interpretation. Third, when several alternative explanations could plausibly be invoked, the one that is most consistent with job or gender models is favoured without adequate discussion. Finally, the search for alternative interpretations is short-circuited. The models offer a ready-made explanation and the researcher follows the path of least resistance.

These distortions are serious enough. An even more serious consequence of the models is that they bias the entire direction of research. As is the case of basic paradigms in science, the job–gender paradigm determines *what* is studied. The models direct attention towards particular issues by defining them as problematic. The job–gender paradigm defines job conditions as problematic for men and family responsibilities as problematic for women, thereby directing research into these areas. The complementary issues, the impacts of specific work conditions on women's responses to work and the relationship of men's family roles to their work attitudes and behaviour, are viewed as non-problematic and, therefore, have not been studied systematically in the mainstream literature.[15]

It is true, of course, that phenomena can be studied even in the absence of a supportive paradigm. This occurs when phenomena become sufficiently visible or widespread that they command public attention. Thus, in response to rising labour force participation among married women, increased research has been conducted on women in specific occupations,[16] and on work–family linkages.[17] However, the research continues to focus on issues that are defined as problematic under the old paradigm. Both types of studies emphasize the strains for women and their families resulting from women's 'two jobs', while giving little consideration to the impacts of conditions of women's employment in specific jobs.

What this suggests is that a new paradigm is needed. Such a paradigm will emerge, perhaps suddenly, as new findings which are inconsistent with the old ones accumulate. In the meantime, we need to engage in a dialectical process of empirical exploration and theoretical development. Pursuit of research which describes and analyses the changing conditions of work will provide an empirical base, while the movement towards a new theoretical paradigm will direct attention towards new questions for research. Our review of the literature and our own research on women clerical workers has suggested to us some directions for theoretical development to take.

First, we need to reconceptualize work. The concept of work needs to be made more inclusive, to cover unpaid as well as paid work. Moreover, it needs to be formulated so that the work people do can be located within the context of their whole lives. The development of separate job and gender models rests on a concept of work which arbitrarily separates paid employment from other work, identifying it as the only form of 'real' work. As a result, other work tends to be treated as 'non-work' and women workers as 'non-workers'.

When considering paid work, closer attention must be paid to the actual conditions of work commonly assigned to women. Understanding women's responses to paid work requires a clearer, more precise picture of their work: again, hours and pace of work, extent of rationalization, kinds of skills, types of work standards. In the absence of such information, attempts to analyse women's responses to employment must continue to rely on stereotypes, not only of female character, but also of 'women's work'.

A reformulated concept of work would also facilitate analysis of the connections between various forms of work and make clearer the distinction between work and 'non-work'. Again, there are beginnings in existing research. Studies of women clerical workers suggest that women's evaluations of the conditions of their jobs are based on comparison with the conditions of housework, as well as of previous jobs.[18] At the macro-level, historical research indicates some important connections between the conditions of paid and unpaid work for women: women's low wages and limited job opportunities in the labour force reinforce and are reinforced by women's disproportionate involvement in domestic labour.[19] This research should be expanded to include the connection between paid and unpaid work for men. The relationship between variation in the extent and type of men's unpaid work and their responses to employment needs to be looked at more closely. For example, responses of men whose paid work is similar, but whose unpaid work differs, could be compared. Parallel historical research needs to be conducted on changes in the types and conditions of men's unpaid work and on shifts in the relationship between their paid and unpaid work.

A second area for major theoretical reformulation is the systematic incorporation of gender stratification into the analysis of work. Because male domination and female subordination have been taken for granted, gender stratification has remained largely invisible and unproblematic in the sociology of work. Changes in the economy and in social life have been accompanied by changes in men's and women's structural and interpersonal situations. As feminist analysts have pointed out, these changes reveal the extent to which gender stratification is socially created, rather than 'natural'. These analysts have begun a detailed examination of the processes by which gender stratification is created and maintained in the family and other socio-political institutions. A similar examination must be made of work and the organization of work.

A beginning is found in recent studies which look at the consequences of differential assignment of men and women to positions in work organizations.[20] This research attempts to show that differences in men's and women's responses to employment are the outcome of their locations in hierarchies, their numerical proportions and other structural features of organizations. The analysis stops short, however. It ignores the ways in which gender stratification, aside from its expression in organizational patterns, is structured into interpersonal relations. Acker and Van Houten's[21] re-examination of the Hawthorne studies points out the different forms of social control imposed on men and women, independent of their organizational positions. For example, the controls imposed on female assembly workers were closer and more paternalistic than those imposed on male assemblers. Some observers have remarked on the parallels between paternalistic treatment of women in the workplace and their treatment in the family and other institutions.[22] A fuller theoretical and empirical treatment of gender stratification would involve detailed consideration of both formal structures and informal processes. An examination of interpersonal behaviour among peers and between superordinate–subordinate pairs would enable us to sort out the impacts of formal organizational hierarchies and informal gender hierarchies, and the interaction between the two.

In what ways would these reformulations enhance the analysis of work? The kind of basic restructuring we have suggested would, we believe, lead researchers to frame different questions, to view as problematic behaviour that they have previously taken for granted. They would, therefore, seek new sources of data because they would be less inclined to rely on unstated and pervasive gender assumptions. The change in questions and in forms of data, in turn, would make it possible for researchers to construct more inclusive, and ultimately more valid, interpretations of data.

Next, let us consider how more systematic attention to gender stratification would have enriched Beynon and Blackburn's analysis of men's and women's work attitudes. An example is their treatment of differences in aspirations for mobility. They show clearly that full-time women, for the most part, do not want to become supervisors, while the men desire such promotions. The difference is reported without apparent awareness that it requires explanation. By failing to analyse the sources of women's reluctance, Beynon and Blackburn leave the impression that their response stems from feminine character or socialization. An analysis incorporating gender stratification of organizations would examine the position of female supervisors in the hierarchical structure, the links (or lack thereof) between these positions and higher positions, the degree of authority these positions command, the responsibilities they entail and the entry points and career paths of those who reach these positions (for example, whether or not they usually come up through the ranks). A comparison of female and male supervisory positions on these dimensions would yield a more comprehensive, and probably more valid, explanation of men's and women's different aspirations for promotion.

Similar detailed analysis of gender hierarchies and norms within the company (and the union) would reveal the sources of patterns of differences and similarities among the four groups of men and women workers in such areas as attitudes towards unions, dissatisfactions with work conditions and orientations towards work.

In addition to enhancing the validity of specific studies, the suggested reformulations would enrich the sociology of work by directing inquiry into new areas. Research and thinking would be directed to aspects of work previously taken for granted, or ignored. The analysis of women's work would include the systematic study of both paid and unpaid work throughout the class structure with careful attention to actual conditions of work and actual behaviour of the workers. The analysis of men's work would involve learning about the kinds of unpaid work men do and the impacts of various 'off the job' concerns (such as family responsibilities or ethnic and cultural values) on their responses to paid work.

These reconceptualizations should also provide points of entry into an understanding of work–family linkages for both men and women. In the introduction, we claimed that, since both men and women work and participate in families, a valid framework for the analysis of work must encompass these linkages on a micro- and macro-level. By reconceptualizing work and incorporating gender stratification, the study of work can be expanded to take into account the complex relationships between the organization of the economy, the labour market, and the conditions of paid and unpaid work and the conditions and structures of family life.

3 Industrial radicalism and the domestic division of labour*

Ian Watt

In this paper I shall provide empirical evidence on some key issues relating to paid work saliency among working women – specifically married women in manual jobs who have children 'on their hands'. The article is particularly concerned with two issues: first, the suggestions made by Taylor in a recent paper pertaining to industrial radicalism among women workers and its effects in the domestic sphere[1] and, second, a discussion of the *peculiar* forms of female industrial militancy, its genesis and potentialities.

The Taylor Thesis

In the latter part of his paper, Taylor endeavours to examine the relationship between paid employment and the propensity to vote for the Labour Party among women. In examining the data he finds an equal 'party identification' between male and female manual workers.[2] This he attributes to the assimilation of beliefs and values in the work setting which Parkin claimed were a decisive factor in 'partisanship' and thus effectively 'radicalized' the women workers. Hence he claims this association between exposure to the industrial culture and party choice will elicit similar attitudes among women and men where the work settings are comparable. Thus he calls into question Parkin's suggestion that this process is less extensive and influential among women. As Taylor has it:

If it can be assumed that the lack of an association reflects the impact upon attitudes of the industrial workplace, then this would imply that working women were as fully integrated into the norms and values of the workplace as were men.[3]

* This chapter is an abridgement of I. Watt, 'Linkages between industrial radicalism and the domestic role among working women', which appeared in *Sociological Review*, **28** (1980) pp. 55–74.

And, more importantly, he goes on to quote Parkin's second argument – that sex is equally decisive in deflecting female voters from the Labour Party:

The fact that women are less prone than men to the attraction of socialism squares well, I think, with the hypothesis. *For it can be maintained that the world of work is a much less salient sphere of involvement to women than to men,* particularly of course in view of the former's primary commitment to domestic life. . . . *It would follow* that even if they were employed in industry – on a full or part-time basis – their assimilation into the value-system would be a less complete affair than the assimilation of men. Women not employed in factory production at all would of course provide the extreme, but not uncommon, case of isolation from an industrial sub-culture.[4] (My italics)

Thus Parkin claims that the primacy of the domestic sphere over-rides the capacity of the workplace to generate deviant behaviour – in the case of women, to direct them towards the Labour Party. Essentially then, the argument runs: involvement in large factories, with distinct separation between workers and managers, will, for a variety of reasons, generate greater identification with the Labour Party among male manual workers. Those not working, due to retirement, or through being housewives, or working in small scale industry, will be more amenable to the 'dominant' ideas in society. Most importantly those *women in paid employment,* despite the influence of factory exposure will still exhibit a marked tendency to vote Conservative because of their prior commitment to the home sphere and the resulting decrease in factory influence.

To counter this, Taylor advances data from Butler and Stokes' 1970 General Election Study, which appear to qualify Parkin's thesis about the respective levels of saliency adhering to the domestic and industrial spheres. He shows that *equal numbers* of paid workers identified with the Labour Party *regardless of sex,*[5] and concludes:

There are some reasons for believing that working women may well have been influenced by their work experiences and less by domestic orientations than Parkin allows for.[6]

This is linked to a consideration of changes in the nature of work for women, away from domestic service towards factory work where:

Work environments were more likely to be conducive to radicalism rather than increasing exposure to 'dominant' norms and values.[7]

Allied to this is what, for the purposes of the article, could only be *speculation*; the suggestion that this radical perspective at work would carry over into the family home, eradicating the more traditional sexual divisions of labour.

The rest of this section is concerned with offering empirical data which question these assumptions – that there is a clear linkage between radicalism at work, and increasing equality in the home, and indeed goes on to suggest that they may be to some degree *discrete*. That is, that a traditional sexual division of labour may obtain in the home, while a radical perspective is held at work.

The qualifications for selection provide information on a particular sector of the working population, i.e., married women, living with their husbands, who have children no older than 16 years and are full-time shop floor employees. These women were chosen because it was felt they *should* possess many of the key traits associated with an equalization of marital roles; an independent source of income, exposure to large-scale production, separation from children and so on.[8]

The setting, a large tobacco factory in the East End of Glasgow, manufactured cigarettes, cigars and pipe tobacco. The area evidenced the myriad influences of urban deprivation – high unemployment, poor housing, low welfare provision/amenities etc. Within the factory itself, forms of work were extremely intensive, utilizing 'continuous process' techniques with staggered meal and tea breaks for all but a few departments, and mainly operating double day shifts which alternated weekly. At shop floor level the factory was completely unionized and paid high wages and, for the immediate area, especially high wages. 'Conditions' – holidays, sick pay, leave etc. were of a similar standing. Thus in the community the factory enjoyed a good reputation and was the major source of employment.[9]

The women had a tradition of working and commitment to work, which was revealed in their consistency and lengths of employment allied to their reasons for leaving jobs. By far the most striking feature is the length of time spent at the factory, with 66 per cent having been there at least seven years in total. Looking more closely at work histories reveals that 82 per cent of respondents had worked elsewhere with 55 per cent having at least four years' employment elsewhere. Perhaps most significantly 61 per cent left their last job for one of three reasons – to have a baby, low pay or poor conditions, or moving home or inconvenience.

A further illustration of commitment is revealed by turnover rate comparison between the two sexes. For men the figure is 7 per cent, for women 14 per cent, but of the actual female figure – 239 – 207 left in the 18–29 age range, the range where most women will leave for one reason – to have children.[10] We are thus in a position to claim the requirements of Taylor's thesis have been fulfilled – longevity of employment, linked to consistency of employment as a basis for female radicalism in both the industrial *and* domestic sphere. The data now provides the basis for deciphering the forms of this radicalism as they enmesh with the home world of the women, and for obtaining an understanding of the linkages – their strengths and limitations.[11] This can best be approached by illustrating the 'radical' at work and then showing that there is no necessary correspondence in the home.

The evidence of radicalism

Beginning with attitudes towards supervision, respondents were asked about the possibility of workers and supervisors having friendly relationships. The evidence suggests that the work culture is deemed by the women to be closely constrained by *power relationships* and by positions in a structured hierarchy. Thus 43 per cent see amicability with supervisors being predicated upon job efficiency. Similarly only 21 per cent evidence any desire for close contact with supervisors. (This attitude was repeated towards managers with over 50 per cent expressing disapproval of worker/ manager relations, the remainder indicated problems arising from a feeling of being 'just a number' and at the mercy of the production process.)[12]

Margaret aged 45, factory 18 years:

Question   Can a worker and a supervisor ever get on well together?
Answer   No, I don't think you can talk to a supervisor the way you can to the girls at the machine . . . maybe it's because we don't come into contact very much . . . the fact she's got the grey coat she's part of the management, they're more for the management than the workers.

Ann aged 31, factory 5 years:

. . . if you're not liked by the supervisor she has the power over you, they think they're a bit better than you and then can tell you what to do.

Table 2 *Workers' desire to be a supervisor*

Would you like to be a supervisor?	
Yes	19
No	38
Strong no	37

Of those answering in the negative in Table 2, 35 said this was because they would 'lose friends', or 'be part of management'.

Table 3 *Unattractive aspects of being a supervisor*

What is unattractive about being a supervisor, would other workers change towards you?	
No longer one of them, lose friends	16
Can't keep everyone happy	17
Having to discipline others	36
No, not if real friends	3

Turning to look at experiences and perceptions of the union reveals 100 per cent membership and 57 indicating a non-interest in holding a trade union post on the basis of 'feeling incapable' (32), or 'having enough to do at home' (25). To the question 'should all workers join a trade union?' 60 said yes and a further 21 stated it was 'up to the individual', but they would 'advise yes'. With regard to a closed shop, 66 women were asked because the union entered negotiations concerning this after interviews had begun. However, of those asked, 57 per cent said yes. It was also felt that, in general, workers should join a union as they 'fought for rises and better conditions' or they gave 'protection against victimization' in 32 per cent of answers. But most markedly of all, 38 per cent answered in terms of 'us and them' contexts. Similarly, 63 per cent readily stated their support for strike action 'if a majority decision', or stressed the importance 'of supporting the union'.

Table 4   *Workers' support for strike action despite personal disagreement*

If the majority were in favour and you disagreed do you still think you should come out on strike?	
Yes, union rules	34
Yes, must stick together	43
No, nothing to do with me	8
No, other	15

Table 4 indicates a strong dispersion of what might be termed radical male attributes.[13] This is particularly true of *solidaristic* beliefs, for example, levels of support for strike action, attitudes towards the closed shop and a 'healthy' awareness of the pitfalls of sectionalism. Combining these with perceptions of management effectively 'fills out' their radical awareness of work relations and intertwines several key variables.

The evidence of traditionalism

A useful entry point, when looking for evidence of traditionalism, is to examine the basic household division of tasks (see Table 5).

Table 5   *Basic division of tasks in the household*

What jobs does your husband do in the house?	
Daily – 'Hoover', dust, shopping, beds, washing, meals, kids	7
Irregular – as above	9
'Only what he had to do by necessity'	33
Regular 'minimum'	18
Nothing	21

The figures reveal a very low level of assistance from husbands, despite the considerable length of time the women have been paid workers and suggests an extremely clear sexual division of tasks. Most striking of all, 71 of the women approved of the levels of assistance given by their husbands since they had begun working. Consequently 30 'agreed strongly' and 39 'agreed' with their husbands' claim that many household tasks were 'women's work'. Also, 53 claimed 'the house/housework and the kids' were 'a woman's responsibility'. As a result 71 respondents dealt with 'all expenses' with 25 husbands handing in pay packets. This unequal division of tasks elicited no great feeling of being overburdened or of the division being anything but 'normal'. However, and crucially, the problem remains of why, given the continuance of marked sexual divisions in the home, an erosion of 'traditional' female orientations takes place at work. It is to this issue that the second part of this paper is now directed.

The play-off between work and home

I want to suggest here that industrial radicalism can survive at work for two very precise reasons. Firstly, the *discrete* nature of radicalism, by which I mean that it has no obvious connection with the domestic world. This is the most important basic point to grasp since it is the clue which allows an understanding of the phenomenon. Thus, I wish to show that *untypical* attitudes and beliefs are *restricted* to those areas at work where the debilitating influences of home hold no ideological sway. The capacity of paid employment to inaugurate radical perceptions is defined by the degree to which these perceptions *elude* the primary and, apparently, more powerful effects of the wider social milieu external to the factory. As Hunt succinctly puts it:

This does not mean that ideology is merely a summary of prevailing social practice . . . at the individual level ideology exerts an independent influence, which can be seen in those cases where individual practice conflicts with prevailing ideology without seriously weakening the hold of ideology.[14]

In the case of women, the exchange between 'individual practice' (being paid workers) and 'prevailing ideology' (women as houseworkers) is a crucial factor in the contradictory mix which results in the workplace.

Verification of this process – *compartmentalized* radicalism, and the *direction of causality* from the home to the factory, emerges if we turn to look at those demands at work which jar with sexual assumptions and the women's images of their role. One obvious question relates to the 'legitimacy' of women being paid employees – to what extent are their rights to work as justified as men's? Of the 46 disagreeing with the question posed in Table 6, only 33 did so because 'everyone should be treated as just a worker' (the rest making reference to the law, or women being 'just as good').

Table 6   *Women's right to work*

If the factory had to pay workers off, should women go first?	
Yes	54
No	46

The linkages between the desire for meaningful and companion-ate activity, and the challenge it presents to crucial assumptions drive an ideological wedge between the rewards of paid employ-ment and domestic peace of mind.

Linda aged 28, factory 3 years:

. . . I think back to when I was in the house, nearly going up the walls and most of the neighbours were working, you're thinking too about being there to give the kids some comfort when you're sitting at the machine . . . I mean when I was younger my mother was always in the house.

As a consequence of this a clear progression emerges between ascription to ideological beliefs about roles and their resolution in acceptance of the double load – paid employment and work in the home.

Turning now to look at those variables which had a 'radicalizing' result according to the theory – existence and length of service, allied to the attendant experiences they carry – we find further proof of the dominance of home in our reworking of the thesis: that radicalism at work exists alongside traditionalism at home. In responding to the question of whether women should go first if the factory had to lay workers off, the dispersion of the replies exhibits no marked difference by length of service. Indeed for those women with over ten years service the figures reflect no more than a 50 per cent split, repeating the same proportions throughout.[15] A further crucial variable, age, reproduces a similar distribution (Table 7). The figures hint at a breaking down of traditional attitudes among only the youngest group, though the small number involved make any conclusions extremely tentative. The variation may be partially accounted for by the heavy financial outlay on house, furnishings and a young child that these respondents may face. This was indicated by many of the younger women as a powerful reason for

Table 7 *Womens' right to work, by age of respondents*

If the factory had to pay workers off, should women go first, by age?		
Age group	Yes	No
20–4	2	8
25–9	3	4
30–4	13	7
35–9	8	8
46–5	17	12
46 and over	11	7

returning to work.[16] In contrast five out of the ten still thought a woman's place was 'in the home' with a baby, further qualifying the picture. Overall 51 per cent agreed with the statement and only worked because of the financial strain or because of the availability of a relative, and a further 13 agreed for a variety of reasons. Taking the foregoing together corroborates the view that previously formed orientations are dominant at work and illustrates the compartmentalized nature of radicalism.

Coming to the second reason for the survival of industrial radicalism, we find the most intriguing possibilities of all. Thus to the effects of plant size and work exposure, I add *role directed* militancy. This relates to the constellation of beliefs about the mothering/wife role and the provision of emotional and, in this case, material benefits as an operationalization of the role. This can be made clearer, first, by looking at 'most important reasons for working', with 78 per cent claiming it was for money for the family/kids, and, very much a poor second, for company – despite the problems of boredom at home.

It appears then, that alongside radicalism generated by the work process, there exists equally potent family centred militancy as an underpinning reason for critical perceptions. However, and most interesting of all, this element of radicalism, the stronger of the two, since the domestic sphere is dominant, is at the same time the most 'flawed'. Because as the women pursue material and representational betterment as role directed activity, they come into conflict with omnipresent ideologically dominant *role divisions* and assumptions. This somewhat nebulous concept can be illustrated by considering the contradictory position the women are placed in with regard to equality of pay and opportunity, since it is here we see the clearest example of the process. Thus 26 thought a bias in promotion selection in favour of men existed and 18 thought the domestic burden a woman faced precluded promotion. These injustices were keenly felt while at the same time the legitimate rights of men as breadwinners was also restated.

Helen aged 28, factory 5 years:

I don't think it's right a woman earning more than a man. Say if my husband and I were working together. . . . It's not very good for a man's morale having to turn to someone and say his wife's getting more than him.

Betty aged 40, factory 11 years:

I know that sometimes I can fight with my husband and say you can go anytime, I don't need you to keep me. . . . I would like to think he could keep me. It's a man's place. I would like to think my man could earn enough to keep me. I still think they should keep the women beneath the men.

Because of increased wages ('equal pay' had been introduced four years earlier), many of the women were earning more than their husbands, thus the image of male as breadwinner as a key ideological construct was being shaken. But alongside this, as indicated, is that strand of role militancy seeking equality which *escapes* the sexual divide, with 61 expressing discontent with the men's attitude towards grievances felt by women workers.

Irene aged 29, factory 6 years:

If we complain about the supervisor or the breaks or some other thing the men just think we're 'daft women', but we're in here from six like them doing a job, they should support us.

Conclusions

The second part of this paper has indicated the parameters within which radicalism and traditionalism at work operate. Radical work attitudes have exhibited many striking and progressive forms but at one level are predicated upon expressions of militancy which do not impinge upon imbibed sexual divisions and understandings of the world.

4 Workers side by side: women and the trade union movement

Pauline Hunt*

I share the view that, in order to understand the position of women in capitalist society, it is necessary to take the physical separation of the family unit from social production as its central feature. In this work, however, a theme of equal importance is the underlying integration of the family unit and social production, in the sense that each sphere constitutes the condition of existence of the other. In fact the contradiction between the apparent separation, but actual integration, of the domestic and industrial arena provides the theoretical framework for the study of gender and class consciousness presented here.

It is to women rather than to men that the task of reproducing and maintaining labour mainly falls in our society. Since in this respect the social situation of women differs from that of most men, we may ask if this difference affects the way women respond as workers at their place of paid employment.

Juliet Mitchell has a reply at the ready:

work as a housewife isn't work – it's 'being at home' (the place of leisure), work in the office or factory isn't work – it's 'getting out of the house for a bit'. Working at home she is isolated, working outside the home she is enjoying some social life. There is no possibility here of comradeship or unity in struggle – the relationship of women workers is simply the counterpart of the loneliness of the home, it is friendliness or its opposite . . . . Their exploitation is invisible behind an ideology that masks the fact that they work at all – their work appears inessential. . . . Cut off from other women at home, going to work 'for the company' she yet brings – at times of crisis – the isolation of the family to bear on the collective possibilities of the work situation, she does not have even a divided loyalty, for where dependence is intrinsic to the situation, loyalty is redundant.[1]

* This chapter is an excerpt from P. Hunt, *Gender and Class Consciousness* (Macmillan 1980), pp. 2, 155–7, 171–9.

As full-time houseworkers women are cut off from the direct experience of class struggle on the shop floor. When such women re-enter the direct labour market they find themselves in the non-career, low paid job sector. It is easy to see how such female labour could represent a threat to the hard won gains achieved by organized labour. However, to present the problem in these static terms is to obscure the actual process involved.

The mothers of school-age children who have been at home for several years, return to the labour market doubting their ability to hold down *any* job for long. The initial desire to serve willingly extends to matters of pay. Norma Wade describes her attitude like this:

Norma   We get equal pay with the men. When I first started here I thought £24 a week, I thought, 'that's great'. Now it's £40, and I still think it's alright.

However, as Norma herself recognizes, the situation changes:

Now I hear of people earning – after seventeen years of earning only pin money I was dead satisfied. But now, I believe I'm worth £40 at least. If they offered me more I certainly wouldn't feel that I didn't deserve it. But it's taken me two years to think like that, I'm afraid.

Expectations concerning pay tend to expand with experience. This is also true of solidarity. Gladys describes the ties that have grown up between women workers in the section of the wire factory where she works:

Gladys   The shop I work in is a closed shop. They don't call it that now, but it's 100 per cent union. Now, a woman came to work there who wasn't in the union. When she came in she was asked, 'are you in the union?'. I didn't ask her, it makes no difference to me. But, see, this was a new shop I'd gone into. The shop I worked in for a couple of years before wasn't a completely union shop. Well, she said she wasn't in the union and everybody downed tools. 'We'll not have a non-union member in this shop', they said. She said she would not join the union. She said it was a waste of money and a waste of time. Well where I'm working there are women who have been there twenty-five years – the biggest majority of them. Apart from me the shortest time someone's done is fifteen years. They've all stuck together through thick and thin. I mean, they've seen more or less what we've fought for. You know, better conditions and more money. Why should one spoil it? You know, break the bond that they've got there. So I thought to myself,

'Gladys, you've either got to join them or be called a blackleg.' Well I went with them. I've got the intelligence to see that they had fought for it. So she was moved to another shop.

It would seem that the docility of the ex-full-time houseworker is temporary. The money they earn represents an important contribution to their families' standard of living, and within a few years they are as determined as their male counterparts to stand up for their rights as paid workers. We also need to know the ways in which women's domestic experiences influence the development of class consciousness.

Production class consciousness

The alienation experienced by houseworkers is closely tied to the privatized nature of that employment and by the lack of public recognition accorded to it. After a period spent as a full-time houseworker the chief desire is often to escape into paid employment, which, apart from having the advantage of social recognition, offers semi-independence financially, company versus isolation and involvement versus boredom. Women's desire to find satisfaction in the work experience finds expression in their concern with working conditions. A woman shop steward working for the General Electric Company (GEC) in Stafford told me the following story which illustrates the point:

In the paint shop last week they changed the paint. They couldn't get the usual one. The women came in and smelt it. They went through the whole day, it takes time, talking among themselves, 'How strong it is getting', and, 'How is it affecting you?' They built up a case among themselves. The next day when they came in they found it just as bad. By the time they got to the point of reporting it to me they knew how many felt sick, and for how long, how many had passed out, how many couldn't eat their dinner. They had a complete picture, which is very useful to have when you're going in to see management.

They had reached such a pitch that management said, 'Yes we recognise the problem, it's terrible. Just stick it as long as you can, go out for fresh air any time you want. Have breaks at regular intervals (this was breaking the normal factory rules where you just have a ten minute break in the morning). Anyone particularly sick can go and lie down in the rest room.'

But the women simply said, 'No. We're not working in it.' The men working nearby said, 'You can't be so unreasonable.' But the women still insisted that the smell had to be put right or they would go home. The management argued that their job was essential to the continuity of production. They still replied, 'We're not working in it.' The men walked away saying, 'They're irrational. They won't listen to reason.'

After a bit management said, 'Alright, go home and we will pay you for the lost production. We will change the paint, and seeing as we are giving you this concession will you give it a try again tomorrow?' The women said that was fair enough, went home and got on with the jobs around the house. While they were at home they had had management running round like wild things. You wouldn't get that happen in a man's shop. I must say I'm proud of them for it.[2]

It is useful to contrast this with the outlook of the chemical workers described by Nichols and Armstrong:

One of the men recalls that when he came to the factory a manager said, 'You've got to expect to put up with some shit you know. This isn't a sweet factory.' And the fact is that though they resent their conditions most men accept the logic of this. . . . 'Nearly thirty-six quid a week. Flat money. So for me, coming from twelve quid a week to three times that amount I'm bloody glad of the job. You know, no matter bloody what. . . .' A minority brag about the conditions they put up with at work. Many more experience a feeling of pride in having withstood what the world has done to them. . . . But above all the Chemco workforce, at least for most of the time, is characterised by the fatalism of men who do not control nor see any way of controlling, the world in which they live.[3]

These men, and most workers, understand that their labour service is a commodity like any other, for which they can but do the same as any other seller – get the highest price. The employers' calculation, like any other buyer, is to pay the least possible. Marx and Engels first identified the impact on social relations wrought by capitalism which, 'put an end to all feudal, patriarchal idyllic relations . . . and has left remaining no other nexus between man and man than naked self-interest and callous "cash payment"'.[4]

As productive workers in the home, women have been less subject to the full force of the calculative relations characteristic of capitalism. In terms of the development of class consciousness this is a drawback. It is, however, also an advantage in that it means that to some extent women have been less adequately socialized into seeing themselves as wage earners above all else. Audrey Wise[5] has come near to expressing this distinction by arguing that when women work in industry they put up a struggle to stay human.

I would say that, as a result of their caring for people in the home, women may well return to work with a greater sensitiveness concerning capitalism's capacity to transform workers into the means to profitable ends. But this sensitivity is reinforced by another factor, noted in *The Sunday Times*: 'More women may be openly admitting what was true all along – that they work for their own satisfaction as well as for money.'[6] Women workers tend to make more positive demands of their work situation than their male counterparts, and if one is concerned with working people having a greater say in running their own lives this tendency is advantageous. Women who are out to find self-satisfaction in their place of work can be more politically assertive than men who see their home as their haven, and who have dismissed the possibility of finding self-fulfilment in industry. It is precisely because women are alienated from the home environment that they are more likely to place greater, more positive, demands on the industrial environment.

The men who deplored the 'irrational' behaviour of the women in the paint shop were out of sympathy, not only with the women's concern with working conditions, but also with their obstinacy.

This obstinacy is partly due to inexperience. As more women come to hold office in the trade union movement, women in general may increasingly learn to play the game according to established rules. The spontaneity and assertiveness of ex-full-time houseworkers may be somewhat curbed. The influence is, however, unlikely to be only one way. One effect of the increased unionization of women over recent years has been to awaken in the unions a concern with working conditions in a broader sense. In addition, the production class consciousness of ex-full-time houseworkers could prove to be an asset in any movement aimed at increasing the workers' control of their work situation.

Since women have more than their fair share of parenthood they also have more of the heartache and more of the satisfaction entailed in that experience. Women, on the whole, are also more involved than their husbands in the management of the home. This sometimes finds expression directly in the way they perform in the labour market. For example when Sarah started work in a bookshop:

Sarah Soon after I'd started there this friend of mine, that I'd known over a number of years came, and we're similar types and a similar age. Well we sort of re-organized that shop. Jobs were done in an easy-going way, so we could re-organize in between, and we got certain jobs done at certain times of the day. I think I just carried on as if I was at home really.

— Women like Sarah return to work lacking self-confidence, but after they have found their footing these women have the challenging aspects of their domestic experiences to fortify them in the world of industry. They have more opportunity than most men to develop a sense of their own worth.

These factors result in women being less adequately socialized into the ethos of capitalist industry. Their resulting behaviour sometimes seems audacious:

Rose Me dog had pups, and I had a couple of days off with her, you know. And I went to work and the boss says to me, 'What's been amiss like'. And I said, 'Well me dog's had pups'. He said, 'Christ Almighty! Don't have any cows off the field!' (Chuckles).

Which just goes to show that despite the line of argument presented earlier, Juliet Mitchell is right: sometimes, women do not have even divided loyalty.

Their involvement in domestic management gives women enough confidence to take matters into their own hands. This is evident sometimes in the behaviour of young women who have not yet started their own family, but who have undergone the lifelong pre-training for that role. Joyce Atkins describes an incident where self-help seemed called for:

Joyce When I first went to Wedgwoods conditions were much worse than they are now. In hot weather we sat with our feet in bowls of water. The girls were sweating and sitting with their feet in cold water. Fancy, putting people under a damned glass roof! I felt very very mad about it. And in the end I got on the glass roof, and I put wet clay on the glass roof to cut the sun out. Of course I got told off for that. I was really stripped off for messing the windows up. But the clay was left up there.

Such action is not in itself indicative of class consciousness. However, it does illustrate a point of view in which productive workers are felt to have rights, and sufficient self-assurance to take action in defence of those rights. If schooled in the class struggle this disposition can give the workers' movement a more assertive dynamic.

I have suggested that ex-full-time houseworkers seek self-satisfaction from their experience of paid employment, and that their management of domestic affairs equips them with skills that can be utilized in an attempt to expand their control of their industrial environment. The question as to which struggles develop class confidence is wider than a consideration of industrial conflict

alone. This question could enable us to situate the political importance of social movements outside industry itself. These movements
are an integral part of the working-class movement to the extent
that they are concerned with extending control over the conditions
for the reproduction of labour. For example, the various campaigns
by women's groups to improve and extend social facilities, particularly in the areas involving the care of dependents and improved
health facilities, are *class* campaigns outside of, but not unrelated
to, the industrial sector. The women's movement to control fertility
through the extension of contraception and abortion facilities represents a direct attempt to control an important aspect of the reproduction of labour power. The Claimants' Union, community food
co-ops, and the organized defence of local facilities represent
attempts by working people collectively to control their own lives.

These developments represent an enlargement of the possibilities
facing working men and women. From taking defensive measures
against the effects of capitalist social relations, working people on
occasions, and perhaps increasingly, adopt offensive measures
through which they can begin to shape their industrial, domestic and
local environment. I have argued that married women who return to
the labour market come with a predisposition to gain satisfaction
from industrial work. As a result, although women as compared
with men are less involved in the trade union movement, when it
comes to offensive struggle at the place of employment women are
likely to be as, if not more, assertive than their male counterparts.

The impact of the working-class struggle is not solely to be
assessed in terms of the concrete improvements secured, but also in
terms of an expansion of the workers' organizing capacities, and in
terms of their ability to relate their particular struggle to the
struggles of producers in industry, and to the struggles of producers
of labour in the home and community.

Since women employees are more immersed in the domestic
arena than most male employees they are better placed than the
latter to formulate demands which relate social concerns and industrial concerns. It was precisely the tendency to isolate 'society' and
'industry' as separate domains, which Nichols and Armstrong[7]
identify as the major factor in the ideological inconsistency, which
characterized the class consciousness of the male working-class
Chemco workforce. Women's involvement in the home and community as well as in industry may go some way towards overcoming
such inconsistency.

5 Militancy and acquiescence among women workers*

Kate Purcell

Introduction

It is one of those taken-for-granted assumptions that women, and particularly women workers, are generally more placid, stable, fundamentally exploitable than men. An unconscious parody of the stereotype involved may be found in an article on industrial disruption by C. Northcote Parkinson.[1] He advised managers wishing to avoid industrial relations disputes to employ a high proportion of women workers on the grounds that:

industrial peace is clearly characteristic of trades in which women constitute a third (say) of the labour force and is still more characteristic of those in which they actually predominate. The reasons for this difference between male and female behaviour are clearly basic, women being more concerned about their children's welfare than about loyalty to a trade union or to the working class. Historically, the trade union is an essentially male institution. . . . The militance of a union has something in common with the enthusiasm which pervades the supporters of a football team. Male emotions are involved in which women share to only a limited degree. As for loyalty to the working class, women are usually without it. They have a sneaking regard for the upper class as is shown by their urge to follow the current fashion in dress. One sometimes sees adjacent doors in a public place labelled respectively 'Ladies' and 'Men'. This usage symbolises the fact that the abolition of the gentleman, a proper trade unionist goal, does not mean the abolition of the lady. To down tools is unladylike – a good housewife would at least put them tidily away. Quite apart from that, to strike on a point of principle (as when coming out in sympathy with others) is something which no woman would advocate. More practical than her husband, she would rather have the money for food and clothes.

Like all parodies and stereotypes, this both reflects and distorts reality. Underneath the humour lurks a covert set of beliefs about

* The full text of this chapter can be found in S. Burman (ed.), *Fit Work for Women* (Croom Helm 1979) pp. 112–33.

the differences between men and women, which is widely held.

It is important that the actual and potential roles of women in employment are not obscured by such stereotypes, since they form, as well as reflect, women's and men's attitudes to themselves and each other. As part of the demystification of patriarchal clichés, I think that it is necessary to re-examine what I will call the passive woman worker thesis. To do this, we may proceed in the following way. First, we look at the cultural scaffolding that supports the thesis that women are more passive employees than men. Second, we examine the composition and distribution of female labour in order to see precisely whom we are talking about when we generalize about women workers. Third, we spend some time looking more closely at the concept of militancy and its relationship to behaviour in, and views about, the workplace. And finally, we reassess the passive woman worker thesis in the light of empirical evidence concerning female action which has been labelled militant, acquiescent or counter-militant.

The myth of the passive woman worker

There are three main sources of supporting evidence for the passive woman worker thesis. The first, and most obvious, is the political invisibility of women workers. Female strike leaders, trade union officials and political activists do exist, but they are a small minority of both women and activists. Women workers are less likely to be trade union members than their male counterparts, and they are less likely to be active within their union if they are members. The evidence for this, and some reasons why it is so, are discussed later, in the section of this chapter that deals with the composition of the female labour force.

The second source of evidence frequently referred to in the matter-of-fact explanation of the passivity of women workers is the general psychological profile of womankind deriving from personality tests and tests designed to measure specific characteristics, such as aggressiveness. King summarizes the psychological material with reference to a widely used personality test, the Sixteen Personality Factor Questionnaire (16PF) and emphasizes the overlap between men and women.[2] For example:

men are more assertive, more aggressive, more competitive, more stubborn, more independent than women (though about 20% of the women are higher on this factor than half the men) . . . women are more careful, more conventional, more regulated by external realities, more practical than men (although about 40% of men are higher on this factor than half the women).

Obviously, we could take virtually every one of the characteristics listed and question both its validity as a concept and the validity of the means used to measure it, but my purpose at the moment is not to challenge either psychological methodology or its specific findings concerning sex and gender: merely to illustrate the sort of findings that emerge from psychological investigations, and to point out that such findings of differences in the *average* scores of men and women become reified as *sex* differences, despite the extensive overlap found between men and women.

The third source of support for the common-sense notion of women workers as passive is the sexual division of labour within the family, wherein the main job for the majority of women is presumed to be that of wife and mother. Any other employment undertaken by women is assumed to be a secondary interest, entered into solely for a little extra money. This being so, women's commitment to work itself is assumed to be much weaker than men's, and their interest in pay and conditions is assumed to be less liable to provoke industrial conflict because their work is seen as temporary, or at least as subsidiary to their main concerns, their earnings being basically an inessential bonus undertaken for what is commonly termed 'pin money'. Apart from their lower commitment to work, the corollary of their greater investment in the family and their role as consumers has been taken to predispose them to be privatized, individualistic and essentially a reactionary brake to working-class revolutionary zeal. According to this thesis, women defuse the pressures built up by social inequalities in two major ways. In the long term, they pass on their privatized, individualistic values to the next generation in their role as the main socializing agents of children; and in the short term, they exert pressure on husbands to avoid militant action which threatens the family income and stability.[3] These beliefs about women's nature and priorities support the impression that the stereotypes of man the breadwinner and woman the homemaker are somehow part of the natural order and any deviation from the gender roles prescribed is a distortion of Nature. In fact, the sexual division of labour does not conform to this complementary, asymmetrical pattern, as an examination of the workforce will indicate.

I should like to emphasize four points concerning women's employment patterns. First, there is a tendency for the majority of women to experience breaks in the continuity of their employment, which are related to family-building patterns and indicate their dual role as domestic workers and members of the labour force. Second, over one-third of women workers work part-time, and this is where the greatest increase in women's employment has taken place in recent years. Third, the majority of women in employment work in the tertiary sector of the economy: they provide services rather than products and represent the greater part of the growth in white-collar employment over the last two decades. It needs to be remembered, too, that a high proportion of the women employed in manufacturing are engaged in clerical and administrative work, constituting the service sector *within* the industry. Fourth, women in employment tend to have lower average hourly earnings than men in the same industry, to be graded as having less skill, and to have less authority. Most women in employment are classified as semi-skilled. Finally, it should be pointed out that there are significant regional variations in the structure and size of the female labour force. According to the 1971 census, female economic activity ranged from 45 per cent in the West Midlands to 36 per cent in Wales, and obviously there is concentration within such large areas, which leads to greater variations between communities, particularly between urban and rural areas. A recent study of the labour force participation of married women[4] concludes that the *demand* for labour in a given region is probably the most influential factor in determining the level of economic activity (which includes counting registered unemployed as economically active): where jobs for women are few, the 'discouraged worker' effect operates and married women do not bother to register as unemployed. It is clear that traditions of female employment and current rates of economic activity affect not only women's activity *per se*, but also their attitudes to, and experience of, employment. The married women I interviewed in Stockport,[5] where female activity rates are 45 per cent[6] and have always been high, define their work as normal and necessary, whereas those women interviewed in the course of a similar exercise in Hull, where the widespread employment of married women is more recent and male unemployment rates are higher, frequently made references to the fortuitous nature of their work, which was mostly badly paid and devoid of obvious intrinsic satisfactions.[7]

Women in trade unions

The final characteristic of women in employment with which we shall concern ourselves is their membership of trade unions. Over one-third of all female employees in 1976 were trade union members, an increase of 58 per cent from 1966. Women comprised approximately one-quarter of the membership of unions affiliated to the Trades Union Congress (TUC) over the same period, and almost two-thirds of new recruits were women. Some unions have recently become more conscious of the membership potential of women workers and have adjusted their recruitment policies accordingly, in line with the current increased interest of the TUC in issues concerning women in employment. The bulk of the increase, however, is explained by developments in the tertiary sector, notably the expansion of white-collar unions in local and central government administration, office work and the National Health Service. As the concentration of women's employment would lead one to expect, women's trade union membership is similarly concentrated. The TUC-affiliated unions where women formed a majority of the membership in 1976 are shown in Table 8.

Table 8   *Women as a proportion of the membership of TUC-affiliated unions*

Union	Female members (per cent)
Union of Shop, Distributive and Allied Workers	59
National Union of Tailors and Garment Workers	88
Association of Professional, Executive, Computer and Clerical Staff (APEX)	55
Tobacco Workers' Union	66
Confederation of Health Service Employees	74
National Union of Teachers	75
Civil and Public Services Association	68
Inland Revenue Staff Federation	56
Ceramic and Allied Trade Union	53
National Union of Hosiery and Knitwear Workers	73
Amalgamated Society of Textile Workers and Kindred Trades	58
Rossendale Union of Boot, Shoe and Slipper Operatives	64
Amalgamated Association of Felt Hat Trimmers and Wool Formers	100

Source: TUC Congress Report, 1976

The most interesting point which emerges from this list is that all these unions except APEX are essentially one-industry unions, so it makes sense to look for an explanation of militancy or lack of it in factors inherent in the organization and character of the industry concerned; the predominance of women in the industry is only one factor.

Militancy

The *Shorter Oxford Dictionary* definition of militant as an adjective is 'engaged in warfare, warring' and as a noun 'one engaged in war or strife'. The media follow this definition loosely, but they almost invariably use 'militant' as an immutable descriptive adjective, as in 'militant miners' leader Arthur Scargill' or as a noun as in 'the militants are opposed to the postal ballot', which implies that militancy is an ideological predisposition which precedes and pre-scribes action rather than a specific response to specific situations. The female shop stewards we interviewed, when asked to define the term militant, were unwilling to discuss it in abstract terms or to make generalizations. Militancy was seen as an aspect of behaviour, but they suggested that one had to consider behaviour in its context, as a reaction to situational variables (as the following quotes illustrate):

I can be militant very much at times. If I had a grievance with the foreman and he was trying to get out of it in a crafty way I would get very annoyed. Militant means strong. I can stick to my guns once I've made a decision.

I can be militant if I know I'm in the right. I wouldn't be militant for militancy's sake. Some people can be fobbed off for quite a long time by management's answers. You have to weigh up whether they intend giving you what you want or whether you're banging your head against a brick wall. Sometimes being militant is the only way to let them see if you are sincere – you've *got* to withdraw labour in some form.

The sociological literature on militancy tends to be confined largely to an examination of trade union militancy, and, with few excep-tions, tends to take militancy as a self-explanatory term which does not itself require examination or explication. There are two excep-tions worth noting. R. M. Blackburn[8] has said that 'militancy is basically the extent to which an organization will go in asserting the interests of its members against employers in fulfilling a *trade union* function', but acknowledges that manifestation of militancy thus defined depends, as well as on the 'character' of the union, on 'opportunities and chances of success of such action, which in turn are governed by the work and market situations as well as by the wealth and completeness [i.e., membership density] of the union . . . and by the need for militancy, since the behaviour of the employer is always an important element in the situation'. V. L. Allen[9] devotes an entire chapter to 'The Meaning of Militancy' and reinforces the relativity of the concept, which he stresses refers to methods rather than aims: 'exploiting fully whatever power or influence they possess'.[10] This does not preclude the making of militant *demands*, which he rightly sees as part of the bargaining process and as such, a means rather than an end. His final definition of militancy is action where:

the aims consist of exploiting market advantages in order to maximise wages and get the best possible working conditions and hours of work. The methods consist of negotiating with employers according to the profitability of their enterprises, using price-leadership tactics to force up wages in the least efficient enterprises and of refusing to accept any unsatisfactory price for labour. A union acting this way will provide the greatest benefits for its members within the capitalist system. It cannot do more without altering the system.[11]

The final use of militancy is that generally implied by much media comment and by the attitudes of some political activists of the left, where little action short of that designed to alter or weaken the capitalist system in the short or medium term is considered to be militant. In this sense, militant becomes synonymous with revolutionary, both as an adjective and noun.

By any of these definitions, it is not difficult to find examples of women's militancy and even of women behaving more militantly than men, both in industry and elsewhere. The Trico strike, the Fakenham Leather Factory work-in, the Leeds Clothing strike, and the strike at Salford Electrical Instruments at Heywood are all comparatively recent examples of women's militancy, in some cases without the support or with the declared opposition of their representative union and/or male fellow workers. Labour history provides numerous examples of women's strikes and women's active participation in the development of the labour movement. Feminist historians are unearthing the hidden women activists of history and it is surprising (although on reflection it should not be) how high the female attendance at Chartist and labour movement demonstrations and meetings was, and how high the female proportion was of those who were charged and imprisoned as leaders and activists.[12]

My own current research indicates that men and women in the engineering and clothing industries in Stockport join and express support for unions and engage in widespread action according to the traditions of their industry rather than according to sex. The attitudes and behaviour of men and women in engineering are more alike than those of women in engineering and women in clothing. Tom Lupton[13] came to similar conclusions in the course of his classic participant-observer study of workers in electrical engineering and rainwear, in so far as day-to-day industrial action was concerned. He found that engineering workers operated collectively whereas the rainwear factory employees were highly individualistic, regardless of gender.

Two observations need to be made to counterbalance the impression that female- and male-dominated industries and unions are radically different with respect to industrial relations conflict. First, although it can be misleading to discuss militancy in terms of recorded industrial action, as far as that aspect of militancy is concerned, it is as well to remember that strikes are not distributed evenly throughout the industries which are labelled strike-prone – such as coal-mining, docks, shipbuilding and motor vehicle manufacture. In manufacturing, 95 per cent of establishments were free of officially recorded stoppages and only 0.1 per cent of establishments had seven or more stoppages in the period 1971–3. Further analysis by industry confirms the point that stoppages are concentrated in a small minority of establishments and that these 'strike-prone' plants are 'distributed among a number of industries rather than being concentrated in a few. There are no industries in which stoppage activity is widespread'.[14] As an example of the extent to which industrial statistics can be misleading, it has been calculated that between 1962 and 1965 in the motor industry, 60 per cent of working time lost from 'within the companies' occurred in one firm alone.[15]

Second, it should be remembered that not all strikes in male-dominated industries are either exclusively or predominantly men's strikes. One of the most famous recent women's strikes was at Fords in Dagenham in 1968, about the grading of women's jobs, where a three-week strike ended in victory for the women. In other words, it is very misleading to take aggregate strike statistics and correlate these with the proportion of females in employment in the industry, as Parkinson did, and conclude that women are less militant than men. The most important correlation is with plant size, with establishments employing over one thousand people being significantly more strike-prone than smaller units.[16] This draws our attention once more to organizational factors.

The passive woman worker thesis does not merely suggest that women are unwilling to engage in industrial action on their own behalf. There is also the implication that women are positively opposed to militancy, and have a pacifying influence on the workforce generally. It is possible to document examples of apparent counter-militant activity by women whose main occupation is mother and wife, such as examples of wives demonstrating against their husbands' strike action; and it is even easier to find examples of women's apparent acquiescence in badly paid work under appalling conditions. It is often argued that the majority of women accept pay and conditions which the majority of men would not work for. Do such examples support the passive woman worker thesis? I will argue that they do not.

The passive woman worker: a reappraisal

If we go back to the definitions of militancy given by Blackburn and Allen, which, like the definitions given by the shop stewards I interviewed, consider militancy as behaviour in specific contexts, it is possible to consider women workers' behaviour in a different light. To do this, it is also necessary to consider the tensions between the family and production and the resultant market position of the majority of women, which stems directly from the domestic sexual division of labour and the ideology that veils it.

Women's market position

The theory that most women's orientation to work is different from that of most men, and that their commitment to employment is lower than men's because their other role of wife and mother is considered by them to be their 'main' job, has frequently been used to account for women's apparent acquiescence at work as manifested, for example, in low involvement in trade union activities. Blackburn, for example, points out that there are clear differences in the class positions of men and women in terms of both work and market situations, since women generally do lower grade routine work for less pay and poor chances of promotion. He considers the important variable in determining militancy to be the degree of commitment to work, which he sees as partly a cause and partly a result of women's lower class position. He suggests that work may be seen as only temporary and often the work itself, with its low status and poor prospects, offers little incentive to higher commitment.

It has been observed in various contexts such as newly industrialising nations that unless commitment is sufficiently high, workers are unlikely to become involved in unions. Thus, skilled workers tend to unionise before unskilled and amongst women it appears to be in occupations offering them some prospects of a career, such as teaching, that unions are most successful in recruiting.[17]

Blackburn concludes that, from the limited evidence available, it seems that variations in union membership among women, as among men, are due to factors determining the level of their commitment to work; and he seems to be talking about factors intrinsic to the job rather than extrinsic orientations. I think that Blackburn is correct in diagnosing women's inferior class and market positions as the basis of their lower rates of union membership and activism, and wrong in setting up the intermediary of commitment to work between them. It seems to me that the crucial variable is the lack of industrial bargaining power of the majority of women, deriving from their own position in the labour market and the market position of the industries in which they are concentrated.

It is not within the scope of this chapter to discuss the reasons for the concentration of female employees in certain industries and occupations, but I will take the sexual division of labour in the workforce as given and ask: are there any reasons why most female-dominated industries should have lower union density and be less subject to militant action, *apart* from the preponderance of women?

There are two distinct categories of female employment: white-collar service occupations, and manual labour in industries characterized by unstable product market conditions. Within these large categories there are distinct sub-categories, and I would emphasize that it is possible to understand militancy only by relating specific manifestations of it directly to the pressures from which they emerge; but I will make a few generalizations which seem to me to be valid, concentrating on the manual labour sector. It has already been stated that white-collar unionization represents the biggest growth area in trade union organization generally as well as in the organization of women, and developments in the industrial relations behaviour of white-collar employees have been discussed in detail elsewhere.[18]

In most of the manufacturing industries where women workers are found in large numbers, the unstable product market conditions of the industries in question make it improbable that industrial action will be perceived as likely to be effective. Indeed, it may well be irrational, so that it is unlikely to be resorted to even where other characteristics normally correlated with militant shop floor behaviour, such as piecework, are present. Clothing and footwear are the two most graphic examples of such industries. They have comparatively unsophisticated technology and operate in a highly competitive market where there is a high turnover of firms and low profit margins. In industrial relations at both national and local levels there tends to be a normative consensus that conflict which interferes with production is to be avoided at all costs. Referring to the footwear industry, Armstrong, Goodman and Wagner[19] comment that 'there appears to be a close and general awareness amongst employees of the relatively fine margin between economic survival and collapse of their employer who in many cases is not a remote impersonal figure but a known individual'.

In addition, many of the female-dominated occupations with low union density – catering, clothing, footwear, distributive trades and some of the service industries – also have other features which are correlated in other industries with a low level of industrial action, independently of the ratios of men and women employed. They are made up of small firms, or at least small units of production, which means that the workforce is scattered and unable to express (or often perceive) common interests. The unions which represent such workers are also characterized by high membership turnover reflecting the high labour turnover of the industries and the difficulty of organizing such a diffuse population. This has a circular reinforcing effect: 'the basic function of trade unions is participation in job regulation'.[20] The more effectively a union is able to fulfil this function, the more successful it is in recruiting members.

The crucial fact to remember here is that women and men in such industries are similarly characterized by high job turnover and apathy towards their unions. Handing in one's notice is ultimately the only effective short-term response to a collective problem where there is no developed collective solidarity. This is the response of many unskilled workers of both sexes in exploitative work situations. Coates and Silburn,[21] discussing poverty, observe that in a slum where the roof leaks, it is a much easier, practicable and more effective solution in the short term to put out a bucket to catch the drips than to organize a petition or campaign for better housing – that is, to adopt the individual as opposed to the collective response. Women workers are often faced with a choice which is analogous to this, and a decision to choose the effective short-term solution rather than the possibly ineffective long-term solution may not be less rational – or less militant.

Women and militancy

This may go some of the way to explaining women's lower levels of union organization as against that of men, but it is also necessary to consider why their activism is lower when they *are* union members. There is a great deal of truth in Parkinson's reflection that trade unions have generally been and essentially are male institutions, and there are numerous documented examples of male hostility to the admission of women members and the support of what are seen as 'women's issues', such as equal pay and the provision of day nurseries. Most of this derives from the historical fact that women's labour has been used to foster competition and depress the value of labour power (in the same way as immigrant labour has), but the result has been that unions have developed as male-orientated organizations. The organization and timetables of formal trade union activities reinforce the sexual division of labour, which implies the provision of domestic services within the family by a more socially passive partner. By this, I mean that it is difficult to be an active member of a trade union without being prepared to spend extensive periods of non-work time on union responsibilities and activities. I have discussed in a previous paper[22] the fact that married women shop stewards whom I have interviewed were generally not prepared to attend evening branch meetings and weekend conferences, but I argued that this was not because they were uninterested, or were less interested in the union than in their families, but because they were prevented from doing so *because of* their family commitments, often mentioning explicitly that husbands discouraged or forbade such activities. They accepted that they had to cook the supper and wash and iron in the evenings, not because they thought such activities right and proper for women, but because they saw no way out of it: their acceptance of the domestic role was pragmatic rather than ideological.[23] It is significant that most active female shop stewards in our sample were either unmarried or childless.

This raises the question of whether militancy and militant *trade union* action are synonymous or even necessarily related. I have avoided discussing the common confusion between militancy and activism, which are distinct though related concepts. I have concentrated on the former to the exclusion of the latter except in so far as activism is *militant* activism. In fact, there are few trade union activists among both the male and female working population, and while gender is not a dependent variable in activism, marriage or motherhood for women may be, as may the 'male club' aspect of trade unionism, which is likely to inhibit women from participating. Trade union movement activists generally have ideological predispositions to behave and react in specific ways, but whereas activism can be independent of the work situation and current work experience, militancy is unlikely to be. Both the Allen and Blackburn definitions of militancy implied rational maximization of outcomes and it is clear that joining a union or operating collectively may not be the way to do this. In many of the clothing factories where I have been interviewing men and women in Stockport, the majority of the employees decided against joining the appropriate union because they considered it ineffectual and felt that they could bargain over piecework prices individually or in groups more effectively than the union would. If we take one factory sample as a case study, only 26 per cent were union members and of the remaining 74 per cent, 72 per cent were neither anti-union nor apathetic but gave specific reasons for their non-membership relating to the reputation of, or their previous experience of, the union. Seventy-two per cent of the non-members had formerly been trade union members and 45 per cent of these were disenchanted members of the appropriate recognized union, the National Union of Tailors and Garment Workers.

The reasons given by most union members in all the industries of which I have experience, when asked why they had joined the union, were along the lines of 'it was the expected thing'. In the light of this response, *refusal* to join may be a more politically conscious decision, or it may be at least a realistic assessment of the appropriately rational behaviour for the circumstances. Research on trade union membership suggests that the majority of employees who join unions do not do so for ideological reasons, except to the extent that 'the union gets us pay rises and I wouldn't want to be a free riding passenger' is an ideological response.

From a consideration of the industries and unions, it seems to me that situational variables can be used to give plausible explanations of both women's militancy and women's acquiescence in industrial relations, which rely very little on sex or even gender *per se*. What about the examples of women's counter-militancy, or even the privatized woman generally, whose main investment in the family has been accused of conflicting with class solidarity? If we make a distinction between offensive and defensive militancy, I think that even these aspects of women's behaviour can be seen as a rational type of militancy in relation to their class and market situation. I define offensive militancy as the struggle to *advance* material well-being and/or political consciousness, and defensive militancy as the struggle to *preserve* material well-being. A high proportion of action labelled by the press and participants as industrial militancy is defensive militancy: for example, the refusal to accept redundancies. For women whose sole or main occupation is mother and homemaker, anti-strike activism and home-centredness can be seen as defensive militancy and rational behaviour on a short-term basis, whether or not they are also seen as manifestations of false consciousness in relation to longer-term interests. Such a paradox is not difficult to understand if we consider contradictions between the ideological pressures upon workers of both sexes and their experience of work and family life. Marilyn Porter[24] has initiated an exploration of the complex relationships between consciousness and experience, particularly what she calls the 'second-hand experience' of industrial disputes that strikers' wives have. She concludes that people who lack direct experience of industry can only make sense of industrial disputes in terms of the effect such disputes have on their own daily lives and any additional information that gets filtered through to them by other individuals and the media. Women's militancy and acquiescence, both at work and in the home can be argued to be a function of their experience as workers rather than as women. Both men and women generally react in ways which seem to them to be rational according to the possibilities of their market situation and the market situation of their employers. Women's market situation is frequently restricted and prescribed by gender, but men similarly situated in the labour market behave in the same way.

6 Women as employees: social consciousness and collective action*

Richard Brown

In the majority of cases where they have not been ignored altogether, women employees have been regarded by industrial sociologists in one of two ways: on the one hand as indistinguishable from men in any respect relevant to their attitudes and actions at work; and on the other as giving rise to special problems, for the employer and/or the families or communities from which they come.[1] Both approaches are inadequate and the adoption of either means that the possibilities of comparative study of the expectations and actions of men and women in industry are generally lost – possibilities which could aid the analysis of some of the central problems of industrial sociology, as well as provide a more adequate understanding of women's position in the labour market and at work.

Social consciousness and collective action

There are two questions to be considered with respect to collective action by women employees: whether they are less likely to take such action than men in comparable employment situations; and if they are, what explanations can be offered for such differences in patterns of action. These questions arise given the assumption that in our sort of society all employees have conflicting interests with their employer and must act collectively to protect and further their interests.[2] Consideration of the actions of women employees may help identify the conditions which affect whether or not such action occurs. I shall discuss the evidence with regard to three areas of collective action: 'regulation' of output under payment by results schemes; trade union membership; and strikes.

* This chapter is an excerpt from R. Brown 'Women as employees: some comments on research in industrial sociology', in D. Barker and S. Allen (eds.), *Dependence and Exploitation in Work and Marriage* (Longman 1976), pp. 33–46.

Regulation of output under payment by results schemes

The Hawthorne Experiments showed very different patterns of behaviour under incentive schemes between the women in the Relay Assembly Test Room and the men in the Bank Wiring Observation Room.[3] An apparently similar finding resulted from Lupton's study of two workshops: women in a waterproof garment factory accepted management definition of their role, emphasized the norm of hard work and 'looking after number one', and did not exercise any 'will to control' even when management was unable to provide the appropriate conditions; men in a transformer assembly workshop had a clear conception of what represented tolerable effort and fair pay, haggled with rate-fixers over the bonus prices, regulated their output to prevent rate-cutting and operated an elaborate 'fiddle' to compensate for management shortcomings in the planning of work, and to stabilize their weekly earnings.[4] Although Lupton does not rule out altogether the possibility that in general women differ from men in their likely reactions to payment by results schemes, or indeed management controls more generally,[5] his explanation of these two cases discounts the importance of the sex difference. This is because the expected reaction to the incentive payments system appeared to characterize each factory as a whole: the men in the garment factory behaved in much the same way as the women Lupton observed; and in the engineering factory 'in general the women had, so far as I could ascertain, accepted the standards set by the men. They haggled with the rate-fixer about prices, and employed methods similar to those employed by the men when booking in work, to minimise the effects of waiting time, and so on'.[6]

Lupton's interpretation is reinforced by Cunnison's[7] discussion of another waterproof garment factory where men and women worked on the same tasks in the same workshop, and both sexes shared the prevailing norm of militant individualism. In the history of the industry this tradition appears to have been passed from men to women rather than the opposite. Klein,[8] who studied an engineering factory where a minority of the operators were women, reported that all of them set a ceiling to output and earnings on the incentive scheme.[9]

The studies cited cannot be regarded as conclusive, but if the suggestion is right that women as such do not differ from men in their willingness to regulate their output according to group norms and in opposition to management's expectations, the problem arises of accounting for the widely held conventional view 'of the women industrial worker as a "sucker", easy to exploit, and with no capacity for collective action, or as women would perhaps say, "women are more conscientious than men"'.[10] This may, of course, merely be part of male ideology serving to justify men's claims to superiority. It may arise because women follow the lead given by men whatever that lead may be. It may, however, reflect the very different occupational and industrial distribution of women manual workers. Lupton's studies suggested that collective action of this sort on the shop floor is more likely to occur given certain technical, economic and social conditions. It is possible that women employees are to be found predominantly in situations which lack these conditions. The operation of the labour market would then become a central part of the explanation.[11]

Trade union membership

The occupational and industrial distribution of women employees is central to any explanation of the patterns of trade union membership. During the post-war period trade union membership in the United Kingdom has increased from over 9 million in 1948 to 11 million in 1970, and after declining slightly from the 1948 peak of 45.2 per cent 'density' (proportion of total employees), the 1970 total of union members represented a density of 46.9 per cent. Within these totals women employees have consistently been less strongly unionized than men; only 24 per cent in 1948, and only 25 per cent of a considerably larger number of women in employment in 1970, were members of trade unions.[12] This difference between men and women remains when manual workers and white-collar workers are considered separately; indeed female manual workers are less likely to belong to a trade union than male white-collar workers. However, the absolute and relative rates of growth of women's trade union membership have been higher over the whole post-war period, and especially in the years since 1964 when most of the increase in white-collar union density has occurred.[13]

It is not possible, however, to conclude from these figures that women employees as such are necessarily reluctant to join trade unions. Writing on the growth of trade unions in the cotton industry, for example, Turner[14] comments: 'Until the First World War, indeed . . . the cotton unions remained the only ones to organise women workers effectively. And that they did in a large way.' But he also goes on to comment on the lower levels of participation by women members in union affairs.[15] Clegg and his colleagues make the membership claim even more strongly, though in a footnote: 'In cotton, women were almost as well organised as men. In 1910 the proportion was 39 per cent compared with 44 per cent for the whole industry.'[16] More recently Blackburn has shown that women bank staff are less likely to join the union but has pointed out that the sex difference also corresponds with differences in the status of the work done.[17] Lockwood is more emphatic in dismissing 'feminization' as a factor in the unionization of clerical workers:

It was Bernard Shaw who said that the two groups most resistant to trade unionism were clerks and women. Women clerks, therefore, might well be considered a most formidable obstacle to the development of blackcoated unionism. . . . The generalisation is not in accordance with the facts. A high proportion of women in a clerical occupation is not universally associated with a low degree of unionisation, nor does unionisation necessarily proceed farthest when women are in a minority. Indeed, if a generalisation is to be made, it is that the proportion of women in clerical unions is usually roughly equal to their representation in the field of employment which the unions seek to organise. Differences in the degree of unionisation are therefore to be attributed to something other than the differences in the sex ratio of the group.[18]

Thus there are suggestions in both historical and contemporary studies that whether or not women join trade unions is to be explained not in terms of their sex, but in terms of the nature of their work situation. The industrial distribution of women employees, as it results from the operation of the labour market, becomes a crucial part of the explanation. Women work predominantly in industries, such as clothing and footwear, and distribution, where firms and plants are small. Trade unionism is strongest where large numbers are employed. On the basis of regression analysis Bain argues that:

The fact that a low degree of unionization is associated with a high proportion of women and that women generally are not as highly unionized as men can be accounted for by differences in the way males and females are distributed across firms. . . . Density of unionization is higher in areas where the average size of establishments is large and employment concentrated than in areas where the average size of establishments is small and employment diffused. . . . The proportion of women is highest in the smaller establishments and lowest in larger establishments. . . .

The proportion of women has not been in itself a significant determinant of the pattern of manual or white collar unionism in Britain.[19]

This finding is based on aggregate data and would not necessarily apply in all situations. It also leaves unexplained the persistent belief that women are more reluctant to join trade unions than men, a belief which can become a self-fulfilling prophecy when it is acted on by male shop stewards or union officials as Beynon and Blackburn[20] described in their discussion of the way the trade union became 'the men's affair'.

Indeed, any adequate explanation of levels of union membership must include consideration of what it means to the actors involved to belong to a union, as well as reference to structural factors such as size of plant. The links between the ways in which the labour market operates, women's actions as 'potential' trade unionists, and women's and men's perceptions of trade unions and of women as possible union members, are probably complex and interrelated. Do men, for example, oppose the employment of women in certain occupations and industries in part because they see them as difficult to organize, and consequently likely to depress pay levels or worsen the effort bargain? If they do, does this help perpetuate the very situation of which they disapprove? Do the different priorities at work held by women as compared with men (for example, hours and conditions) mean that their main concerns are given second place to men's (for example, overtime) in male-dominated workplace union organizations, which thus continue to fail to attract their interest and support? Does women's experience of being excluded from certain areas of work by male trade unionists encourage them to see union membership as not for them – and thus reinforce the men's prejudices? The labour market operates as it does partly because of the choices and preferences and definitions of the situation of the actors involved, but these in part reflect experience of the way it operates. Exploration of such interconnections might not only provide a more complete explanation of the pattern of union membership among women, but contribute to our understanding of union membership in general as well.

In the case of strikes there are, so far as I am aware, no statistics of the actions of women employees as compared with those of men, not even approximate figures like those of union membership. The most strike-prone industries in Britain, however, in the post-war period – the docks, coal-mining, motor vehicles, shipbuilding, metal manufacture, construction, and so on – are industries in which women are not employed in any numbers. In addition one of the best-known attempts to explain inter-industry differences in strike proneness appears to assume that women are less inclined to strike:[21]

If the job is physically easy and performed in pleasant surroundings, skilled and responsible, steady, and subject to set rules and close supervision, it will attract women or the more submissive type of man who will abhor strikes.[22]

Such assumptions about women employees' strike activity cannot go entirely unquestioned. In a review of strikes in the inter-war period and in the years before the First World War, Knowles certainly denies that women as such are less inclined to strike:

Although there is no quantitative evidence here, it is clear that women – having regard of their numbers in industry – have played an important part in strike movements. True the relative youthfulness of women workers and the other consequences of their 'mortality by marriage', as well as the hostility of the established men's Trade Unions to the organisation of the exploited minority, did for a long time inhibit the large-scale organisation of women, but it is doubtful how far these things have restrained women from striking.

Possibly their very lack of economic opportunity and responsibility has influenced them in the opposite sense. Women, wrote Barbara Drake, have never been backward in strikes: 'They are, on the contrary, more often accused by their officials of being too forward, so that they "down tools" for frivolous reasons and often drag the men after them. It is a fact that the courage and loyalty of unorganised women in supporting organised men have been among the principal factors in deciding the latter to organise them.' The authoress had in mind, of course, the great women's strike movement of the late 1880s and of 1911–13, which opened and closed the sweated trade agitation.[23]

In his study, Hyman[24] cites some more recent examples of strikes in which women have been involved. He argues that although indust-rial conflict among women workers may manifest itself in alterna-tive ways (for example, high labour turnover), it 'does not mean, however, that women are never prominent in industrial disputes'. But he, in some contrast to Knowles, concludes, 'Women tend to be employed in industries and occupations where collective organiza-tion is least strong, and they strike far less frequently than men.' In a study of the motor industry, Turner and his colleagues[25] could find no relationship between the proportion of women employed in motor car factories and their relative strike proneness. More recently the night cleaners' campaign, the Ford machinists' strike in 1968, the Leeds clothing strike and the work-in by women in Fakenham have been well publicized examples of women employees' willingness to take strike action; and the fifth issue of *Red Rag* (no date) was able to include a long list of strikes in which women employees had been involved during 1972 and 1973.

Thus, as in the case of other forms of collective action, the situation appears to be one where it is not possible to claim that women employees as such are unwilling or unable to strike. But women do work predominantly in industries and occupations which are less strike prone (and may be part of the reason for this?); and they do share characteristics like lower levels of union membership and higher rates of labour turnover which are associated with a lesser propensity to strike. What might be most illuminating, in terms of the more general question of explaining manifestations of industrial conflict, would be research which studied in comparison with other situations those where women have taken collective action. In such situations one could perhaps see more clearly than elsewhere the ways in which changes in conditions of action and changes in 'consciousness' are combined and interrelated and lead to collective action.

7   Unions: the men's affair?*

Huw Beynon and Robert Blackburn

The unionization of the workers at Brompton had begun among the
men; the impetus coming in the first instance from the men on the
night shift. This was predictable and can be explained in terms of the
greater centrality given to work in the lives of the men and con-
comitantly their previous involvement with the traditions of trade
unionism. Given this, however, the unionizing process within the
Brompton factory had consequences for the ways in which men and
women related to the trade union.

Roy,[1] among others, has indicated that the union organizing
campaign within a factory entails quite severe tensions between
workers and management and also among workers, and he shows
how the campaign involves a number of dedicated active trade
unionists within the factory organizing support with which to confront management. This process was in evidence in the Brompton
factory, where the senior stewards were concerned to obtain a union
shop. Shop-stewards were sponsored by these senior stewards – a
potential steward being someone who either took an immediate
interest in the union when he arrived or who came into the fore-
ground during a sectional dispute. The potential steward was
appraised in terms of his dedication to developing a union organization in the factory and the main demand upon him was that he
obtained full membership on his section.

This process at Brompton was complicated by the presence of the
women. The senior stewards firmly believed that the women could
not be organized. Most of the men supported this view and justified
it by the claim that the women either worked for 'pin money'[2] or
were waiting around to get married. This belief had its greatest
consequence upon the trade union organization on the night shift.
Here, in combination with the relatively high level of union

* This chapter is an excerpt from H. Beynon and R. Blackburn, *Perceptions of Work* (Cambridge University Press 1972).

membership achieved on the shift and the identification of their work as 'women's work', this belief in the fact that women could not be organized reinforced the social isolation of the shift described earlier in *Perceptions of Work*.

An example of the consequences of such isolation is demonstrated by a strike that took place during the summer of our fieldwork. The company had employed students for the summer holidays, and some of these had been put on the night shift. These students were under the age of 21 and so were not paid the full night-shift rate. The shop-stewards had long understood that no one under the age of 21 would be employed on the night shift. The issue was a complicated one and was seen by the stewards to have far-reaching implications. 'The thin end of the wedge' was frequently mentioned. While we cannot, at this time, examine the strike in any detail, we can fruitfully relate two of the main tactics adopted by the night-shift stewards which were strongly supported by the men. The first related to the students. It was seen to be important for the students to realize that the strike was not against them. In fact this feeling was an important reason for the strike being articulated in terms of 'full rate for all night-shift workers'. This slogan served to unite the interests of both the night-shift workers and the students. The second tactic was of more fundamental importance. Although the issue could be seen as one which potentially affected all workers at Brompton, and although a number of stewards on the day shift emphasized this and indicated that they could 'pull a strike in support of the night shift', the night-shift stewards insisted that it was a 'night-shift affair', and that 'we can handle it better ourselves'.[3] These two tactics taken together are interesting. The stewards on the night shift were able to argue that it was important that the students appreciated the issues involved. They were all extremely pleased when a representative of the students addressed a strike meeting and expressed strong support and approval of the strike. The senior steward on the night shift recounted this event on a number of occasions, pointing out how the action itself was important as it fostered a greater understanding between students and workers. In spite of this, however, the men and shop-stewards on the night shift were not prepared to see the situation as one in which the support of the women could be obtained. There was no attempt made to 'open the eyes of the women' or even to keep the women informed of events. During the two days of the strike the interviewer casually discussed the strike with several women, none of whom had any idea of what was involved.

While it is important that too much is not drawn from this particular example, it does indicate the extent to which the 'image' of women held by the men in general and the night-shift stewards in particular affected the way in which the union developed at Brompton. Granted that women tend to be less involved in work and less committed to a trade union, the fact of the men organizing themselves had further consequences for the relationship between the women and the union. For the women the union became 'the men's affair'. No women attended the branch meeting. Even the women stewards insisted that the branch was the place where the men discussed things. It can be seen, therefore, that the belief in the inability of women to be committed union members can take on elements of a self-fulfilling prophecy. Once the involvement of women is so defined by the men who organize and increase their power, the definition becomes sustained through its institutionalization. It will be useful during this chapter to examine some of the consequences of this process and to question the validity of the particular image of women workers adhered to by the union organizers at Brompton.

Before we look at this in any detail it will be of interest to look further at the way the workers perceived their union by considering their reasons for joining or not joining.

Reasons for joining or not joining

Once we had established whether or not respondents were in the union, the first question we asked of members, which specifically related to trade unionism, was 'How did you come to join the trade union at Brompton?' Non-members were asked whether there was a specific reason why they had not joined. The responses are presented in Table 9.

A high proportion of all union members stressed ideological reasons for joining the union.[4] Over half the men, 32 per cent of the full-time women, and 43 per cent of the part-time women members gave responses of this type. In general these responses laid stress upon the need for the worker to rely upon collective action. Frequently they were loosely formulated: 'You need a union don't you'; 'We'd get nowhere without a union – I've always been a union man'; – but occasionally members were more explicit. 'The unions

Table 9   *Reasons for membership or non-membership of the union*

Union members	Day men	Night men	Full-time women	Part-time women	All
				(percentages in brackets)	
'Ideological' unionist	22 (51)	18 (53)	12 (32)	10 (44)	62 (46)
'Business' unionist	7 (16)	4 (12)	6 (16)	1 (4)	18 (13)
Problem	2 (5)	2 (6)	6 (16)	— (—)	10 (7)
Everyone else joined	7 (16)	9 (26)	10 (26)	10 (44)	36 (26)
Asked to join	5 (12)	1 (3)	3 (8)	1 (4)	10 (7)
Other	— (—)	— (—)	1 (3)	1 (4)	2 (1)
Total	43(100)	34(100)	38(101)	23(100)	138(100)

Non-members	Day men	Night men	Full-time women	Part-time women	All
				(percentages in brackets)	
Anti-trade union ideology	4 (19)	1 (8)	1 (1)	6 (11)	12 (8)
This union is no good	3 (14)	2 (17)	14 (20)	4 (7)	23 (14)
Ex-member	8 (38)	7 (58)	18 (25)	4 (7)	37 (23)
Never been asked	4 (19)	1 (8)	17 (24)	25 (46)	47 (30)
No need to join	— (—)	— (—)	17 (24)	12 (22)	29 (18)
Other	2 (10)	1 (8)	4 (6)	4 (7)	11 (7)
Total	21(100)	12 (99)	71(100)	55(100)	159(100)

have got the worker everything that he's got today. Above all they've given him his self respect. I'd say a lot of things against them – especially this one here – but we just couldn't think of being without one. A bad union is better than no union at all', was a response from an operator on the day shift. Responses of this order indicate the influence of working-class history and tradition in the area. Membership is precipitated by wider considerations than the position of the individual worker in the firm; it draws upon the whole history of experience shared by the worker, his family and his class.

On a more instrumental level we have the 'business unionist' response. Unlike the ideological union member, the business unionist tends to stress the economic advantages that he, as an individual, receives by virtue of his union membership. Strike pay, insurance, sick benefits, were all quoted here, together with the protection that the union could give him in his job. Thirteen per cent of the membership gave this type of response. With these we may link a further 7 per cent who joined because of some specific individual problem. There is, of course, a point where 'business unionism' in the form of collective means to individual ends merges with ideological unionism, with a common stress on collective solidarity, but it is generally meaningful to distinguish quite sharply the practical reasons from the ideological.

Reasons for membership appear similar for all groups, except for a tendency for ideological considerations to be of greater importance to the men while the women were more susceptible to social pressures. Nearly half the part-time women and a third of the full-time women joined because the other members of the work group joined, or because they were asked by a shop-steward. On the other hand, only a quarter of the men had joined for these reasons. This trend is also revealed in the proffered reasons for non-membership; the women, particularly the part-time women, were far more likely to say that they had not joined because they had never been asked.[5]

When we look more closely at this pattern among the Brompton workers, we find it was not so much a result of different orientations of men and women as of previous contact with unions.[6] Only three of the women were union members in their last place of employment (each of these had been a member of the Union of Shop, Distributive and Allied Workers (USDAW) branch at the local co-op) and almost all of the rest had not been working where unions were available; in fact many of the women were either school leavers or housewives and only a handful of them had prior experience of factory work. Large proportions of the men, however, had been previously employed in unionized work situations. In fact 41 per cent of the day men (even though a quarter of all the day men were school leavers) and 59 per cent of the night men had been members of a union in their last place of employment. Given this distinction it is instructive to examine in detail the men who quoted social reasons for their membership or non-membership of the union at Brompton. Sixteen of the day men and eleven of the night men either joined for 'social reasons' or claimed that they had never been asked to join the branch at Brompton. Of the eleven night men, only two had been union members previously; one had decided not to pay his dues at Brompton because he 'hadn't been asked', while the other claimed to have joined because his mate, who moved to the plant with him, intended to continue with his membership. Of the remaining nine workers, four had been previously employed as clerical workers, another four as retail workers and the remaining one as an unskilled manual worker. A similar pattern is revealed in the sixteen day men who indicated social reasons. Here only one man was a member when he arrived, nine were school leavers and the remaining six divided evenly between clerical and retail workers. The pattern is a definite one. Men who gave social reasons for joining or not joining the trade union tended to be those who had little or no direct experience of trade unionism before they came to the plant. Men who had past experience of union membership were much more inclined to give definite, specific reasons for joining the union at Brompton.[7] This relationship between responses and union background suggests quite dramatically that attitudes towards trade unionism tend to be hardened and made specific by the direct experience of trade unions at work.

This relationship may help to explain the fact that 23 per cent of the women non-members thought that there was 'no need' to join the union at Brompton. However, the fact that none of the men gave this response is also important. This points further to the fact that, for the women, involvement in the employing organization centred around the work group,[8] and the union at Brompton had little influence upon these groups. Only a minority had been recruited so any contextual effect would not encourage belief in the union's importance, and as we noted earlier there was a tendency among men and women to see union matters as men's affairs.

It is important to appreciate that there were quite fundamental differences in the types of responses given by the two groups of women. Our previous analysis would lead us to expect that although similar proportions of both groups were members of the union, the full-time women would be more likely to give specific criticisms of the union as reasons for their non-membership. This in fact was the case – 45 per cent of the full-time women who were not members of the union quoted specific discontents with the union organization at Brompton as the main reason for not joining, or for not continuing as members of the union. Over half of these – a quarter of the non-members – were ex-members who were almost all extremely critical of the union. In responding to the questions on the trade union, the full-time women who were critical of the union were often extremely articulate and answered the questions at much greater length than they answered many of the others they were asked. This was particularly the case in the large packing block – Big Block – where a number of the work groups had staged walk-outs recently over errors, or suspected errors, in the calculation of their pay under the newly introduced 'grading system'. It is worth looking at a rather large sample of the responses to demonstrate this point:

We went on strike over 'waiting time'. We didn't gain a thing. The union wouldn't help us. He just told us to go back to work. Just like a foreman he was. It doesn't seem like a union here. They do nothing for you. They're all talk – they just keep putting things off.

They don't seem to do much for us. They don't seem to be for the workers; they're more on the firm's side. You need to have *good* people in charge of the union. These here – they just talk round the questions you put to them – you never get a straight answer.

They don't do anything for the girls. I went to the strike meeting that they had – they just tied you up in knots. They'll do nothing until you walk out of the building. You need to do something pretty drastic before they'll take any notice. They've lost an awful lot of members. The union here is in Gourmets' pocket.

They don't do a lot for you. Most of the time they do nothing. I left – we all left together – because of the night men. We were sick and fed up of the state they left the belt for us to come in to in the morning. The union man did nothing. Apparently he was laughing at us.

The union here is just a waste of time. I can't see what it's supposed to be doing. Two or three of us just dropped out. It was a waste of time. You complain and they do nothing about it. We went to the table (the senior stewards sat at a 'union table' in the canteen) about a dozen times once and they did nothing for us.

I didn't mind joining in the Co-op. It was a strong union there; it does something for you. Here, they back down when management look at them. I'd begrudge paying my half a crown a week to this lot.

Compared with these responses from the full-time women the part-time women were quite mild. In fact a much smaller proportion of the part-time women were at all critical. The critical responses taken together with the ex-members only amounted to 15 per cent of the non-members. As we would expect, among the men the proportion of non-members expressing specific criticisms was even higher than among the full-time women.[9] However, these men were substantially fewer in relation to the number of members. Almost four times as many men were members compared to those who explained non-membership on grounds of disapproval of the union, whereas the full-time women members barely outnumbered the critics. Similarly, the ratio of members to ex-members was about five to one for the men and two to one for the full-time women. Looking at it another way, of all the non-members who quoted these critical types of response, over half were full-time women.

The relationship between the worker and the union, therefore, tended to be closely associated with the patterns we have developed elsewhere in *Perceptions of Work*. The part-time woman, because of her lower involvement, was likely to be neutral towards the union. The night man, because of his general satisfaction with his economic rewards and the more flexible organization of the night shift (itself related to the development of the union on the shift), was likely to be more involved in, and less critical of the union than other groups. However, the day men and full-time women, although revealing different types and degrees of involvement, were much more likely to be critical of this aspect of the control system than the other two groups. A particularly large percentage of the full-time women were severely critical of the union and often gave this as a reason for non-membership. The day men on the other hand were less inclined to take this criticism to the extent of not joining or of leaving the union.

Commitment to unionism

In Table 10 we have widened the discussion to a consideration of trade unionism in general, rather than as a specific feature of the individual's work experience. Here workers were asked to consider whether or not all workers should be in a trade union. This question attempts to get at the worker's attitude towards unionism as a principle rather than as an aspect of his present job.

The dramatic feature of this table is that the majority of the sample, members (86 per cent) and non-members (72 per cent) alike, believed that all workers should be in a union. A few of the

Table 10 *Should all workers be members of a union?*

Members	Day men	Night men	Full-time women	Part-time women	All
			(percentages in brackets)		
Yes:					
Working man needs a union	18	17	15	8	58
Worker more powerful	9	6	6	6	27
No point 50/50	6	—	6	1	13
Non-members benefit	6	9	1	4	20
	39 (91)	32 (94)	28 (74)	19 (83)	118 (86)
No:					
Free to choose	4 (9)	2 (6)	10 (26)	4 (17)	20 (14)
All members	43(100)	34(100)	38(100)	23(100)	138(100)

Non-members	Day men	Night men	Full-time women	Part-time women	All
			(percentages in brackets)		
Yes:					
Working man needs a union	3	3	16	19	41
Worker more powerful	10	3	18	12	43
No point 50/50	1	3	15	12	31
	14 (66)	9 (75)	49 (69)	43 (78)	115 (72)
No:					
Free to choose	3	1	13	3	20
No need for unions	4	2	9	9	24
	7 (33)	3 (25)	22 (31)	12 (22)	44 (28)
All non-members	21 (99)	12(100)	71(100)	55(100)	159(100)

non-members felt that unions were a bad thing, while rather more of both members and non-members argued that the individual should be free to please himself about membership. In general, however, the replies expressed a marked pro-union ideology.

Somewhat surprising is the large proportion of women who thought that all workers should be union members. About three-quarters of them expressed this view, with hardly any difference in the proportions of members and non-members. In contrast, the union members among the men were significantly more likely to answer that all workers should be in a union, as many as 92 per cent supporting this view, compared with 70 per cent of non-members. Indeed the proportion of male non-members was slightly (though not significantly) lower than the proportion of women non-members, though the position was clearly reversed for members. Among the members it is possible that the greater readiness of the women to say workers should be free to choose was due to a reluctance to imply criticism of their many workmates outside the union.[10] Nevertheless, the overall feeling was one of positive support for unions.

An interesting example of the lower involvement of the part-time woman was revealed here, when many of this group answered that they thought all workers should be in a union, but not part-time women. Some of the part-time women, it seems, did not perceive themselves as being 'workers'.

A relationship between the workers' work experience and assessment of unionism is further revealed by the fact that large numbers of women felt that unionism was a good thing, 'because there is no point being half in and half out'. A typical response of this type was given by an 18-year-old packer who was not a union member.

If there's got to be a trade union everyone should be in it. There's no point being half in and half out, that just leads to ill feeling. We all need to be united then we'd be more powerful. Even on some of the belts you've got some girls in and some of them out. That's not right!

This type of response is almost certainly related to the increase in the conflict potential that is caused within the work group when some of the women are members and some are not. In this context it is significant that many of the women members joined the union as a direct result of social pressure.

Commitment to the union at Brompton

Many of the responses, however, reveal a dichotomy between the workers' relationship with the union branch at Gourmets and trade unionism in general. We have already mentioned the part-time women who 'opted out'; many other respondents indicated that although they were in favour of trade unionism in general they saw little point in joining the branch at the firm. Further indication of this trait is revealed in Table 11.

Table 11 *How would you feel if your trade union were unable to continue?*

Response	Day men (per cent)	Night men (per cent)	Full-time women (per cent)	Part-time women (per cent)	All (per cent)
Very badly	25 ⎫ 56	25 ⎫ 67	15 ⎫ 48	14 ⎫ 36	79 ⎫ 49
Quite badly	11 ⎭	6 ⎭	37 ⎭	14 ⎭	68 ⎭
Wouldn't mind all that much	12 ⎫	8 ⎫	19 ⎫	23 ⎫	62 ⎫
Wouldn't mind at all	15 ⎬ 44	7 ⎬ 33	27 ⎬ 52	14 ⎬ 64	63 ⎬ 51
Be pleased	1 ⎪	— ⎪	— ⎪	— ⎪	1 ⎪
Don't know	— ⎭	— ⎭	11 ⎭	13 ⎭	24 ⎭
Total	64	46	109	78	297

Because of their lower involvement in the union, about 13 per cent of the women were unable to say how they would feel in the hypothetical situation of the union being unable to continue. Of all groups, the men on the night shift would feel most badly about the absence of the union – two-thirds of them would feel either badly or very badly, while 56 per cent of the day men, 48 per cent of the full-time women, and 36 per cent of the part-time women would feel the same.

A number of the respondents who gave these committed responses justified them in strong ideological terms. One man on the night shift, for example, replied, 'What! . . . . If the union packed up, I'd pack up.' Others, mostly among the men, insisted likewise – they wouldn't wish to work in any place where there was no union organization. More typical, however, were responses which stressed the ambivalent nature of commitment to the union at Brompton. A number of responses will make this point more explicit.

A 40-year-old male operator on day shift:

The branch here is not a lot of good, but I'd hate to think what would happen without it. They'd have a field day. The whip would really come out then.

A 53-year-old belt worker on the night shift:

At least there's some protection if you're in a union. They could do all sorts if there was no union. They could go all the way home.

A 17-year-old packer:

Well this one don't do a lot for you, but it's better than nothing. They are at least *supposed* to be for the workers. I think we'd be worse off without one at all.

It is important to note that the committed men on the night shift were much less likely to give such ambivalent responses than their counterparts in the other three groups. Frequently these men replied that 'the union has got us what we've got out of this company' and that the union was important as it 'kept the men together' and prevented management from 'getting it all their own way'.

A large proportion of all four groups, therefore, believed in a trade union ideology, and were positively committed to the trade union organization at Brompton. However, the commitment of the night men appears much more definite than that observed in the other three groups. Although workers may have been critical of their own branch, frequently this criticism was tempered by the belief that some form of union organization is essential as a check upon the indiscriminate use of power by management. It is of further interest in this respect that no respondents made specific reference to the 'instrumental rewards' of union membership in justifying their commitment to the union.

On the other hand, it is important not to lose sight of the fact that a substantial proportion of our four groups would clearly not grieve the departure of the union from the Brompton factory. If we take the bottom four responses in Table 11 to indicate a lack of positive commitment to the union (i.e., including those who answered 'don't know'), we find that 33 per cent of the night men, 44 per cent of the day men, 52 per cent of the full-time women and 64 per cent of the part-time women lacked such a commitment. Of the respondents who showed least attachment to the union – those who 'wouldn't mind at all' and the one man who would actually be pleased – two-thirds came from the full-time women and the day men.

Many of the uncommitted respondents had previously indicated a firm belief in the principle of trade unionism and, in keeping with this, few of them justified their responses with anti-unionist beliefs. The most frequent replies were either rather neutral ones which claimed that they were unsure of what the union did, but that it hadn't had much effect upon their lives and so they couldn't see how they would miss it, or, less frequently, full-blooded criticisms of the trade union organization as it existed in the plant. As we would expect, these latter responses were most likely to come from the full-time women and the day men, the women again tending to be most forthright. Typical comments of this sort were:

They are no good . . . no bloody good at all. For all the good they do they'd better pack up. I wouldn't miss them.

It would be different if they did something. I've told you though, they don't. They do nothing. I can't see what difference it would make if they left. Except to them that is.

These responses again, therefore, tend to confirm the pattern that we have noted throughout. It will be useful to examine further the responses recorded in Table 11 by relating them to union membership. Taking the first two responses – that they would feel badly or very badly – as indications of commitment and the others as indicating no commitment, we get the distributions of Table 12.

The most striking thing about this table is the low association between commitment and membership. To be sure it is always in the expected direction, but is very weak among the women, and even among the men it is fairly low – phi = 0.33 for night men and 0.32 for day men.[11] What this means is that attitudes towards the union were poorly related to actual membership. The implications of this are twofold, as indicated by the substantial proportions in the two discrepant cells – the top right and bottom left corners – for each group. First, we see that quite large proportions of the union

Table 12   *Commitment to the union at Brompton by membership*

| | Membership (percentages in brackets) | | | | | |
Commitment	Members	Non-members	Total	Members	Non-members	Total
	Day men			Night men		
Positive	29 (67)	7 (33)	36	26 (76)	5 (42)	31
None	14 (33)	14 (67)	28	8 (24)	7 (58)	15
Total	43(100)	21(100)	64	34 (100)	12 (100)	46
	Full-time women			Part-time women		
Positive	23 (61)	29 (41)	52	11 (48)	17 (31)	28
None	15 (39)	42 (59)	57	12 (52)	38 (69)	50
Total	38(100)	71(100)	109	23(100)	55(100)	78

membership in the plant lacked any firm commitment to the union organization. This is most noticeable among the groups of women but a third of the union members among the day men also lacked such a commitment. Second, many of those who expressed a commitment to the union organization were not union members. This was particularly so in the two groups of women, where only a minority of those who expressed a commitment to the union at Brompton were in fact members of the union. This bears out our earlier evidence suggesting that the women workers at Brompton were a much more fruitful source of union members than the recruitment strategy of the union organization would lead us to expect. We see that, unlike the men, they were more likely to be positively committed than to be members.

Thus the low relationship between membership and attitudes to the union was the result of two factors. The general dissatisfaction with the union was coupled with a widespread belief in the need for a union so that, as we have seen, some workers joined on principle without any commitment to their particular union while others were unwilling to join but nevertheless felt the union was necessary. On top of this conflict between ideology and immediate experience was the belief that the union was the men's affair. This meant that more women, with favourable attitudes, could have been recruited.

8 Unity is strength? feminism and the labour movement*

Michèle Barrett

For some time now the labour movement has faced a feminist assault on its strategies and organization. Feminists have shown there to be conflicts of interest between working men and working women and have forcefully pointed out that the labour movement has – actively and not just by default – fought for the interests of men at the expense of those of women.

To a certain extent this challenge has been accepted. Some trade unions, and some political organizations on the left, have taken the issue seriously and have not only encouraged much more participation from women but have also tried to rethink their demands and internal power structures in the light of feminist issues.

We have now to assess how far this process has gone and whether these developments are simply lip-service paid to a militant feminist presence or whether they indicate more far-reaching changes. The present political situation makes this extremely difficult, creating real tensions and divided loyalties for those who support both the struggle for socialism and for women's liberation.

Many socialist feminists feel that the weight of feminist arguments has been mainly critical in pointing to the overbearing preponderance of men on decision-making bodies, blatant sexism in men's attitude towards women at work, policies that are aimed at improving men's conditions of work and exclusionary practices through which men have sought to defend their superior bargaining power. After a while, these criticisms, however justified they may be, can often be seen as undermining ones.

These charges of undermining working-class struggle are particularly forceful and emotive at the present time. A barrage of criticism directed at the labour movement at a time when it is reeling from the Tory onslaught and attempting to patch up intractable internal rifts, can only seem quite gratuitously destructive. Just as the movement

* This chapter is from M. Barrett, 'Unity is strength?', *New Socialist*, no. 1 (September–October 1981), pp. 35–8.

struggles manfully to its feet, it gets a further blow – this time a righteous knee in the groin – from the very feminists who might be helping it up. Those who think feminism has always been diversionary and divisive see this as proof that they are right.

This reaction is understandable, but ultimately misplaced: it construes the whole problem of the relationship between feminism and the movement as one of political goodwill and trust. The issues at stake, however, have a more solidly material basis. One way to look at this is by considering the alternative political and economic strategies currently being put forward as a possible programme for a future Labour government.

It is obviously true that the left needs a set of coherent policies on which we can mobilize to reverse the appalling impact of current Tory policies; it is obviously also true that this right-wing offensive has had a particularly retrogressive effect on women's lives and opportunities. Does this mean that the alternative strategy now put forward by the left is one that will benefit women? Or will socialist feminists have to develop an alternative strategy of their own?

The Alternative Economic Strategy (AES) has as its primary objective the reflation of the economy through public spending, with a view to planned expansion and the restoration of full employment. A series of controls on foreign trade, prices and wages are usually envisaged to combat the twin dangers of flight of capital and an inflationary spiral. These would be complemented by judicious nationalization, particularly of key financial institutions, with production in general carefully planned in conjunction with a high level of industrial democracy.

I do not want to go into the question – important though it is – of whether such a strategy could succeed against the degree of capitalist resistance it would inevitably encounter.

For feminists, prior questions must be considered, and I mention only two examples. First, what is meant by full employment? In a situation where women have not in our recent history ever had full employment it is somewhat ominous to speak of the 'restoration' of something women never had. Is the full employment of which we speak therefore full male employment?

To tackle the problem of women's right to work in a situation where over 40 per cent of women workers are part-time, we need a fundamental reconsideration of why women have traditionally not participated fully in wage work – the responsibilities of childcare and running a home. If by full employment we refer to women as well as men, we need some specific proposals as to how the organization of family responsibilities is to be changed and the labour of childcare divided more equally.

The demand for a shorter working week, 35 hours, often accompanying the AES is a step in the right direction; if men's jobs allowed more time and flexibility for them to take a responsible part in childrearing, things could be easier. But we should be watchful that this takes place in the form of a shorter working day rather than a shorter working week.

A second example is the concept of industrial democracy. Like full employment, all feminists would in principle support the objective – but in practice what is this notion of industrial democracy? Essentially it is the idea that the workers involved in production should play an active role in decision-making and take a share in the responsibilities of planning. This is fine, but it necessarily restricts democratic participation to the workplace and those able to be involved.

The example often cited of creative workers' planning geared to community needs is that of Lucas Aerospace. It is no criticism of this valuable work to point out that such a project is hardly likely to emerge from the situation of non-unionized women outworkers in the East End rag trade. The concept of industrial democracy presupposes not only full employment but an organized workforce: where workers are not equal in this respect, the system will be more democratic for some than for others.

It is not that there is anything wrong, from a feminist point of view, with these alternative strategies – they contain no explicit anti-feminism and no explicit appeal to workers as men. Feminist doubts would not be answered by clauses asking combine committees to bear in mind the ideological incorrectness of having pin-ups on the walls. The real difficulty lies in what is *not* said – in the silence on how women are to participate fully when they are still unequal as workers, unequal as trade unionists and unequal in the political parties and organizations of the left.

The underlying question is the family. Although there can be no doubt that women are discriminated against at work and in the labour movement, we cannot get to the root of this without looking at the institution of the family, the means by which this discrimination is usually justified. Many trade unions, particularly those in the skilled sectors with a certain amount of bargaining power have in the past defended the ideal of the 'family wage' – that a man's wage should be set at a level which enables him to support a dependent wife and children. This principle is now less secure, as it is widely recognized as being incompatible with equal pay for women and increasingly irrelevant to the majority of families who simply cannot live on the man's wage.[1]

Yet there is still considerable support for an idealized and romanticized notion of the working-class family. Many socialists, for example, routinely argue that Tory policies are crushing working class families, exacerbating the poverty of poor families, depriving children in poor families. Of course this is correct, but we need to question whether the interests of children really are best served by preferential wages and welfare policies that are geared to the family.

The numbers of children now being brought up outside the confines of the nuclear family, let alone arguments in favour of women's independence, suggest that we cannot just sink into the rhetoric of defending 'the family' against the inroads of unemployment and spending cuts. We need instead, as some feminist groups have argued, to push for precisely the reverse – 'disaggregation' of the family unit – so that we can tell what *individual* needs are not being met.[2]

The labour movement has as yet remained deaf to this call for disaggregation of the family as a waged and taxed unit. Indeed it seems likely that the implications of the demand have simply not yet registered. In order to rid ourselves of the myths about men as breadwinners and women as by nature suited to housework and childcare, we need to make sweeping changes. These would affect conditions of work, pay structures and differentials, income tax, the social wage and welfare policies.

Many socialist feminists believe that the labour movement can play an important role in making such changes, but the abolition of even the grossest inequalities between men and women as workers (let alone the longer-term and broader aim of women's liberation) is still not a concrete part of socialist strategy. Feminists may have a certain support from socialist men of goodwill, but what are the changes this goodwill should be directed toward? There are three major areas where feminist demands directly affect the labour movement.

First, there is the question of major inequalities between women and men at work. As is well known, equal pay legislation by no means brought equal pay. In 1979 women's average gross weekly earnings amounted to only 63.6 per cent of those of men. The main reason for this is that by and large the labour force is so clearly divided into 'men's jobs' and 'women's jobs' that no comparison of like work can be made as required to operate the act. To achieve equal pay, it would be necessary to break down this job segregation so that women as well as men were found across the whole range of occupations and industries, and across the whole range of grades within them.[3]

Some of the present inequality is undoubtedly the product of mechanisms over which the movement has little control, such as an employer's manipulation of vulnerable groups of workers, or biased systems of education and training. But some of it is the result of explicitly male interests – practices excluding women from skilled work and attempts, often successful, to define the work that men do as skilled and the work that women do as unskilled. Such practices, and the assumptions on which they are based, are blatantly anti-feminist and must be challenged.[4]

Furthermore, the labour movement has been unusually passive in its response to these inequalities. It is comforting to point to capital's tendency to divide the workforce, its need for cheap or part-time labour and its immoral exploitation of women. Yet there is more that the movement could do, though current debates on the role of positive discrimination in union strategy (as recommended by the TUC's Women's Advisory Committee) show that this is being given more thought. Trade unions could bring pressure to bear on employers' recruiting and grading policies in the light of sex discrimination, and we could work towards a system of workplace control of job opportunities for women.

Second, the movement can play a role in breaking down the actual or assumed dependence of women on men's wages – and this means a more equal sharing of childcare between men and women. Recent support from the unions and left parties for feminist demands on abortion plays an important role, since the ability to control fertility is a central prerequisite of women's independence.

But women will only be equal at work when the burden of the 'double shift' is lifted. And in order to achieve this we would need a complete restructuring of the basis on which *men* are employed. When a child is ill and off school, fathers as well as mothers must cope with the problem. The working day will obviously need rethinking. And it is not enough to campaign for workplace nurseries where women can leave their children – they are also needed at Ford and British Leyland.[5]

Third, we can expect the labour movement and the left to take a clear position on sexual politics. It has so far shown little sign of throwing its weight behind campaigns to counter sexism in the media and advertising. It has no public voice on sexual harassment at work and issues of male violence.

Comrades who beat up their girlfriends, sabotage the political lives of their wives or refuse to do any work in the home, are passed over in silence or thrown to the feminists to be dealt with. The left press has had virtually nothing to say about the Yorkshire Ripper, and, though we might not have expected *The Yorkshire Miner* (a paper notorious among feminists for its defence of *Sun*-style nudes) to take the lead on this, it is telling that nowhere on the left have we seen any serious reflection or analysis of the political issues raised by this case.

Why should the labour movement take feminist politics seriously? As I have suggested, doing so means more than simply generous gestures – it requires a major rethinking of strategies and struggles that are held dear. It is often said that feminist issues are marginal and that struggle around them will not provide the strength we need to advance socialism.

In some ways this argument can be very forceful. The miners, for instance, demonstrated last autumn that the present government is not invincible and could be made to back down – an achievement scarcely likely to result from industrial action by secretaries or social workers. In a very real sense the traditional centres of working-class resistance offer more hope of political breakthrough than the armies of women workers whose position in the workforce makes them correspondingly weak in industrial struggle.

Yet to conclude from this that socialist support for feminism is purely a matter of choice would be wrong. No progressive movement can retain its integrity if it is riding on the back of an oppression conceived of as someone else's problem.

When the labour movement is called upon to correct both explicit racism in its practice and implicit racism in its failure to protect the specific interests of black workers, then a lack of response calls into question its overall project and undermines its credibility. So too with feminist demands. Furthermore, the fragmentation and sectionalism of the labour movement and the political organizations of the left – the chief obstacle to making progress – is profoundly structured through divisions of race and gender.

It hardly needs repeating that a divided working class is a weakened working class. But it does need stressing, at a less rhetorical level, that these divisions between men and women will not simply disappear in the magic of solidarity. If we are serious about overcoming them, we shall need some concrete and practical changes in strategy.

Part Two

Women and electoral politics

Women and electoral politics

9 Introduction

Challenging existing traditions of analysis from the vantage point of women's experience is not simply the presentation of 'another point of view'. To insist that political science and political sociology fully acknowledge and treat seriously women's engagement in politics is to insist on a thorough search into the corners and foundations of our understanding of political institutions and political processes. To discover that women's political views and practices have been less rigorously or sympathetically researched, and to discover that women's political stance cannot readily be embraced by an analysis of politics developed with reference to men, is to provide the groundwork for a more adequate and comprehensive political analysis.

In this section, we present a variety of challenges to the orthodox portrait of women in political science and political sociology. The first two articles, by Bourque and Grossholtz, and by Goot and Reid, examine the research practices and interpretative assumptions which have given rise to a misconception of women's political capacities and interests.

Bourque and Grossholtz find four categories of distortion in studies of political participation and political socialization. The practice of 'fudging the footnotes' results in statements concerning women's political orientations which are either unsupported by the references cited or misleading simplifications of the original arguments. The tendency to assume men influence women's political opinions, but not vice versa, leads to interpretations of women's political attitudes as shallow reflections of those expressed by husbands or fathers. Distortions also arise from the unquestioned assumption that the political attitudes, preferences and style of participation characteristic of men define mature political behaviour. Thus, when women do not match men's political characteristics, they are said to be either apolitical or politically naïve. Finally, women's political contribution is argued to be located within their role as mothers. Such a view constructs and promotes a constrained vision of women's political potential.

Equally disturbing distortions are uncovered by Goot and Reid in their extensive review of voting studies and women's alleged greater conservatism. Together, these two articles survey a vast amount of literature. They dispute the 'mindless matron' profile of women in political science and political sociology, and illustrate how it is often the product of a misconceived analysis of politics and political life. Moreover, they reject explanations which suggest women wilfully place themselves in a marginal relation to matters political. When women's political involvement is less than men's, Bourque and Grossholtz, and Goot and Reid, persuasively argue this as an indication of the degree to which political parties, political issues and the norms of political participation do not resonate with the concerns, needs and opportunities of many women.

The next four articles take the assessment of the existing literature outlined above a step further, presenting new evidence and new interpretations of women's and men's political activities and orientations.

Hills, arguing against claims to the contrary, shows that during the last two decades, women have voted in British elections at the same rate as men, and that women's alleged greater support for the Conservatives is really an age, rather than a sex, difference.

Taylor tests Parkin's argument for women's lower attraction to socialism. Even when in paid employment, Parkin argues, women are not assimilated into an industrial subculture, and this renders them more vulnerable to Conservative views. Taylor finds, in his analysis of the party identifications of female and male manual workers, equal support for the Labour Party and suggests women's employment is as salient as men's in forming their political orientations.

The tendency for women to personalize politics to a greater extent than men, to be 'personality' rather than 'issue' oriented, is investigated by Shabad and Anderson. By reconceptualizing evaluations of political candidates, they present not only a more robust analytical framework but show women and men to be equally sensitive to a variety of dimensions in their candidate evaluations. Furthermore, as Shabad and Anderson emphasize, attention to personal qualities, such as integrity and reliability, in the assessment of political leadership is not, as some would have it, a trivial or apolitical concern.

The final presentation of new evidence is Jennings and Farah's cross-cultural comparison of women's and men's translation of political thinking into political action. Presenting data for both conventional and unconventional forms of political activity, they find only one instance (out of ten comparisons) of a significant difference between women and men. Interestingly, women and men are most similar in translating political thinking into unconventional political protest and action.

The new evidence presented in this section stresses the similarities in the political orientations and activity of women and men. It is meant as a small corrective to the overwhelming tendency, within political science and political sociology, to concentrate on 'sex differences'. However, we cannot conclude, even on the basis of this new evidence, that women and men have identical political experiences, nor can we conclude that the involvement of women in electoral or protest politics simply doubles the number of participants without any implications for (or challenges to) the modes of organizing or political concerns. The concluding contributions in this section offer distinctly competing views on the implications of women's political engagement for the shape and texture of political life.

Sanzone concentrates on women in positions of political leadership in Britain, France and Germany, and her assessment of the political positions they adopt indicates that policy is indeed related to the sex of the decision-makers. Thus, although the pursuit of politics as a career is primarily a male prerogative, Sanzone finds the minority of women in the upper echelons of government to be not simply 'honorary males'. Despite reservations about Margaret Thatcher, Sanzone sees promise for the advancement of women's rights in the greater presence of women in government.

The final selection presents a different view. Wainwright locates the possibility of an egalitarian society, and the realization of the demands of the women's movement, in the direction of socialism. However, the traditional strategies and forms of organization within existing socialist groups do not, as Wainwright argues, meet all requirements. Socialist organizations need to combat the depoliticizing effect, for both women and men, of the division between the 'leadership' and the 'led'. Towards this end, Wainwright draws attention to the alternative forms of organizing and political action within the women's movement, and to its aim to support and encourage all its participants to become, in some sense, political leaders.

New forms of political action and understanding render old forms of political analysis and explanation obsolete. The contributions included in this section provide insights into the issues and possibilities of alternative explanations and interpretations for the contemporary features of the political life of women and men.

10   Politics an unnatural practice: political science looks at female participation*

Susan Bourque and Jean Grossholtz

That politics is a man's world is a familiar adage; that political science as a discipline tends to keep it that way is less well accepted, but perhaps closer to the truth. This paper addresses itself to both concerns: the sexual definition accorded to politics and the manner in which the discipline of political science perpetuates this definition. We argue that in the choice of data to be analysed and in the interpretation of that data, the discipline insists upon a narrow and exclusive definition of politics which limits political activity to a set of roles which are in this society, and many others, stereotyped as male. Since society assigns roles by sex, this differentiation is carried over into political roles.

The tendency for political scientists to explain disparities in the political participation of certain groups (women, blacks, minorities, those of low income and status) as a reflection of their social position and purported innate proclivities, has provided a justification for those disparities and relieved the discipline from the need to seek alternate explanations which would question the distribution of roles, status and power, as well as the very definition of politics. The conclusion reached by this sort of orientation is that the fault lies with the excluded group who simply will not get organized and participate in the ways open to them. We agree with Bella Abzug on this point:

I suggest what is really ludicrous is a political structure that denies representation to a majority of its population and then winds up fingering the victims of this situation as somehow responsible for it because of their personal inadequacies.[1]

By accepting the behaviour of those who presently exercise power as *the* standard of political behaviour, political science explains the

* The full text of this chapter, with more extensive examples, can be found in *Politics and Society*, 4 no. 2 (Winter 1974), pp. 225–66.

failure of others to participate by their inability to approximate that behaviour. Unfortunately, political scientists do not go on to ask why or if this *should* be so, or how to overcome the impediments to 'proper' behaviour. Nor does the discipline ever deal adequately with the ramifications of this standard for the political system itself and for such other values as equal participation and government by consent.[2]

We argue in this paper that we have misconceived politics (pun not intended) and political life, and that the exclusion of women and numerous others may be a product of that misconception. Consequently, we should set ourselves the task of redefining the study of politics to adhere to the unqualified and uncorrupted demand and expectation of equal participation. We maintain that women, as women, can never be full participants in politics as presently defined by political scientists given the assumptions made about the nature of politics and the necessity for sex role differentiation in society.

This paper illuminates the content and pervasiveness of these assumptions. We have not developed, in this analysis, specific alternatives. Rather, we define the problem. We look first at the way women are treated in some classic studies, and then at the basis of the statements which are made about the participation of women in politics.

We found that we could sort our findings into four categories of distortion of the participation of women in politics. Some studies fell into only one category, others fit into all four.

Our first category, 'fudging the footnotes', comprises those statements of female political characteristics, attitudes or behaviour which are not substantiated in the material cited as the source. Misuse of the data of earlier studies usually involves removing all the qualifications and careful language of the original study, thus misrepresenting and in some cases falsifying the data.

Our second category is 'the assumption of male dominance'. This comprises the most pervasive expectation about sex differences in politics: that men will occupy dominant political roles and control political decisions. There is no doubt that males hold the vast majority of public offices at every level and control influence at every level as well. That political scientists report this cannot be faulted. What we find unacceptable is the failure to question this occurrence, to ask why this happens and to worry about the implications.

The reason for this is simply that it has been asserted and

accepted, without proper evidence, that men dominate and women are dependent at the primary level of community life – the family. This asserted dominance of the male is then extended to a wider realm. For example, women's political attitudes are assumed to be reflections of those of the father or husband. This unwarranted assumption about family life and its relationship to the broader community is doubly damning because it suggests that it is women's preferences which give men control of politics. Moreover, whereas it is quite clear that males are dominant in politics, it is often asserted on the prior basis of assumed family relationships, not on the basis of evidence.

The third category of distortion is the acceptance of 'masculinity as ideal political behaviour'. This refers to the unexplained and unexamined assumption that those stereotyped characteristics held up as the masculine ideal (for example, aggressiveness, competitiveness, pragmatism, etc.) are the norms of political behaviour as well.[3] The distortion is most frequent when discussing explicit political behaviour (candidate preferences, issue preference and saliency). Rational political behaviour is defined by the male pattern: it is by definition the expression of male values, and irrationality is by definition the expression of female values.

The fourth category of distortion we have called 'commitment to the eternal feminine'. In this sense feminine political behaviour is explained as a direct product of a woman's social role as wife and mother and her mythical status as purity personified. This distortion involves an assumption that women's present weak political position is necessary and functional. Society relies upon the services provided by women in the social realm, therefore there must be no corruption of that role and no change in it. We must tolerate limited participation by women in order to assure that we have wives to nurture our leaders and mothers to preserve the race.

Studies of political participation

We examined in detail three of the frequently quoted studies of political participation which summarize the question of sex differences: Angus Campbell, *et al.*, *The American Voter*; Gabriel Almond and Sidney Verba, *The Civic Culture*; and Robert Lane, *Political Life*. These studies are, in turn, cited by the students of childhood and adult political socialization as the source of their knowledge of sex differences in participation. Here is the picture of female participation that we found in each.

Campbell *et al.*'s *The American Voter*, written in 1960, is a study of voting: the influences on turnout and partisan choice.[4] It concluded that there is an average difference of about 10 per cent in the turnout rates of men and women. The authors' examination of sex differences in turnout revealed that at succeeding levels of education the similarity of rates increases. At the upper end of the scale, male and female rates approach one another. Among the young, the single and the married without children, they found 'no average difference in turnout between men and women across categories of education and age, outside the South'.[5]

What then, apart from age, accounts for the difference in turnout rate? According to Campbell *et al.*:

Mothers of young children, however, are consistently less likely to vote than are fathers of young children across all levels of education. . . . Furthermore, this dip in participation among mothers of small children does not appear to be matched by a slackened political involvement within this grouping. . . . The presence of young children requiring constant attention serves as a barrier to the voting act.[6]

Here we find direct evidence of the relationship between female social roles and limited political participation. But rather than suggesting that this impediment to female voting might change through some new division of childcare responsibilities, the authors conclude that the situation is hopeless:

Our analysis may be brought to bear on our expectations for future female participation. If primary responsibility for young children leads to some reduction in turnout potential, this effect is likely to leave a permanent discrepancy in participation between the sexes.[7]

This is the eternal feminine in action.

Campbell *et al.*, also report a difference in the degree of political efficacy sensed by men and women. The data on differences in political efficacy supposedly demonstrate:

Men are more likely than women to feel that they can cope with the complexities of politics and to believe that their participation carries some weight in the political process. We conclude, then, . . . what has been less adequately transmitted to the woman is a sense of some personal competence *vis a vis* the political world.[8]

The authors of *The American Voter* found an explanation for this lower sense of political efficacy among women in the sex roles that prevail in this society:

The man is expected to be dominant in action directed toward the world outside the family; the woman is to accept his leadership passively. She is not expected, therefore, to see herself as an effective agent in politics.[9]

The authors are building an explanation on an assertion that males are expected to be dominant. This is a case of *assuming* male dominance.

The authors imply that men's and women's expressions of political efficacy are rational for both, given the societal sex roles. By the same reasoning it is irrational for a woman to express a sense of political efficacy comparable to a man's. But the fact is, under these criteria there are a large number of irrational women in this sample. Among the women polled, 68 per cent of the college educated, 40 per cent of the high school and 14 per cent of the grade school, expressed high efficacy, in contrast to 83 per cent, 47 per cent and 32 per cent of the men, respectively.[10] Obviously there are differences between men and women but an explanation based on societal sex roles is inadequate.

One might offer the alternative hypothesis, that given the very limited number of issues that citizens can effect, the lower sense of political efficacy expressed by women is a perceptive assessment of the political process. Men, on the other hand, express irrationally high rates of efficacy because of the limitations of their sex role which teaches them that they are masterful and capable of affecting the political process. In fact, few of us have any political influence in any case.

This second interpretation of the data will not be taken seriously as long as male political behaviour is considered the standard by which all other responses should be measured. Furthermore, the second hypothesis rests on granting women a degree of political cynicism, realism, sophistication, and understanding greater than that of men. This is something that these authors are unwilling to do.

In choosing to use Robert Lane's *Political Life* we wondered if it would be fair to criticize a book published in 1959 before some of the more comprehensive studies of voters had appeared. However, when we consulted the 1964 paperback edition of *Political Life* we found in the preface the author's assurance that the book had 'weathered well' and that he had 'modified the relevant comments on changing patterns of electoral participation'.[11]

Lane reports that there is a high degree of political agreement among members of the same family. But there are disagreements, and what happens then?

> What evidence we have shows that conflict between husband and wife, when it occurs, produces a greater degree of discussion than political conflict in other groups [here he cites Maccoby 1954] followed usually by the wife's being 'persuaded' on the point. The wife is 'persuaded' rather than the husband partly, at least, because her role is culturally prescribed as less political; she loses less by yielding.[12]

Here Lane finds his pattern of male dominance. He argues that wives are 'persuaded' to adopt their husband's position, or when failing to do so, decide not to vote.

Lane's comments on the effect of political conflict among married people were probably triggered by a section in the Maccoby article in which the amount of political discussion in various groups is compared. Here is what the original study found:

> we find that people who prefer the same party as their fellow workers tend to talk politics with them quite a bit while those who have a different political position than their fellow workers less often engage in political discussion at work. The opposite situation tends to hold true in the home of the young married couples: when they disagree on politics they discuss them extensively, while with agreement, politics become a less central subject of discussion.[13]

There is no indication here, or anywhere in the article, that wives are 'persuaded' because it is somehow less costly for them to do so. On the contrary the authors conclude quite the opposite:

> our data suggest that the husband–wife team is a cohesive group and that political agreement is important to the smooth functioning of the group, so that disagreement produces discussion and *mutual influence*.[14] (Our emphasis)

The data presented by Maccoby and her colleagues cannot be said to substantiate the conclusions drawn by Lane. However, a more recent study by Kent Jennings and Richard Niemi supports the Maccoby findings.[15] The authors describe two different models of husband and wife political behaviour:

In the measure that participation in matters political represents an instrumental action *vis a vis* the outside world, then clearly the role differentiation model points toward fathers rather than mothers as the chief actors. . . . Conversely the role sharing model suggests that fathers have no necessary monopoly on instrumental and adaptive behavior, that sharing may occur within a family or that patterns vary from family to family.[16]

As Jennings and Niemi point out, the predominance of one of these models over the other has deep ramifications for the position accorded women in politics.[17] The authors studied 430 conjugal pairs who were parents of high school age children. Their conclusion was that 'the evidence for the role sharing view of political participation is rather marked'.[18] And they argue that forces are at work pushing in the direction of even greater overlapping.[19]

Lane's treatment of this data suggests a case of fudging the footnotes to fit his assumption of male dominance.

A more subtle effect of these images, however, in Lane's terms, is that they perpetuate a moralistic or reform orientation towards politics among women. He notes that this moralistic orientation has its roots in the female responsibility to engender morality in the young. There are, in addition, other factors which lead to this orientation, and these, in Lane's view, have some rather important consequences for female political behaviour:

the more limited orbits of women, their more restricted contacts in society and narrower range of experience may tend to reinforce the view that the values they are familiar with are the only values – a lack of cultural relativism.[20] The evidence of the somewhat greater intolerance of women seems to support this view.[21]

The net effect of this moralistic orientation has been not only to provide an ineffective and relatively 'ego-distant' tie with political matters but also, as Riesman has remarked, to limit attention to the superficial and irrelevant aspects of politics.[22] Furthermore, such an orientation gives an illusion of comprehension because it is relatively easy to compare political acts and statements with moral symbols to assay moral worth, while it is difficult, indeed, to ascertain causes and estimate results. Finally such moralism may account for the relatively greater candidate orientation of women,[23] since persons – as contrasted to issues – are even more clearly perceived as 'good' or 'bad'. Hence, women, more than others contribute to the personification of politics both in the United States and abroad.[24]

What Lane appears to be saying is that the limited roles open to women lead directly to their greater intolerance, an ineffective tie to political matters, and an interest in the superficial, irrelevant aspects of politics. Women may appear to understand politics because of their manipulation of moral symbols, but they have actually missed the deeper currents, and more critical concerns.

Lane concluded that the moralistic orientation of women towards politics had led them to limit their attention to 'the superficial and irrelevant aspects of politics'. Here he cites page 58 of an article by David Riesman. On this page Riesman cites three incidents in which women or women's groups have been aroused about corruption in the political process. This he takes as an indication of their greater political conservatism and lesser sophistication. One example from Riesman will suffice:

I recall the grimness of my own reception when I spoke several years ago to a politically active women's organization and criticized Kefauver and his TV hearings as a lure for the unpolitical, a mobilization of the indignants, and a distraction from more important issues . . . a men's group of like education, perhaps worldly wise and cynical, would have gotten the point more easily – perhaps too easily.

It is clear the Lane believes that masculine behaviour is ideal political behaviour. But he does not pause to speculate on the consequences of this view of politics for the participatory political life he sets up as ideal. However, when he turns to his suggestions for improving participation he does consider the implications of change. One of the suggestions is to politicize the female role. Here is his assessment of that remedy:

Politicize the female role. Since the rate of political interest, knowledge and activity of women is generally lower than that of men, it is appropriate to consider how to relieve this depressed area of politics. Broadly speaking, political affairs are considered by the culture to be somewhat peripheral to the female sphere of competence and proper concern. Would it be wise to reinforce the feminist movement, emphasizing politics on the women's page along with the garden club and bridge club news, and making ward politics something like volunteer work for the Red Cross or the hospital auxiliary? No doubt something along this line could be done, *but it is too seldom remembered in the American society that working girls and career women who insistently serve the community in volunteer capacities, and women with extra-curricular interests of an absorbing kind are often borrowing their time and attention and capacity for relaxed play and love from their children to whom it rightfully belongs. As Kardiner points out, the rise in juvenile delinquency (and he says, homosexuality) is partly to be attributed to the feminist movement and what it did to the American mother.*[25] (Our emphasis)

Better to have 50 per cent of society operating in their political behaviour with only an 'illusion of comprehension' than to risk more juvenile delinquency and homosexuality.

Even Lane, after all his dire descriptions of female political participation (or perhaps he meant images), is reluctant to make any changes in the social roles of women that might change their assignments in the sexual division of labour. This is the eternal feminine response. In it women are caught in a damned if you do and damned if you don't situation: they do not behave politically like men because of their social roles – and as a result they do not behave very well; but you cannot change their social roles because, if you did, the fabric of society would be torn asunder.

The Civic Culture, a comparative study of political attitudes in the USA, Britain, Germany, Italy and Mexico, makes several important departures in its analysis of the political behaviour of women. At times the authors do not seem to be aware of the dramatic departures they have taken from the standard interpretations of the political behaviour of American women. Their opening statements match the interpretations we have previously discussed:

Wherever the consequences of women's suffrage have been studied, it would appear that women differ from men in their political behavior only in being somewhat more frequently apathetic, parochial, conservative, and sensitive to the personality, emotional and esthetic aspects of political life in electoral campaigns.[26]

The authors claim that their data are consistent with previous findings in the literature,[27] and their figures support this except in the American case. In the US data the differences between men and women, it is claimed, are not impressive and suggest a remarkable degree of similarity between the sexes, given the rather different political roles that are open to them.[28]

Almond and Verba point out the comparatively high rate of female participation in the United States and devote some attention to the importance of the role of women in determining the shape and direction of a society's political culture. Since political culture consists of an orientation to action, women are important in shaping political behaviour. The authors note that other studies of the role of women in politics have erred in treating sex as simply another demographic category.

What they have overlooked is the fact that the great majority of adults are married; that they create families, raise children and help to 'socialize' these children into their adult roles and attitudes. Thus the political characteristics of women affect the family as a unit in the political system and affect the way in which the family performs the socialization function.

It makes a great deal of difference whether women tend to live outside the political system in an intra-mural family existence, . . . or within the political system . . . which tends to be the case in the United States and Britain.[29]

In a refreshing admission of the limitations of their data, and the frequent propensity to make assertion without evidence the authors go on to say:

While our data do not permit us to demonstrate it directly and explicitly, we are suggesting that in the United States and Britain the family tends to be a part of the political system, that events and issues in the polity tend to be transmitted into the family via both marriage partners, and that political discussion tends to be frequent and reciprocal, rather than male dominated.[30]

While this flies in the face of the assertions of both Lane and Campbell and his colleagues, Almond and Verba give it scant attention. It may be an indication that their assessment of the literature on this question indicated it did not merit refutation.

Almond and Verba conclude that as a result of the family unit 'being in' the political system, which is a direct result of women 'living-in' the political system:

that the problems of family life, the needs of women and children are more directly and effectively transmitted into the polity through this kind of politically open family. The esthetic quality and emotional tone of political life are probably also affected by the political competence and activity of women in the United States and Britain.[31]

As they see it, women in the US, and to a lesser extent in Britain, make their greatest political contributions in their roles as wives and mothers. It is in the home, through the political attitudes they instil in their children and the atmosphere of political discussion in which they participate, that the civic culture is passed on from one generation to the next.

Thus, Almond and Verba present a new view of American women, one that accepts the notion of comparable levels of political interest, involvement and competence between men and women. But, at the same time, this view underscores and praises the traditional sexual division of labour and uses that division to justify the exclusion of women from the leadership levels of political life. This is a case of commitment to the eternal feminine combined with an assertion of male dominance.

Studies of political socialization

The study of sex differences in political socialization is confined almost exclusively to childhood. The studies of childhood socialization show very few significant differences between the sexes although there is wide disagreement in the profession about the evidence.

The classic modern study of childhood learning about politics is that of Fred Greenstein, *Children and Politics*,[32] which includes an entire chapter on sex differences.

Greenstein collected information by questionnaire for children in grades four to eight and found differences between boys and girls in his sample on the following items:[33]

1 amount of political information;
2 ability to name an interesting news story;
3 naming a news story that was political in nature;
4 interest in national news.

Amount of political information was measured by the number of 'reasonably accurate answers' to questions asking the names of the incumbent mayor, governor, president; the duties of such officials and of legislative bodies. Although, as Greenstein reports, the amount of such information held by the children in the sample was 'infinitesimal', boys were significantly better informed. When asked to name an interesting news story boys were more likely than girls to be able to do so and furthermore were significantly more likely to name a story that Greenstein classified as 'political'.

The sex differences reported in Greenstein all hang on what is meant by political. When asked, for example, 'if you could change the world what would you do?' girls are likely either not to respond at all or to give 'a distinctly non political response' such as 'get rid of all the criminals and bad people'. We have no examples of what the 'political' responses of boys were.

Another sex difference used by Greenstein in his study to show the natural enthusiasm of boys for politics involves children's attitudes towards the Second World War. This difference is based on a study of twenty-one children between the ages of 6 and 7, which was conducted during the war. Although the sample was small, only twelve boys and nine girls, the differences were strikingly clear cut, Greenstein reports. 'When asked which of a series of pictures they preferred nine of the boys and none of the girls picked war pictures.' A look at this study shows that on other measures as well, the sex difference exists. In general, the attitude of the boys was classified as enthusiastic or excited about the war in eleven out of twelve cases, while only two girls were so classified.[34] Seven girls but only one boy were indifferent to the war. The exception among the boys was described by the authors as:

almost a genius in mathematics and music, reads at the fifth grade level and has unusual ability in spelling. He is the most immature member of the class socially and engages little in group activities.[35]

It is worth noting as well that part of the measure of interest was taken to be the report of three boys that they actually read the newspaper to get their news of the war while girls relied on conversations with their parents or the radio.

A major part of Greenstein's orientation, if not explanation, relies upon Lewis M. Terman and Leona E. Tyler, 'Psychological sex differences', a review of the literature on sex differences among children published in the *Manual of Child Psychology* in 1954.[36]

They find sufficient evidence of aggressive behaviour on the part of boys, although some part of that difference they assign to teacher bias in reporting.[37] On emotional differences they report a study which shows girls rating their own response in thirty-four situations more emotional than boys, but they caution that girls and boys are not equally willing to confess emotion. They also note that girls get credit for more moral superiority than they possess.

From the basis of this data Greenstein argues that the demonstrated differences in aggressive and dominant behaviour means that more men are willing to express hostility and engage in controversy.

He also relates this finding to the fact that 'women are more pacifist in their issue positions'. These relationships must remain speculative as must the following:

In a field as controversial as politics, it also seems possible that differential aggressiveness would affect the degree of participation.[38]

The tendency of women to have 'an absorbing interest in persons and personal relations' that Terman and Taylor report, is related by Greenstein to the fact that 'adult women are more likely than men to be candidate oriented'.

In conclusion, Greenstein argues that some factors inhibiting the participation of women in political life (such as having small children at home to care for, low levels of education, etc.) can be changed, but there are other 'less malleable psychological causes of political differences such as "deeply engrained sex roles" and the female dependence on males'. Greenstein quotes, with obvious pleasure, what he calls Duverger's charmingly Gallic remarks:

While women have legally ceased to be minors, they still have the mentality of minors in many fields and particularly in politics, they usually accept paternalism on the part of men. The man – husband, fiance, lover, or myth – is the mediator between them and the political world.

Greenstein says that his data give him no basis for final conclusions as to the explanation of adult sex differences. None the less, the data 'cast doubt on theories which suggest that such sex differences will disappear in the near future', that is, changes in educational level, work experience and so on that adults experience will not have any significant effect because differences in political involvement and orientation by sex emerge early in life.

An adequate theory must account for the psychological underpinnings of political sex differences, understood in terms of sex roles in society, how they develop, and what maintains them.

Further research is needed to discover what these underpinnings are. In part they may be curiosity, interest, and other related positive drives, channeled from tender age in one direction for girls and in another for boys. Politics, although not of deep interest to children of either sex is resonant with the 'natural' enthusiasms of boys.[40]

Like the designation 'political', 'natural' is also in quotes, and never defined so we do not know why politics is natural for boys. Greenstein has accepted without question masculinity as ideal political behaviour.

The not so hidden basis for sex differences in politics

The first conclusion we can draw from this research is that there is a high level of distortion in this literature. Much of the conventional wisdom on sex differences in politics is based on what we have called 'fudging the footnotes'. Consider the notion that women are more intolerant than men. This is consistently repeated and assigned to evidence presented by Samuel Stouffer.[41] On the question solely of the right of communists or communist doctrine to a public forum, Stouffer found 'women tend to be somewhat less tolerant'.[42] However, he goes on to point out that despite this attitude women are far more likely than men to be tolerant of deviance in their children. There is no evidence in the Stouffer study for the statement in Lane referring to 'the somewhat greater intolerance of women' about politics generally.[43] In the same pages Lane cites another source which, upon investigation, also notes that women are more likely to defend their children from 'patriarchal legalisms' and insist on the right of their children to be idiosyncratic.[44]

A second set of distortions result from the political scientists' acceptance of a sexual division of labour and function in the society, and their transference of that division of labour to politics. We disagree with this both on the basis of the assumed immutability of the sexual division of labour and on the basis of the validity of its transference to political behaviour. Despite the fact that differences between males and females, as shown by the research cited in this paper, are modest, i.e., that many women act just like men, these political scientists have assumed a fundamental difference between masculine and feminine political behaviour. The sexual stereotype of females as more emotional and sensitive is used to describe the contribution of women to political life. The forum for female participation is still the family and the primary function of the politically competent woman is to socialize children and to filter the needs of home and family into the political system.

The hidden message that femininity precludes politics becomes, in the hands of political scientists, a curious weapon. They seem unduly concerned that the attitude be assigned to women's self-evaluation, to her free choice. A widely used text published in 1967 put it all together:

The political inactivity of women evidently results mainly from the view widely held in our society that a woman's proper business is caring for her home, her husband, and her children, and she should leave the rough and dirty world of business and politics to her menfolk. As one woman respondent put it, 'Woman is a flower for men to look after,' and another, 'I have never voted, I never will . . . a woman's place is in the home . . . leave politics to men.'[45]

Significantly the source of these quotes came from women respondents in the Merriam and Gosnell study, forty-three years earlier.

Nowhere in the literature is there any attempt to treat seriously and systematically the exclusion of women from political leadership roles. Almond and Verba, conscious of the importance of women to the creation of civic sentiments, make it clear:

The significance of the political emancipation of women is not in the suffragette's dream of women in cabinets, parliaments, at the upper levels of the civil service, and the like. . . . [Greenstein] points out, correctly, that there are inherent limitations in the adult female role, which set an outer boundary to political participation for the great majority of women.[46]

Campbell, *et al.*, Lane, and Greenstein all explicitly adhere to the assumption of male dominance. All the elite studies implicitly support this assumption. Many of the supplementary sources we have used in this paper also accept this assumption. Let the reader be clear, we firmly believe that political life in the United States is dominated by males. But we also believe that the character and explanation of that dominance has never been explored or tested by political scientists. On the contrary, the distortion arises from the political scientists' acceptance of male dominance without questioning why that should be a social fact, or if it is a valid explanation.

The clearest expression of commitment to this belief involves the explanations for the fact that conjugal pairs usually vote alike and hold similar political opinions. From this it is concluded that women vote according to their husbands' dictates.

A variation of this distortion is the notion that male dominance exists because women lack interest. This notion is buttressed by some unexplained and undocumented assertions, such as Greenstein's 'deeply engrained sex roles', or female dependence on men, or the assertion of 'a set of norms that women hold that they should not be as participatory as men'. We have not found in any of the literature cited in these studies, or anywhere else for that matter, a study of female socialization and political attitudes that supports this assertion.[47] Rather, it appears that political scientists have very clear and decisive beliefs about adult women's attitudes and roles which they are using in lieu of evidence.

The second and most basic conclusion we can draw from this research is that politics is defined as a masculine activity. The basis for assertions of male political dominance and the unwillingness to take female participation seriously, derives from this definition of politics. Those characteristics and enthusiasms which supposedly sway men (war, controversy, electoral manipulation) are defined as specifically political, while those characteristics and enthusiasms which supposedly sway women (human needs for food, clothing and shelter, adherence to consistent moral principles, the pre-emption of national by human concerns, a rejection of war as rational) are simply not considered political.

A 'political' response becomes by definition a male response. Note the ease with which Lane and Riesman are willing to relegate some political concerns, such as morality in public life, to the irrelevant category. In the same way elite studies, such as Presthus[48], find that women in the elite are concerned with 'community improvement of a welfare kind' which really carries no weight in 'politics'. This is an arbitrary judgement which is used to support the image of women in political life that the author has in mind. We do not argue that in the reality which Presthus describes his assessment of the importance given to 'community improvement of a welfare kind' is incorrect, only that to deem this less political is to adopt a limited and strange notion of that classification.

One of the sources often cited as evidence of sex difference in political attitudes is the catalogue of public opinion polls compiled by Hadley Cantril and Mildred Strunk for the period 1935–46.[49] The belief that women have fewer opinions than men is based on the fact that women are said to give 'don't know' responses more often than men. Greenstein, for example, cites the following questions in Cantril and Strunk on all of which women gave more 'don't know' responses than men:

Would you approve or disapprove of a speed limit on open roads? Do you think the Russians are planning a world revolution or do you think they have given it up? If there had been a Liberal candidate (in the British election of July 1945) would you have voted for him? Are you in favor of a union of Western nations? Do you know what workers councils are and what their task is? (asked of a Czech sample in 1946). It has been said that quarreling among political parties has interfered with Canada's war effort. Do you agree or disagree? (asked of Canadians in 1942).

On the basis of the percentage of 'don't know' responses women are assumed to be less willing to take a controversial stand and also, it is presumed, to have less information.

However, in the same volume we find that women, more often than men, said they thought the people should be consulted before any declaration of war (in both 1935 and 1939); women, more often than men, opposed capital punishment; women, more often than men, were willing to continue food rationing in order to feed hungry Europeans and even the defeated Germans. Women also expressed strong opinions about draft laws, divorce law reform and women in high office. On all these issues there were no significant differences by sex on the 'don't know' responses. These opinions we submit are 'political'.

In short, it is not a question of women not having opinions on controversial matters, it is a question of which matters one takes as being most important to politics. It is clear that the assumptions being made here exclude those interests about which women are most concerned.

Fundamentally those things which society defines as stereotypically masculine (aggressiveness, pragmatism, etc.) are considered to be the norms of politics. One must have these characteristics to be a 'real' man and to be a 'real' *politico* one must have these same characteristics. Our response to that message is that we must redefine politics and political life in terms that will allow political science to treat human persons as necessarily participatory in the collective decisions that shape their lives. Furthermore, the definition of human persons must not be restricted by stereotypical images of what human beings are all about, whether they are male or female.

The implications for political science

There is in our view a distressing compatibility between the stereotypical model of politics that political science has accepted and the denial of moral values and acceptance of pragmatic political expediency that the Watergate scandal represents. There is as well, a frightening similarity between assumptions that war is exciting and glorious, that aggressiveness and controversy are politically mature and the long and bitter blood letting in Indo-China. We would not argue that women would bring anything different to politics in the present circumstances. Rather, women who enter this polity carry the same ideals, norms and orientations as men. As the material in this paper makes specifically clear – there are relatively few differences between men and women in politics. This is a tragedy in our eyes for it means that women have accepted the masculine ethos in politics.

But there *are some differences* in the political behaviour of men and women. Paradoxically it is the discipline's treatment of these differences which demonstrates the problem. What we see in the treatment of women is a symptom of a larger problem in the discipline – a willingness to either avoid questions of power and justice by blaming the victims, or to substitute explanations based on societal norms while at the same time ignoring the political system's role in the maintenance of those norms.

Perhaps if political scientists had subjected the data they found on these differences to more searching analysis, and avoided the assumptions that they have used as explanations, they might have found some interesting hypotheses about our political life and even some suggestions as to where it goes awry. Let us illustrate with some examples.

Women were found to have a moralistic orientation towards politics. We think the evidence cited is not striking, although there are significant but small differences between men and women on those things which political scientists label moral positions. This classification is never truly explained but at times seems to consist of women's application of individual moral principles to political life, at other times it seems to deal with women's assessment of government officials as doing their job, or with the need to obey the law, or with pacifist notions. But the most difficult problem and the most revealing factor in this entire category of difference is the fact that political scientists who assume the category is real and who believe it is a view held by women more often than men, deem this a concern with the irrelevant, and a lack of sophistication. Clearly politics in the United States has been conducted as if moral concerns were irrelevant, but should political scientists accept this as mature political style? Are we satisfied with an assessment of political life which calls a concern for consistent principles, obedience to the law and concern for human life irrelevant?

Another example is women's attitude towards elections. Women do not see much difference between the parties, preferring instead to search out candidates they can believe in. Might this not be interpreted as a realistic appraisal of conventional political life? Women, like Lipsitz's poor, may well have grievances, and when allowed or encouraged to voice them come forth loud and clear.[50] But those who determine which issues will be discussed and which emerge in party platforms are not women.

Initially, in our own research, we thought the treatment of women in political science could be explained by the assumption of social roles as determinant and the acceptance of this assumption as legitimate justification for low levels of participation on the part of women. This view holds that both men and women have come to accept certain divisions within the society (of labour, status, behaviour) along sex lines and these have been translated into politics. But as we read the literature, looking critically at both the data and the interpretations which were offered, we came to a rather different conclusion. If politics was to be the man's realm, then at the levels that political scientists measured political involvement, women were not getting the message. Women turned out to vote at about the same rate as men, except when the care of small children kept them at home. Moreover, they had about the same level of interest and involvement in politics as most men. Many of the differences in the political orientations of men and women were created by the political scientists out of their own notions of what should be the case.

What happens to our understanding of political life and our very definition of 'politics' if we assume that women are as interested in and competent to exercise political power as men?

11 Women: if not apolitical, then conservative*

Murray Goot and Elizabeth Reid

Introduction

While it is often suggested that the enfranchisement of women has had little or no impact on politics[1] and that this, in hindsight, could have strengthened women's claim to the vote,[2] it is also argued that a variety of chancellors, presidents and governments owe office to the votes of women: Adenauer and de Gaulle;[3] Eisenhower;[4] and several conservative administrations in Britain,[5] Italy[6] and Australia.[7]

Either way (or both), it may come as something of a surprise to find on turning to the academic literature, that the political behaviour of this half of the electorate has been the object of little in the way of questioning or systematic research. Thus, in Philip Converse's recent list[8] of 'priority variables in comparative electoral research' all the 'face sheet' items used in surveys are included – except sex. Prior to Amundsen,[9] the most recent monograph on *The Political Role of Women* had been compiled (at the behest of UNESCO) in the early 1950s by a team led by Maurice Duverger.[10] And it is symptomatic of the status accorded women by the political science profession that this report should have had to record, among the difficulties the project encountered, 'a certain degree of indifference. The political scientist . . . often tended to regard its purpose as a secondary one of no intrinsic importance'.[11] For Dahl[12] and Sartori,[13] among others, a state's claim to being a 'democracy' is in no way impaired by its withholding the vote from women altogether. Even Lipson can scarcely be said to be dissenting from such a judgement when he remarks in passing, that 'only one democracy today, namely Switzerland, persists in its curiously old-fashioned ways on this topic'.[14]

From the view that politics is at least primarily to be left to men one does not have to traverse any great distance to come to believe

* This chapter is an excerpt from M. Goot and E. Reid, *Women and Voting Studies: Mindless Matrons or Sexist Scientism?* (Sage 1975), sections 1, 4, 5, 6, and 8.

that such is the only conceivable state of affairs, or that only men are in fact involved in politics, or that only the male electorate is worthy of note. Much of the empirical work within the profession, including some of the most prestigious, comes perilously close to making one or other of these moves; and some come even closer. Take the major research technique: questionnaires. Nordlinger, for instance, in his discussion of working-class attitudes to political authority and leadership poses a choice, at one point, no wider than that between a peer's son and a clerk's son on the one hand, and an Eton and a grammar school man on the other.[15] Abrams asks his respondents which of the parties they would consider 'most satisfying for a man with ideals'.[16] Almond and Verba print a table headed: 'Per cent who say the ordinary man should be active in his local community', and conclude that, except for the USA, 'Participatory norms . . . are more frequently held by men than by women';[17] and so on.[18] Of Almond and Verba's American findings, Barber has commented, archly, that 'women who score high on citizen duty questions, may simply mean that their *husbands* ought to be active citizens'.[19] This may simply mean that the interviewees are more sensitive to what the question asks than are the researchers.

If techniques of research represent one side of the enterprise, the culling of respondents represents another. Among the more notable is Robert Lane's exploration of the *Political Ideology* of Americans,[20] based on fifteen interviews, all with men. His *Political Thinking and Consciousness*,[21] again without so much as a word of explanation, is a study of twenty-four 'courageous and insightful young men'.[22] Even where the initial sampling embraces women they can, when it comes to analysis, be readily cast aside. Thus Abrams: 'Since a claimed interest in politics is largely concentrated among men we have in the rest of this account of the survey restricted ourselves to the replies from the men in the sample'[23] (in fact, 43 per cent of the women had said they were interested or very interested as against 60 per cent of the men). Or Davies,[24] from the proposition that there are 'definite' (but unspecified) 'age and sex patterns of political interest, knowledgeability and participation', concludes: 'Politics is a game, in one simple sense, for middle-aged men'.[25]

While the political behaviour of women has been the principal concern of very few voting studies it remains an incidental concern of many. Women are of interest only in so far as they resemble, or fail to resemble, men.[26] Beyond that, women count only by virtue of the utilitarian, reliable and stable qualities of the 'sex variable'.[27] As a matter of course almost any questionnaire records the sex of the interviewee as a 'background' variable. Since the sex distribution of the population is usually known the sex distribution of the sample provides a means of assessing the representativeness of the sample. In addition, a person's sex (unlike, for example, a response to an opinion item) is a datum which can hardly be impugned. In the eyes of a science which is inclined to regard the 'subjective' as a pollutant, sex becomes an important part of a person's ontological status.[28] It occupies a similarly privileged position within causal analyses: that sex determines belief and behaviour is, after all, generally more plausible than the reverse. Sex, then, is usually included among the background variables in behavioural research. It is largely with analyses of the relationship between sex and voting behaviour by British, American and Australian social scientists, especially political scientists, since the Second World War, that this paper is concerned.

To date, even analyses of the political situation of the woman voter by social scientists sympathetic to the women's movement have been marked more by their endorsement of the 'findings' of survey research than by their questioning of them. Iglitzin's thesis[29] that the 'total conditioning process' accounts for the image of women that this research constructs, is so widely accepted that where the elements of a different view can be glimpsed, they are as unintended protrusions, salutary only as contradictions of the dominant theme. Amundsen, in particular, is guilty of arguing, on the one hand that by way of the 'socialization process . . . women inevitably come to internalize the general disesteem in which they are held' so that under 'the impact and pervasiveness of sexist ideology one cannot expect that the majority of American women will express any interest in changing . . .'; and on the other, suddenly endorsing Schattschneider's interpretation of non-voting as a sign of a 'rejection of the political system', and similarly suggesting that what might happen if (non-voting) women were to vote 'staggers the imagination'.[30]

While such interpretations build on the findings of the profession, they do not build on all of them. On occasion, one or two have been firmly denied.[31] But the process has stopped well short of a full-scale critique. It had to. For the assumption that girls are conditioned, from the time they see pink to accept, for example, that 'politics is a man's world' fits well with the image of women in the voting literature. (So well, that it is often the explanation ventured in the literature itself.) Among these feminists, then, such findings are destined to be greeted as (alas) terribly true.

Our own position is different. In terms of theory, we reject 'internalization', 'socialization', and so on, as the only possible ways to account for the political consciousness of women. In terms of method we argue against the adequacy of questionnaires which are structured on the principle that they 'speak for themselves'. In addition, we shall argue against the image of the woman voter as an apolitical being – founded as it is on the belief that she is merely concerned with morality and insulated from work and politics – as arbitrary on the one hand and untrue on the other.

Even where questionnaire methods have been appropriate, but where feminist positions (of the kind outlined) have provided no incentive to check the results, much of the data does not support the conclusions derived from them (for instance, the conclusion that more women are conservative than not, or at least that more women than men vote conservative). Too often, where voting studies have actually looked at women voters, prejudice has posed as analysis and ideology as science.

That women are more conservative than men

'There is overwhelming evidence that women are more conservatively inclined than men' (Pulzer).[32] In one obvious sense we have the makings of a contradiction between this view and the view that a wife's vote is a husband's vote times two. Yet there is another sense in which those who accept Pulzer's proposition do not always present women in so very different a light from those who see them as politically beholden to men. For the 'conservatism of women' is often regarded as yet another indication of the apolitical temperament of women.

However familiar expressions such as 'women are more conservative (or less interested, and so on) than men' may be, their ambiguities, however unintentional, are easily overlooked. That the proportion of women voting conservative is greater than the proportion of men is a statement about differences only. That women, on balance, vote conservative but not men is but one of three possibilities – plus a variation.

1   First, the variation: that more women than men support the Conservatives *and* more women than men support the Labour Party. There is evidence which fits this.[33] That such a possibility even exists is principally due to the fact that men rather than women might abstain from voting, vote invalidly, vote for another party or even say 'don't know' to the appropriate item on the questionnaire. Almost all the evidence, however, indicates that in so far as there is a difference between the sexes in turnout, etc,[34] it is the women rather than the men who exercise such options.[35]

2   Occasions in which majorities of *both* men and women have favoured the Conservatives, have, clearly, been more frequent. This has certainly been true of middle-class British voters on occasion.[37]

3   The same data suggest, predictably, that most men and most women in the working class prefer Labour. Similarly, on occasion, this is true of men and women in the British electorate as a whole: notably in 1945 and the early 1950s,[38] and in 1964.[39]

4   Indeed, the distribution of preferences which might be expected on a 'strong' interpretation of the claim that more women than men vote conservative, namely most women voting conservative but most men not, as in Belfast in 1966[40] has not occurred more frequently than the above possibilities. In Britain as a whole it seems to have been true, since the war, in 1951, 1955 and 1959[41] and 1970.[42]

In the last surveys the differences between male and female support for the Conservatives averaged 7 per cent while in the surveys noted in (2) and (3) the corresponding margins ranged from 1 to 8 per cent. We have so far established then, that where more women than men vote conservative, the differences between the two are small; and that only in some cases are the differences such as to make conservative voting typical of women but atypical of men. More than this, that on one occasion at least, while it was true to say that more women voted conservative than men, it was equally true that more women than men voted Labour. But we can go further. The literature throws up cases in which the sex differences have virtually disappeared.[43] Just's secondary analysis of data from Almond and Verba's 1959 and Butler and Stokes' 1963 surveys of Great Britain reveals no direct relationship between sex and partisanship.[44] But Bone and Ranney had already declared that there appeared to be no 'significant sexual differences in political preferences'.[45]

This is only to encourage a situation where one sexist (behavioural) orthodoxy replaces another. For there is evidence that women preferred *Labour* to the Conservatives in 1945,[46] and again in 1964.[47] Between these dates researches in several British constituencies produced samples[48] or sub-samples[49] in which this was true. Again in the USA, women in 1948, 1964, 1968 and 1972 voted Democratic rather than Republican.[50] And it does not stop here. A Belgium survey shows more women than men supporting the Socialist parties in some regions.[51] There are further studies in which the sex difference is reversed; i.e., where more *men* than women favour the conservative parties. In America Campbell *et al.*, report that in 1948 and 1952 somewhat fewer (2 per cent and 4 per cent respectively) women than men supported the Republicans.[52] This also seems to have been the case in 1958 and 1972.[53] British Gallup data of 1945 covering lower professionals suggest that 'the women were distinctly more favourable to Labour'.[54] In Australia a 1972 constituency study[55] found more women than men favouring Labour, while two investigations of groups with tertiary education[56] indicate a higher proportion of Labour voting among wives than among husbands.

Women's conservatism: social and economic explanations

Oddly enough, almost no effort has gone into trying to explain this phenomenon. We know that the old are disproportionately Conservative, and also that there are more old women than old men . . . beyond this all is supposition and hypothesis. (King)[57]

Thus King is echoing Blondel[58] when he states that a greater proportion of women than men vote Conservative (1959–70) in Britain. Commentators in Australia,[59] America[60] and Britain (of whom Milne and Mackenzie[61] might claim to be the first) argue that differential death rates are a factor, but differ on their importance. What other explanations have been advanced?

Lane argues that the answer lies in the essence of femininity: being a socialist is incompatible with being a true woman since it signals a 'confusion of sex role'.[62] Thus, joining the Communist Party allowed 'women with sexual confusion' to adopt masculine roles. At the same time it allowed passive or homosexual men to 'slough off the masculine role of an independent and responsible (family) leader'. But this is simply to wed a biology which is false (genitalia determine behaviour) to a politics which is repressive (the personal as political being replaced by the political as merely personal).

A much more popular and plausible line of attack is through religion. The correlation between 'religiosity' (for the most part part church attendance; sometimes believing in God), conservative voting, and sex has often been noted.[63] But how are we to interpret it? It can hardly be regarded as some have been tempted to do,[64] as self-explanatory. Churches have been associated with particular parties or have instructed their flocks to vote in particular ways. And interpretations along these lines have been advanced[65] with particular reference to France and Italy and the role played by the Catholic Church in directing its congregation – most of whom are women – not so much to vote for conservative parties as to vote against socialist and communist parties.[66]

In Protestant countries, however, it has been argued (or assumed) that the dominant or established church and the conservative parties embrace similar values – values which are distinctly non-Labour. Explanations derived from factors such as these have met their baptism of fire where women are disproportionately conservative.[67] Whether, in turn, they apply in those cases where the men are disproportionately conservative has never been explored.

Women 'work less' than men (Aitkin and Kahan):[68] we are now at the bottom of most explanations of women's conservatism. But in its simplest terms, it is a false bottom – one might even say a bustle. Women, for the most part, probably work more than men.[69] The vast majority of women electors are married, and though Stacey may be misleading about wives in general, she is surely right about housewives in particular:

A wife cannot resign from her work without breaking from her husband and children, nor can she leave her husband without losing her job. Her occupation is rightly returned as 'married woman'.[70]

All the work done by housewives and a major part of the work done by women with 'two careers' is unpaid labour, not non-work. Moreover, the entry of women into the market economy over the last twenty years has proceeded apace. In America, more than 31 million adult women are now gainfully employed. They constitute about 40 per cent of the paid workforce.[71] In Britain and Australia the situation is not dissimilar.

Heinz Eulau, in his study of *Class and Party in the Eisenhower Years*, decided that housewives (as well as farmers and 'other occupational groupings') could not be 'properly classified', so he simply dropped them and wrote his monograph without them.[72] Yet this is only one of the strategies adopted to deal, in whole or in part, with women. Most women, whether married, unmarried, deserted, deserting or widowed, whether gainfully employed or housewives, are fed into the computer under the occupation of their father or husband or male head of household, be the man retired or still in the workforce, dead or alive. Thus:

The standard of living of the economically inactive wife depends on that of her husband. The wage of the working wife usually constitutes an additional salary which does not change the family's social position; besides, in economic life, women generally occupy a lower position than that of the men. As for young girls, they are in the same social class as their brothers. Widows quite often live in very difficult material conditions; yet from the psychosocial point of view, they remain attached to the socioeconomic milieu in which their late husband belonged. One must not, therefore, search in the economic field for an explanation of the difference between men's and women's political behavior.[73]

The third way of dealing with women is to omit them altogether. What is unusual about the fact that 'a nationwide survey designed to provide a first approximation to delineating the social stratification of Australia' should be based on a survey 'of Australia's adult male workforce'[74] is not that it should be confined to the male 'workforce' (which has a long tradition)[75] but merely that this should happen without so much as a footnote.

What is it about working that might increase the likelihood of a Labour vote? 'We may say' says Blondel quite insensitively

that women, most of whom still do not go out to work, do not experience the difficult conditions of life in factories and that in any case many more work in offices where work is clean and generally more pleasant.[76]

But if work situation and status (and not their market situation)[77] were the politically relevant features of their employment, and if cleanliness, pleasantness and the ease of conditions were crucial, we might well expect women who did *not* go out to work to be equally inclined to Labour. We might, in turn, not be surprised to find that, according to a view Rose once espoused[78] but appears since to have rejected,[79] 'the increase in the number of women working [sic] . . . does not seem to have influenced their voting behaviour'.

Since 'to work' has so consistently been identified with 'going to work', the potentially relevant political similarities between work at home and outside have mostly passed unremarked. Similarities between work situations may of course go well beyond the kind mentioned by Blondel.

There is also the market situation of women to be considered. Women earn less than men. We would not expect this to increase their propensity to vote Conservative, as Aitkin and Kahan seem to maintain,[80] but (other things being equal) to increase their propensity to vote Labour. Women tend to receive less formal education than men and have fewer paper qualifications. Again, Aitkin and Kahan notwithstanding, this clearly places them in an inferior market position, and should statistically make a Conservative vote less rather than more likely.

But the political consciousness to which a woman's market situation (including income, job security and mobility) gives rise, remains virtually unexplored. On the rare occasion that the problem is glimpsed, it comes as an apology at the end of the research, not as a problem of method or theory at the beginning. Thus Benney *et al.*:

The contrasts in social experience (and hence in knowledge) between men and women are more varied and complex than these passing speculations indicate. But we cannot pursue the problem further with the data available to us.[81]

Indeed not. And being dependent on them, neither can we.

Are women traditionalists, fickle or what?

Only in one sense does the 'conservatism of women' refer to their tendency to vote for conservative parties. In their study of Leeds/ Pudsey voters during the 1959 British general election, Trenaman and McQuail discovered that more women than men preferred Labour and that in the course of the campaign the movement away from Labour was less marked among women than among men:

The explanation of Labour's support amongst women, and of the slight movement measured by the Gallup Poll may be a greater solidarity among women supporters, a reluctance to abandon a former allegiance, rather than a positive pro-Labour movement. In a time of movement away from the left, women's traditional conservatism may in fact not operate in favour of the Conservative Party.[82]

Similarly Rose's suggestion 'that the conservatism of women has made them more likely than men to retain traditional attachments to Labour'.[83] In other words: heads, women are conservative; tails, women are not non-conservative.

When the swing is in the opposite direction, from Conservative to Labour, but again less marked among women than among men, their inertia looms as more of a piece. Thus Burns:

Women under thirty-five remained predominantly Liberal. Their femininity was politically stronger than their youth. . . . It was only among those over fifty-five that the political coerciveness of sex began to fade . . . women were more given to voting because of *habit* when they were not meekly following their husbands.[84] (Emphasis in the original)

Sears[85] on the other hand, seems to believe that whichever way the swing goes it will be confined to men. For women 'seem to reject innovation, deviation, and conflict'.

Should the data show that, contrary to their traditionalist image, the proportion of women changing their preference is greater than the proportion of men doing so, not everyone need despair. For prejudice here has played its hand impartially: it has provided an alternative prop for analysts to lean on. Thus we learn of the 'fickleness'[86] or 'political immaturity' (IPSA Report)[87] of women. Conversely Tiger[88] invites us to believe that phenomena such as 'political loyalty . . . may be viewed as activities on their own and as exhibiting . . . the male bond'.[89]

First cousins to these 'fickle' and 'immature' women hover in the background, providing the occasional comic backdrop to the otherwise dullish presentation of survey results. Thus, Rose's sole example of an 'accidental reason' for voting Conservative: 'A woman because a nice young Conservative had offered her a ride to the polls.'[90] A sole example, but certainly not an isolated one. It is indeed striking how often reasons regarded as silly[91] just happen to emanate from the mouths of women.

Now, in certain circumstances women clearly do 'change parties more often than men',[92] i.e., the proportion of women changing exceeds the proportion of men. Equally, however, the contrary is sometimes true.[93] Other evidence comes down on neither one side nor the other, or fails to detect any sex differences in the matter[94] at least in the rate and intensity of party identification.[95]

But were all the evidence to fall on one side rather than the other, the labelling would still need to be justified. For one can stick to an initial preference for reasons other than traditionalism, just as one can switch without being fickle or immature. After all, men are seen to swing or stay for other reasons. The absence of any attempt to define immaturity, much less embark on a systematic attempt to justify the application of such terms (as against instructing research assistants to hunt through interview schedules for illustrative material) tells us something extra about the researchers but nothing more about their ostensible subjects.

Politics, political and passive

The husband bring[s] to his politics a certain patina of realism, and in an interview a certain dialectical facility, while his wife remains a femme couverte at best able to repeat his views, without qualification or critique. (Riesman)[96]

An alleged preoccupation of women with the superficial or irrelevant, is just one aspect of the image of the woman voter as an essentially apolitical person. The idea that women follow the politics of the dominant male is another. A woman who votes the same way at successive elections is simply conservative by nature. A woman who changes her vote is not responding to changes in the world or her position in it; she is simply being fickle. Where women pass judgements on the political world they are not necessarily passing 'political' judgements. Men are the people who involve themselves in politics, and political judgements are masculine ones.

Let us consider the notion of politics first. Berelson, *et al.* stated, 'Women are less politicised than men – they follow the vote of their SES level less than men.'[97] This begs several important questions. Just which American men and women do share the same socio-economic status? By what criteria is the vote appropriate to a given 'SES' set? Of greater pertinence here is the question: what are the grounds for saying that someone who conforms to their SES level is political while someone who does not is not political? Ten years

later, Berelson (in collaboration with Steiner)[98] unveils the other
side of women's politics as a 'moralised political orientation' which
'tends to focus female political attention upon persons and
peripheral "reform" issues'. The source quoted is Lane[99] who in
turn cites Riesman:

Louis Harris presents evidence . . . as to the greater political conservatism
of women, or more precisely their relatively apolitical outlook on politics
which led them in recent years to voice a greater fear of corruption and
suspicion of malfeasance among the Democrats in Washington than their
menfolk did. He suggests that the homebound political feet of many women
made Eisenhower, the candidate 'above politics', appealing enough to lure
them to the polls. And the kinds of efforts . . . which have been made in
recent years to get out the vote often bring the uninformed and indifferent
to the ballot box when . . . they should have been . . . counted as 'don't
knows'.[100]

But if it is naïve to think that a presidential aspirant could be 'above
politics' it is doubly naïve to think that such a judgement could itself
be apolitical.

What is being cited in the name of political science is a conception
of politics every bit as narrow and misleading as the one being
assailed. Here, politics appears to be restricted to material interests
jockeying for advantage in a tough-talking world of wheeler-
dealing, cost-benefits, and compromise. A masculine world.
Women's 'demands' are seen as soft, unimportant, at best unreal;
women are dumb to the 'needs' of politics (as Lane states):

the female vote as a 'reform' vote, that is, impersonal and detached from
personal gain, qualitatively different from the male vote, which is imbued
with matters of self-interest . . . gives an illusion of comprehension because
it is relatively easy to compare political acts and statements with moral
symbols to assay moral worth, while it is difficult indeed, to ascertain causes
and estimate results.[101]

And, notwithstanding the fact that 'women with little interest feel
free not to vote, while men with little interest still feel called on to go
to the polls',[102] the transition from the view that women are
concerned with moral issues to the view that women only vote
because voting *itself* is just such an issue is readily made. Lane
comments:

It is via this moral route [*viz.*, the sense of citizen duty] that they [women] come to the polls, not because of their interest in elections, nor because of their ambition to see certain policies put into effect. As the moral custodians of the family and the community, women now find that they must include citizenship among their other duties.[103]

Most amazing of all, are remarks like Robert Lane's about the 'illusion of comprehension' attendant on a moral outlook, without so much as a mention of the McCarthyite or Cold War periods in which 'moral symbols' – created not by women, but by men – constituted the hardest political currency of the time.

Similarly with explanations of the political interest of women, their knowledge of politics (principally their ability to name party members and party policies), their feelings of political efficacy, and the extent of their political participation (especially beyond voting). The fact that at each point women as a whole score slightly or even considerably (in the last case) less well than men has been fairly continually,[104] but by no means universally,[105] attested. Most explanations, of course, centre on sex role socialization, while some include education[106] and diminished leisure time.[107]

Unlike Rose,[108] who describes as 'similar' the proportion of women (40 per cent) and men (54 per cent) who are 'very or quite interested in politics', the above writers do at least acknowledge the existence of sex differences. But the explanations they offer are at best one-sided. Schattschneider's words seem to have made the guardians of the profession none the wiser:

It is profoundly characteristic of the behavior of the more fortunate strata of the community that responsibility for widespread nonparticipation is attributed wholly to the ignorance, indifference and shiftlessness of the people. . . . There is a better explanation. Abstention reflects the suppression of the options and alternatives that reflect the needs of the nonparticipants. It is not necessarily true that the people with the greatest needs participate in politics more actively. *Whoever decides what the game is about decides also who can get into the game.*[109] (Emphasis in the original)

In so far as political parties have ignored women as voters (for example, by keeping abortion reform and childcare off the agenda, or by not recognizing how many are wage-earners or are conscious of food prices, or by accepting that a 'worker' cannot include a housewife) and as potential power holders, they can scarcely be said to have promoted women's interest or participation. Might this not account for Trenaman and McQuail's suggestion of a link between the higher rate of abstention among women and their inability to choose among the parties?[110] Women who are put down or who remain politically invisible are, quite understandably, likely to feel less than politically efficacious. Almond and Verba celebrate women as 'trustful of their social surroundings' and as taking 'a pride in the political characteristics of their nations'.[111] But, in the circumstances, such trust and pride might better be read as a sign of widespread delusion rather than robust good health.

Not only is the political world seen as not impinging on women directly – immortalized in the proposition that the 'relatively unedu-cated' women who live an 'intra-mural family existence' actually live 'outside the political system'[112] – but even under indirect exposure to it (via men) women emerge as almost totally passive. The accepted view is that they do not engage or interpret for themselves that which does get through to them, they merely accept it. The images of women we have encountered, from uncomplaining followers of their husband on the one side to fickle or arbitrary decision-makers on the other, all take this for granted. As Davies claims: 'the interviews with girls (as with adult women) suggest a listening mode: a way of making up one's mind by absorbing different active opinions'.[113] The corollary, as Nordlinger makes clear, is that women are of no (independent) account even in an explicit analysis of the future political stability of Britain:

since one of the study's major goals is to suggest certain inter-relationships between non-elite attitudes and the contours of the political system, the data relating to the male manual workers is far more relevant . . . if women were included in the sample the data concerning them [would] be of less significance for understanding the operation of the political system. . . .[114]

Among those sympathetic to feminism[115] the docile accommoda-tion of women to men becomes, not just another piece, but the most fundamental piece of evidence of the extent to which women are dominated by men. They too, along with their unsympathetic colleagues, subscribe to the 'passivity' of women, although for different reasons. First, the mode of explanation to which most of the voting literature subscribes is a non-interactionist version of the social-psychological. On this view, opinions 'originate' by being absorbed by one person from another. The emphasis is on face-to-face communication (spouse, other workers, etc.) with the information thus received being taken in in lumps rather than worked up anew. And the two are related. For it is the mass media, notably television (for example, the news) and the press, but also radio (for example, talk-back programmes) which – whatever their biases – act less like 'socializers' pressing a line and more as disgorgers of information which individuals forget, revise and interpret largely on their own.[116] The fact that the 'isolated' housewife reads newspapers, listens to the radio and watches television, perhaps somewhat less,[117] perhaps somewhat more[118] than her husband, has occasionally been noted. But to little effect. Likewise, the direct political and work experience. For to get at the effects one must study in detail the experiences of women and the qualities of their political thought. The pre-coded, superficially quantitative ('Do you get a little/a lot of political information from newspapers?' 'Do you work?') questionnaire items commonly employed merely reflect the weakness of the theory while ensuring that such data as might expose the theory cannot emerge.

But this is as true of the account of male behaviour as it is of female. What extra factor, or twist, explains the peculiar passivity of women in the literature? What reason, for instance, has Burns for maintaining there is something qualitatively different between husbands following their workmates and wives following their husbands?[119] What seems to happen is that the model of general passivity is, quite arbitrarily, relaxed for men in the 'presence' of women. Like most 'value-neutral' research, much of the work we have reviewed simply assumes the dominant values of the dominant groups of society. The values taken for granted here are the values of the (male) researchers operating in a male-dominated society in which they too are numbered among the beneficiaries. The electorate is passive, but some are more passive than others.[120] In so far as anyone constructs a world of politics or work the builders are men. This is the ultimate insult accorded the woman voter. But it is not, as we have endeavoured to show, the only one.

12   Women and voting in Britain*

Jill Hills

Voter turnout at [British] general elections has more or less continuously declined from the 84 per cent of the period 1950 to 1964 to 73 per cent in 1979.[1] Women's contribution to this state of affairs has been little studied by political scientists, who have concentrated upon class, age, environment and political socialization as the primary explanatory variables in British voting behaviour. In general, however, women have been said to vote less often than men, and, until 1979, were said to be more Conservative than men.[2]

Because people do not admit to non-voting, a problem with data collected from questionnaires after an election, is that it always over-represents the turnout in that election. In a study which attempted to outflank that problem, Crewe, Fox and Alt found that in four elections between 1966 and 1974, non-voters were not a discrete section of the electorate, and were likely to resume regular voting in the future. Once those aged 75 and over were excluded from the analysis, the 3 per cent superiority of men in turnout narrowed to 1 per cent, reflecting the disproportionate number of women in the older age group. They concluded that 'the well known tendency for women to vote in Western liberal democracies in smaller proportions than men is not only statistically insignificant in British elections, but attributable more to their greater longevity than to their sex'.[3] Their conclusions are confirmed by those of Lansing.[4] At least since the 1960s British women have voted at the same rate as men.

Besides attributing women with failure to vote, political scientists and journalists have also attributed post-war Conservative victories to women's suffrage. Women have been presented as more Conservative than men and, in particular elections, such as that of 1970, have been considered directly responsible for a Conservative victory.[5] Yet to talk of a 'women's vote' in contrast to a 'men's vote'

* This chapter is an excerpt from J. Hills 'Britain', in J. Lovenduski and J. Hills (eds.), *The Politics of the Second Electorate* (Routledge & Kegan Paul 1981) pp. 8–32.

is a nonsense, because women's voting pattern, in the mass, is affected by the disproportionate number of elderly women in the electorate.[6]

Given the attributed importance of women to electoral outcomes it seems surprising that it was not until the late 1970s that the concept of the 'Conservative woman' was specifically examined. Then, Lansing founded that contrary to the myth, young women voted Labour in the 1964 election at a higher rate than young men. Although women seemed to become more Conservative in the older age groups, those over 60 years old were almost identical in their Conservatism to men in the same age group. She concluded that the apparent Conservative bias among women was no more than a generational artefact.[7]

There is evidence to show that, between 1970 and 1976, women's support of the Conservative Party declined.[8] This decline might possibly have been related to the increased numbers of middle-class women in public sector employment – education, health and social work – to which the Conservative Party was less sympathetic than was the Labour Party. By 1979 even male political scientists could not ignore the evidence. Writing just after the election, with reference to the 'typical Conservative advantage among women' Crewe acknowledged that, in 1979, women in general were not more Conservative than men. He said of the election: 'the last minute surge of male chauvinism predicted by some never appeared, on the contrary, men swung much more strongly to the Conservatives (9.5%) than did women (3%)'.[9]

The 1979 election data in Table 13 shows that in the largest age group within the population, that between 30 and 59 years old, both men and women voted in similar proportions for the three major parties. In the youngest age group, from 20 to 29 years old, women supported both the Labour Party and the Conservative Party more than did young men, the difference being made up by less support of the Liberals by women. Only in the age groups over 60 years old was there, among women, both less support for the Labour Party and more support for the Conservative Party. Hence, once again, only in the elderly age group can women be said to be more Conservative than men. Even then, possibly attracting women to the Conservatives, a woman potential prime minister may have complicated this voting pattern. If British women ever were more Conservative than men, they apparently no longer are.

Table 13 *Sex difference by age and party vote, 1979 (percentage of total sample)*

Age	Sex	Conservative	Labour	Liberal
20–9	Men	25	27	21
	Women	30	30	13
30–59	Men	39	32	11
	Women	41	33	12
60–75	Men	40	36	8
	Women	46	32	10
Over 75	Men	40	26	12
	Women	52	18	3

13 The party identifications of women: Parkin put to the test*

Stan Taylor

The theory of working-class voting patterns advanced by Frank Parkin[1] is one of the more notable contributions to the large literature on that subject. The core of his general argument was that working-class voting should not be treated in isolation, but regarded in terms of the macro- and micro-social contexts in which partisanships were 'determined'. The macro-context in Britain was that of an advanced capitalist society in which values and norms appropriate to the maintenance of the existing social, economic and political order were 'dominant' and disseminated by the commanding institutions.[2] The extent to which these values, rather than those associated with radical change, were held by the population at large was a function of the degree to which the micro-social context – the immediate environment in which the voter lived and worked – was 'open' or 'closed' to the influence of the dominant institutions. Where, among the working class, a voter lived in a socially-heterogeneous community, and worked in a small factory where the relationship with the employer was of a 'paternalistic' kind, he would tend to interact with middle-class people who supported the 'dominant' norms and values. Where, on the other hand, he lived in a traditionally working-class community, and worked in a large plant where employer–employee relations were 'rational-bureaucratic', he was likely to imbibe radical social and political orientations contrary to those dominant in society as a whole. Between the servant in the Oxbridge college and the miner, various combinations of work and community milieux could be associated with appropriate degrees of support for or deviance from conservatism.

A relationship was then posited between locations on the continuum of 'conservative'/'socialist' attitudes and support for the political parties. In the context of the 1960s, it was reasonable to

* This chapter is an abridgement of S. Taylor, 'Parkin's theory of working class conservatism: two hypotheses investigated', *Sociological Review*, 26 (1978), pp. 827–42.

argue that workers whose attitudes tended towards the conservative end of the scale would support the Conservative Party, and those who held opinions 'deviant' from the 'dominant' values would be more inclined to Labour. Parkin reviewed the available literature on patterns of party choices between workers in various micro-social contexts and found considerable support for the general interpretation. This part of the theory has been extended and confirmed in the later study by Jessop.[3]

Parkin then imaginatively extended his analysis to suggest explanations for the associations between two what may be termed 'proxy' variables and party choices among the working class.[4] An association between sex and partisanship, women voting for or identifying with the Conservatives disproportionately compared with men, had been found in a number of studies but attracted relatively little in the way of interpretation. It was suggested that the difference may have reflected the fact that women who did not work outside the home did not have the protection of the workplace sub-culture against the 'dominant' values, and thus were more amenable to Conservatism. Further, even among those women who were working, the workplace would be a less salient part of life than to men, given the primarily domestic orientation of the former:

The fact that women are less prone than men to the attraction of socialism squares well, I think, with the hypothesis. For it can be maintained that the world of work is a much less salient sphere of involvement to women than to men, particularly of course in view of the former's primary commitment to domestic life. It would follow that even if they were employed in industry – on a full or part-time basis – their assimilation into the value system would be a less complete affair than the assimilation of men. Women not employed in factory production at all would of course provide the extreme, but not uncommon, case of isolation from an industrial sub-culture.[5]

A similar argument is advanced to account for the association between age and partisanship found in many surveys, which is presumably what Parkin meant when he claimed that 'almost universally higher rates of Conservative voting [are to be found] . . . among retired men compared with those who are still employed'.[6] In this case removal from the social milieux consequent upon retirement means greater exposure to the 'dominant' values and, logically, a switch from Labour to Conservative. Younger workers were held in the Labour camp by virtue of their participation in manual work.

These hypotheses have not directly been analysed empirically. If Parkin's hypothesis concerning the explanation of sex differences among the working class could be validated, then this would explicate the nature of a relationship which has puzzled British political scientists for some time.

The working class was, for present purposes, taken to be manual workers and members of the families of manual workers who either were employed inside the home or were employed outside the home in manual occupations. The dependent variable used to indicate party choice was that of party identifications, which may represent general orientations more accurately than vote and thus be more suitable for testing the hypotheses. As the major concern of Parkin's thesis was to predict the distributions of preferences between Conservative and Labour, workers reporting that they identified with other parties or had no definite partisanship have been excluded.

Table 14 *Party identification of the working class by whether or not they participated in manual work outside the home*

	Percentage whose party identifications were Conservative	Labour	Total	Number (N)
Non-participants	42	58	100	283
Participants	31	69	100	488
			Total	771

In the sample, 33 per cent of workers identified with the Conservatives, the other two-thirds with Labour (Table 14). If Parkin's general contention, that whether or not a worker was engaged in manual work outside the home, is critical in 'explaining' partisanship, then at a minimum it would be expected that non-participants in such work would be rather more inclined to identify with the Conservatives than participants. The latter were defined as those respondents who worked full- or part-time in a manual occupation, and the former, those who had retired from a manual occupation or did not have a job outside the home. The expectation was confirmed by the data. The association was significant at the 0.01 level, but fairly small in magnitude with Yule's $Q = 0.22$.

There was a slight difference in the distributions of party identifications between men and women in the sample. Thirty-nine per cent of the women identified with the Conservatives (N = 333), compared to 31 per cent of the men (N = 368).[7] The association was significant at the 0.05 level, and fairly small in magnitude at 0.17. If, as suggested, the association was a compound of the lack of experience of the industrial workplace among women who worked inside the home, and the lesser salience of the world of work to those who did, compared to working males, then it would be anticipated that if the overall association was disaggregated, the highest rates of Conservatism would be found among 'isolated' women, the next highest among women working in manual occupations and the lowest among male manual workers. In order to test this, women who were housewives or other members of the families of manual workers who were not employed outside the home were combined as 'non-participants', and their patterns of party identifications compared with those of women who worked, full- or part-time, in manual occupations and with those of male manual workers (Table 15). The levels of Conservatism between the two female groups, and between female non-participants and males, were along the lines suggested by Parkin. The difference between the two female groups was significant at the 0.05 level, the value of Yule's Q for the magnitude of association was 0.24. The second difference, between female non-participants and males, was significant at the 0.01 level, with a strength of association of 0.25. The comparison which was not in line with Parkin's speculations was that between men and women who were manual workers; these identified between the parties in the same proportions. If it can be assumed that the lack of an association reflects the impact upon attitudes of the industrial workplace, then this would imply that working women were as fully integrated into the norms and values

Table 15 *Party identifications of women and men by whether or not they participated in manual work outside the home*

Sex	Participation or non-participation	Percentage whose identifications were Conservative	Labour	Total	Number
Female	Did not participate	41	58	99	212
	Did participate	31	69	100	121
Male	Did participate	31	69	100	367

of the workplace as were men. The industrial workplace may then be rather more salient to women employed outside the home than has been thought, and this greater influence reflected in the comparability of party identifications between such women and male manual workers.

14 Candidate evaluations by men and women*

Goldie Shabad and Kristi Andersen

Generalizations abound concerning women's political orientations and behaviour. One of these is that women tend to personalize politics and politicians. Women, it is said, are more likely than men to be interested in a candidate's personal attributes – style, character, looks, and family background – and to evaluate a candidate on the basis of such personal qualities rather than on issue positions. Moreover, this presumed concentration on the candidate rather than on the issues is considered to be 'irrational', 'apolitical', or 'naïve'. This particular generalization about women and the normative implications drawn from it are widely accepted in the social science literature. However, while statements claiming that 'women are more candidate oriented than men' or that women are 'more interested in candidates than issues', are often found in studies of mass political attitudes and behaviour, particularly those based on survey research, these studies offer neither systematic evidence to support these conclusions nor persuasive arguments to justify the conceptual and normative distinctions made concerning citizens' evaluations of candidates and political leaders more generally.

The purpose of this paper is twofold. The first is to determine whether an analysis of the available US survey data tends to support the claims made about women being candidate-oriented. The second is to suggest alternative and more precise ways of conceptualizing *both* men's and women's responses to and assessments of political leaders. The open-ended 'candidate likes and dislikes' questions on the Michigan election studies provide us with a set of data about voters' candidate evaluations. But while these data have been mined fairly extensively to study individuals' level of ideological thinking,[1] responses dealing with candidate attributes have generally been ignored or treated as a relatively unimportant residual category.

* The full text of this chapter can be found in *Public Opinion Quarterly*, **43** (1979), pp. 18–35.
Copyright 1979 by The Trustees of Columbia University.

Background

Before proceeding with our own analysis of the validity of the argument that women tend to be more candidate-oriented and less issue-oriented than men, it is of some interest to trace how this notion came to receive such widespread acceptance among social scientists. Jacquette, in her introduction to *Women and Politics*, asserts that 'a number of studies have shown that women are more interested in candidates than issues'.[2] That there is a body of congruent findings on this subject is implied by a number of other writers as well.[3] However, a careful examination of citations indicates that all the empirical evidence in support of this generalization actually comes from one source only: Campbell, Gurin and Miller's *The Voter Decides*.[4]

In their study, Campbell, Gurin and Miller divided the sample into categories based upon the number of responses to open-ended questions on likes and dislikes of presidential candidates in a 1952 election study that referred to a candidate's personal qualities. These responses ranged from statements about the candidate's ability to deal effectively with Congress to replies like 'he's wonderful'. They found that women, who constituted 53 per cent of the sample, made up 61 per cent of those who gave four or more 'candidate attribute' responses. Women were over-represented by only five percentage points in the next category (three candidate-oriented responses) and under-represented by only two percentage points in the lowest (no candidate references).

There was a somewhat larger difference between men and women with regard to the number of 'issue' responses to the open-ended questions. But in general, sex differences in terms of both types of responses are not very substantial. Moreover, because the term 'candidate orientation' is used in the study in a rather imprecise and unspecified manner (a fact readily admitted by Campbell, Gurin and Miller),[5] one is left with the impression that women, in being 'more candidate-oriented', tend to personalize politics and politicians by focusing on a candidate's personality, family, and so on.

Contrary to the conclusions drawn by Campbell, Gurin and Miller, other studies which examine the same question assert that sex differences with regard to evaluation of candidates are 'too small to be significant',[6] or are not always in the same direction.[7] Only a few scholars have been cautious in formulating generalizations on these rather precarious and contradictory findings – Sears, for example,[8] says women were 'more candidate-oriented and less issue-oriented than men in *1952*' (italics added). It appears, then, that a single table in *The Voter Decides* has become the basis for a body of social science literature.

One of the reasons this myth may have been so easily accepted, despite limited empirical evidence, is that it seems to be theoretically consistent with socialization studies which portray girls as having a more 'personalistic' orientation to politics than boys. The work cited most frequently in this respect is that of Hess and Torney.[9] Girls, Hess and Torney found, tend to 'personalize' the political system more than boys, as indicated by their more frequent choice of the president as the symbol of government and as a source of national pride, by the extent to which they believe the president runs the country, and by their slightly greater degree of affection for political figures. This seems fairly straightforward – there appear to be small but consistent differences between young boys and girls on a few measures of this type. But Hess and Torney attempt to go beyond this set of findings to say something more general about the socialization process and how it facilitates the personalization of politics on the part of women. For example, Hess and Torney remark that 'there was some tendency for girls to make a higher assessment of the influence of rich people and labor unions in determining laws'. Despite what the reader may think, this is not taken by the authors as an indication of political sophistication; rather, 'this may be another expression of the tendency of girls to personalize governmental processes'.[10] The source of this personalization, the authors suggest, lies in the fact that 'experience with their (girls') major role model (mother) is a more personal one and because authority figures deal with them in more expressive and personalized ways'.[11] The causal explanation is not too different from the one cited in a 1960 article on women's voting behaviour in the *New York Times*. This piece stated that the reason women tend to be more candidate-oriented and less issue-oriented than men stems from the fact that 'most candidates and all serious presidential aspirants are men. The analogy between choosing a candidate and choosing a mate can be strained, but there is probably more than coincidence for the attributes taken seriously by women in both cases. They want to be wooed, not persuaded.'[12] In neither case is the causal link demonstrated empirically. None the less, the existence of such links has been assumed by many who cite the Hess and

Torney study, despite the fact that several more recent studies have found only minimal, if any, sex differences among children on political attitudes similar to those examined by Hess and Torney.[13] Thus, along with the findings of *The Voter Decides*, those of Hess and Torney have become a pillar of support for the candidate-orientation myth.

Together with the acceptance of the myth of female candidate-orientation, there is often, in the voting behaviour literature, the tacit argument that evaluating candidates on the basis of criteria other than issue stands or party identification is 'irrational'. Elshtain,[14] Bourque and Grossholtz,[15] and Goot and Reid,[16] among others, have recently argued rather convincingly that political science as a discipline has demonstrated certain biases, so that whatever attributes are found to characterize women's political attitudes or behaviour, those characteristics are then defined as 'apolitical' or 'unpolitical' or 'naïve'.[17] It may be going too far to argue that the notion that choosing a presidential candidate on the basis of personal qualities is the least desirable, least rational way gained currency because the myth of female candidate-orientation was widely accepted in the discipline. But we may suggest, at least, that its wide acceptance may have discouraged careful theoretical and empirical analysis of the various and equally plausible ways by which ordinary citizens evaluate political leaders more generally.

Sex differences in candidate evaluations

In this section we will present a simple analysis of men's and women's candidate evaluations at numerous points in time, based on placing those responses into 'personal', 'issue', and 'party' categories. The classification by Campbell *et al.* of individuals according to how many responses of these three types respondents gave seemed to us rather arbitrary. A more direct method of assessing differences and similarities between the sexes in this regard is to simply compare the proportion of 'personal', 'issue', and 'party' responses given by men to the proportions given by women.

Three problems arise immediately in dealing with these particular data, each of which has several reasonable solutions in addition to the ones we arrived at:

1   How should the responses be categorized? Here we followed what appears to be standard operating procedure in the literature,

classifying the responses as they are grouped in the Election Study codebooks into the very general categories of 'candidate personal qualities', 'issues', and 'party connections'.

2   Should all possible mentions be used? In our analysis, we chose to use only the first responses to the 'like–dislike' questions. The proportion of the sample giving responses to the subsequent probes falls off rapidly,[18] so that by summing across and combining all possible responses one is giving disproportionate weight to the articulate, politically involved portion of the population.

3   Should the denominator be the opportunities to respond, once second and subsequent responses are ignored, or only the 'non-missing', responses (i.e., responses other than 'don't know', 'have nothing to say', and the like)? We chose the latter alternative, while recognizing that there is a slight tendency for women to have more 'missing' responses (don't know, or refused to say).

Thus, the percentages presented in Table 16 represent the proportions of the valid responses of men and of women which focused on candidates' personal qualities, on issues, and on candidates' party connections. There are several obvious points to be made on the basis of this table. First, there are few substantial differences in the response profiles of men as a group and women as a group.[19] With the exception of 1960, which will be discussed below, none of the differences appear to be substantively interesting (though they are in the expected direction).

Second, the changes in the relative frequency with which personality, issues, and party are mentioned occur at the same rates and in the same direction for men and women. The fact that men and women, as groups, appear to be responding in similar ways to changes in the political environment and to different election campaigns provides no evidence to confirm the argument that women structure their political world substantially differently than men.

Third, the version of the myth that 'women mention candidates more often than issues' is true for *both* men and women. In all years except 1972, when issue mentions achieved approximate parity with candidate mentions, both male and female respondents gave more responses pertaining to the candidate than to the issues.

Let us look more closely at the 1960 data, which seem to come closest to supporting not only the general myth but the more specific one that women are particularly attracted by Kennedy's family,

Table 16 *Percentages of personal, issue, and party references in candidate evaluations of men and women, 1952–76*

| | Numbers of References in candidate evaluations | | | |
	valid responses	Personal (per cent)	Issue (per cent)	Party (per cent)
1952				
Men	1772	60	16	22
Women	1977	61	16	22
1956				
Men	1821	64	18	17
Women	1944	68	17	15
1960				
Men	1187	60	21	18
Women	1312	71	14	12
1964				
Men	1837	48	41	10
Women	2241	50	39	10
1968				
Men	2462	50	33	11
Women	2980	52	29	10
1972				
Men	1291	43	49	6
Women	1586	47	45	7
1976				
Men	2303	62	25	14
Women	2813	65	23	11

Percentages do not always add up to 100 because of errors due to rounding-off and because in some years there were a number of unclassifiable responses (for example, 'miscellaneous other'). This number was significant only in 1968, when many people were recorded as giving 'an emphatic no' to the questions of what they liked about the candidates.

looks, wealth and charisma. It should be noted that, in 1960, women voted slightly more heavily than men for Nixon. Further, it has been shown elsewhere that the mobilization effect which the 1960 election appeared to have on women was confined primarily to those who identified with the Republican Party and who were Nixon voters.[20] But to address the myth more directly, we can isolate all the candidate evaluation responses which seem to fall into pure personality, social background or physical attribute categories. Examples of such responses include references to Kennedy's being well educated, his wife, his 'likeability', his age, and his coming from a 'good family'. It is obvious that JFK did appeal to people on these dimensions. But the percentages of male responses and female responses falling in these categories are exactly the same. The greater proportion of so-called 'personality' mentions by women actually reflects a slightly greater tendency to mention Kennedy's competence, trustworthiness, reliability, and leadership qualities. This raises the question of the appropriateness of the traditional conceptualization of candidate evaluation as consisting of three dimensions (personality, issues, party).

Dimensions of candidate evaluations

In order to specify the dimensions along which various candidates are evaluated and to determine the relative impact of these types of evaluations on the vote one might, like Miller and Miller,[21] subject these (and other) responses to a factor analysis. Alternatively, one can *specify* the dimensions which one expects voters to use in evaluating the candidates and investigate the extent to which they appear to utilize those dimensions. We have taken the latter course, and in a rather preliminary way have derived a categorization of responses which goes well beyond the more common threefold classification and specifies more precisely the criteria used by the electorate to evaluate presidential candidates. The categories are as follows:

1   Political party as a basis for liking or disliking a candidate.
   a   *Party references*   Respondent prefers the candidate because of his party or because of his association with other party figures, etc.
2   Issue positions as a basis for liking or disliking a candidate.
   a   *Issue references*   For example, 'I agree with him on civil rights.' 'I like his attitude towards the Soviet Union.'
   b   *Group references*   The candidate will benefit (or hurt) particular social or economic groups, in particular issue areas.
   c   *Ideological references*   To a candidate's liberalism, conservatism, 'socialism', etc.
3   Candidate attributes as a basis for liking or disliking a candidate.

Responses with little or no explicitly political content.

   a   *Personality*   Respondent sees the candidate as warm (or cold), likeable (or not), religious, kind, outspoken (or too critical); indicates a positive or negative response about the candidate's family; feels the candidate is hard to understand or appears attractive or unattractive on television.

b   *Background*   References to candidate's education, family, background, age, etc.

Responses with explicitly political content.

c   *Specific competence*   What the respondent perceives to be the candidate's specific areas of competence (or incompetence): how the candidate would handle various international trouble spots, how well the candidate could communicate with various groups in society, how experienced or inexperienced the candidate was in dealing with specific problems.

d   *General competence*   Respondent's perception of the candidate as being experienced *in general*, or in politics, as having a 'good record', 'well qualified for the job', etc.

e   *Leadership*   Positive or negative responses about the candidate's ability to lead the country, referring to his strength, his confidence, decision-making ability, inspirational qualities (or the reverse of these).

f   *Reliability*   Is the candidate viewed as hardworking, realistic, pragmatic, careful, capable of handling the job? Or is he lazy, impractical, erratic?

g   *Trust*   The respondent's views on the candidate's integrity, principles, and ideals. Is the candidate perceived as honest, dishonest, sincere, insincere, etc.

In general, the responses we classify under the headings trust, reliability, leadership, and general and specific competence have all been considered responses dealing with 'personal attributes'. Furthermore, the use of these criteria in the evaluation of candidates has typically been considered, at least by implication, a politically unsophisticated mode of behaviour.[22] But given that the president's role can be plausibly seen as equally concerned with symbolic leadership and policy direction, and in the context particularly of our recent political past, it does not seem unreasonable to evaluate presidential contenders on the basis of their perceived honesty, competence, experience or leadership abilities.

Table 17 *Percentages of valid first responses containing specific personality, leadership, competence, trust, and issue references in the candidate evaluations of the population and of men and women, 1952–76*

	Number of valid first responses	Person-ality (per cent)	Com-petence (per cent)	Leader-ship (per cent)	Trust (per cent)	Issues (per cent)
1952						
Total	5923	7	38	2	6	9
Men	2801	5	40	3	6	8
Women	3122	10	36	2	7	8
1956						
Total	6411	15	26	3	7	12
Men	3101	12	29	3	7	11
Women	3310	19	23	3	8	11
1960						
Total	6315	9	26	3	5	16
Men	2998	8	25	3	4	16
Women	3317	10	28	4	6	16
1964						
Total	6886	11	15	2	7	28
Men	3175	7	17	2	7	28
Women	3711	13	16	3	7	26
1968						
Total	9866	9	13	5	10	20
Men	4494	7	14	5	11	21
Women	5372	12	12	5	9	18
1972						
Total	3189	4	14	6	10	35
Men	1433	3	13	7	9	38
Women	1756	5	14	6	9	33
1976						
Total	5125	8	17	9	15	15
Men	2312	6	17	9	15	16
Women	2813	9	18	8	14	15

Table 17 shows that details of candidates' personalities and lives do not form a very large component of the public's evaluation of them. The proportion of pure 'personality' responses among valid first mentions ranges between 4 per cent (in the issue-oriented 1972 campaign) and 15 per cent (in 1956). These types of evaluative remarks, however, are certainly overshadowed by the public's reliance on competence, trust (especially in later years), and issues (especially in 1964 and 1972) as yardsticks with which to measure candidates.

The differences between men's and women's evaluations are small, just as they were when the three broader categories of responses were used. In only six out of thirty-five instances in Table 17 do men and women differ by more than four percentage points in the proportion of their responses falling into a particular category. Moreover, the percentage differences never exceed 7 per cent. In four years (1952, 1956, 1964 and 1968), women more frequently than men mentioned personality criteria by 5 to 7 per cent. In 1956, men mentioned competence more often than did women; and in 1972, 38 per cent of men's responses had to do with issues, compared with 33 per cent of women's responses. There does not seem to be any consistent trend over time with regard to these differences, nor is there a strong pattern of differences which asserts itself similarly year after year.

Conclusion

Several conclusions can be drawn from our analysis. We have found no confirming evidence to support the myth that women tend to be consistently more personality-oriented and less issue-oriented than men in their assessments of presidential candidates. There are few differences between the two sexes in this respect. Indeed, our analysis of male–female evaluations of candidates from 1952 to 1976 indicates that, when viewed as aggregates, men and women tend to respond to their political environment in a similar fashion. This suggests that one should be wary of attributing to women, or to any group, certain unique and fixed political characteristics.

However, although we find little that argues for the perpetuation of this myth, we would not want to conclude on the basis of these data alone that there are no significant differences between men and women in the ways they view and come to orient themselves to the political world. Even if we knew that individual men and women had given similar responses to survey questions of the type used here, this similarity might well mask significant variations in the process by which they came to respond in common ways.

We have argued that both women and men view and evaluate presidential candidates in a more multi-dimensional manner than previous analyses, by virtue of their conceptual framework, have suggested. Most works on this subject conceptualize the criteria used by the electorate to evaluate candidates as falling into three categories: those based on the partisan connections, the issue stands, and the personality of the candidate. Generally, far more attention is given to the first two categories, with assessments based on a candidate's personal qualities treated as a residual category. By lumping together rather diverse candidate attributes, such as looks, style, family background, prior experience, and leadership capabilities, and by referring to this category as 'personality characteristics', these analyses imply that such evaluations are generally concerned with trivial and politically irrelevant matters. As a consequence, these analyses obscure other personal dimensions of political leadership which are known to be significant for effective performance and which are perceived as such by both the mass public and political elites.

15 Gender, levels of political thinking and political action*

M. Kent Jennings and Barbara Farah

In this discussion we will compare the way men and women relate their levels of ideological thinking to political action. Our main theoretical concern is to determine if men and women translate conceptual sophistication into political action in the same manner.[1] We begin with conventional participation and then move on to unconventional activity.

Respondents in our cross-national survey[2] for the early 1970s indicated whether they often, sometimes, seldom, or never performed the following seven activities:

1 Read about politics in the newspapers
2 Discussed politics with friends
3 Tried to convince others to vote in the preferred direction
4 Worked with others to solve community problems
5 Attended political meetings or rallies
6 Contacted public officials
7 Worked actively for a party or candidate.

Voting was omitted because it was nearly universal in the continental countries.[3]

Eight-point Guttman scales were constructed from the response patterns for each country. It will come as no surprise that men participate more than women in all countries, but there is a dramatic range in that margin. The *tau-c* correlations were 0.39 in Germany, 0.28 in Austria, 0.27 in the Netherlands, 0.19 in Britain, and 0.17 in the United States.

In order to assess whether men and women convert ideological conceptualization into conventional participation at the same rate we use least squares regression analysis for each group. Unstandardized slope coefficients (bs) are used as the statistical measure of the

* This chapter is an excerpt from M. K. Jennings and B. Farah, 'Ideology, gender and political action: a cross-national survey', *British Journal of Political Science*, 10 (1980), pp. 219–40.

relationship because they allow us to gauge the strength of the linkage for the two groups and provide an interpretable way of indicating how equal the conversion rates are for men and women across the five countries.

Table 18 *The relationship between ideological sophistication and conventional participation in politics (unstandardized regression coefficients)*

	Nether-lands	Austria	Germany (FDR)	United States	Great Britain
Women	0.43*	0.47	0.24	0.58	0.54
Men	0.45	0.51	0.43	0.52	0.46

* All entries are significant at the 0.005 level.

Table 18 shows, as expected, very strong associations between ideological awareness and participation. The strength of the relationship varies somewhat between men and women across the countries. In Britain and the United States ideological thinking serves to motivate women to political action slightly more so than it does men. In contrast, men receive an advantage in the three non-Anglo-American countries. Only in Germany, however, is the difference in the coefficients statistically significant. Inspection of the detailed analysis for Germany reveals a widening gap in the motivational pattern between men and women. Whereas the distribution for men follows a steep and monotonic course, for women it begins at a lower level, follows a much more gradual rise, and then tapers off at the upper end of the scale. As regards conventional participation, then, we find only one case where the translation of ideological thinking differs in a meaningful way for men and women. We now turn to unconventional participation to determine whether the same pattern emerges.

The epidemic of political activity outside the mainstream, stretching from the early 1960s (in the United States) to the early 1970s, prompted students of political participation to re-examine prevailing assumptions. As a consequence of the relatively great numbers of the mass public either taking part in or approving what were often illegal and usually unorthodox activities, the standard lore about the modes of participation, the socio-economic correlates, and elite responses came into question. The study from which our data are drawn had as a major objective the conceptualization and measurement of unconventional as well as conventional modes of participation.

A chronic problem in assessing unconventional behaviour in mass publics is that – almost by definition – insufficient numbers of respondents in typical cross-section surveys fit the criteria. Partly in anticipation of this and partly for theoretical reasons, the parent study treats unorthodox behaviour in terms of a readiness or potential to engage in what are called acts of protest. As stated by Kaase and Marsh, 'the actual involvement in protest behaviour may be contingent upon strong and hence infrequent stimuli . . . but the *potential to participate,* the individual readiness to be mobilized, is an abiding property of a wide sector of the whole political community, whether currently active or not'.[4] Whether or not the spread of the idea of unconventional activity as a legitimate way of seeking redress is a new or revived concept in Western societies, its appearance in contemporary times suggested that ways had to be found for assessing its distribution in mass publics.

The final protest potential scale developed in the parent study (see above and note 2) combines the two elements of affect and behavioural intention with respect to the following activities: signing petitions, demonstrating lawfully, boycotting, withholding rents and taxes, occupying buildings, blocking traffic, and striking unofficially. For each item the respondents indicated whether they 'have done', 'would do', 'might do', or 'would never do' the activity; they also indicated their level of approval of the activity in terms of a four-point approval scale. Affirmative responses – have, would, or might do – were joined with the 'strongly approve' and 'approve' responses and scored positively. All other combinations were scored negatively. The resulting measures were then combined to

Table 19 *The relationship between ideological sophistication and unconventional participation in politics (unstandardized regression coefficients)*

	Nether-lands	Austria	Germany (FDR)	United States	Great Britain
Women	0.37*	0.26	0.25	0.41	0.36
Men	0.37	0.34	0.30	0.31	0.34

* All entries are significant at the 0.005 level.

form an eight-point Guttman scale of protest potential. Sex differences in protest potential are smaller than in conventional participation. *Tau-c* correlations are 0.21 in Austria, 0.20 in Germany, 0.18 in Britain, 0.14 in the Netherlands, and 0.10 in the United States.

Applying the same procedure used for conventional participation, we find that the rate of 'conversion' of ideological thinking into unconventional action differs only marginally between the sexes across the countries (Table 19). There are no differences in the Netherlands; in Germany and Austria women gain slightly less than do men; and in the two Anglo-American countries women derive marginally more benefits from increased levels of ideological thinking. However, in no country are the differences significant at the 0.05 level. The pattern we find for unconventional participation mirrors that for conventional participation. The cumulative score is impressive in so far as only one case out of ten reveals any significant difference between men and women in the translation of ideological thinking into political action.

16 Women in positions of political leadership in Britain, France and West Germany*

Donna S. Sanzone

Women have traditionally been excluded from high-ranking positions in both government and politics. In recent years, however, more women have achieved positions of political influence, and several women have been appointed or elected to high executive positions in the governments of France, Britain, and West Germany.

France

Although there is an underlying tradition of egalitarianism in France, stemming from the French revolution, women have suffered from inferior status written into the Napoleonic Code of the early nineteenth century. Progress for women has been slow and difficult, as evidenced by their failure to win basic political and legal rights until the end of the Second World War. Interestingly, two women served as ministers of state in the Popular Front government of 1936, even before women won the right to vote. The first full woman minister – Germaine Poinso-Chapuis – was appointed to the Ministry of Health in 1947 under the Fourth Republic government of Robert Schuman. However, there were no women ministers in the governments of the Fifth Republic until the election of President Valéry Giscard d'Estaing in May 1974.

There were no women ministers in President Charles de Gaulle's Cabinet; nor were there women state secretaries until his last year in office, when he appointed one woman to share a state secretarial position with a man. President Georges Pompidou retained most of de Gaulle's ministers and kept the only woman state secretary, Marie-Madeleine Diensch, in the Ministry of Health.

At the time of his inauguration on 24 May 1974 Giscard d'Es-

* This chapter is taken from D. Sanzone, 'Women in politics: a study of political leadership in the United Kingdom, France and the Federal Republic of Germany', in C. Epstein and R. Coser (eds.), *Access to Power* (George Allen & Unwin 1981) pp. 57–52.

taing appointed a woman, Dr Simone Veil, as Minister of Health and two women to state secretarial positions: Dr Hélène Dorhlac as Secretary of State to the Minister of Justice for Prison Conditions, and Dr Annie Lesur as Secretary of State to the Minister of Education for Preschool Children. In addition, in July 1974, Giscard d'Estaing created a new ministerial office concerned with the status of women and appointed the co-editor of the newsweekly *L'Express*, Françoise Giroud, as Secretary of State for the Status of Women (*Secretaire d'Etat à la Condition Feminine*).

Although Giscard d'Estaing was convinced of the need to include women in his government, Premier Jacques Chirac was reluctant to concede any real power to them. The premier confided during a private meeting that it was 'undoubtedly not the President's best idea, but there was nothing to worry about'.[1] Women were given impressive titles, but they were in fact excluded from the government's inner circle of power. For example, the rich and powerful social security system was removed from Dr Veil's ministry and placed under the Ministry of Labour. Hélène Dorhlac was relegated to an office outside her ministry's building. To dramatize her exclusion from the centre of government activities she addressed the National Assembly in her raincoat. After several weeks she was given an office in the building.

The case of Françoise Giroud is perhaps the most revealing. Not only was her new post of Secretary of State for the Status of Women deprived of an independent budget, but there were also fundamental questions concerning the status of the new office and its authority. In addition to opposing the idea of creating a ministry for women's affairs, Chirac also objected to Giroud on the political grounds that she had supported François Mitterrand, the opposition candidate, during the presidential elections. In the end, however, Giroud was confirmed in office and empowered to 'move toward integration of women into contemporary society and advance them on every level of responsibility'.[2]

Giroud made considerable progress during her two years in office. By February 1976 she had submitted 111 proposals to the premier designed to eliminate the most obvious forms of inequality in French law. While in office she succeeded in initiatives changing divorce laws, outlawing job discrimination on the basis of sex or family status, and setting up measures to improve the condition of widows, unmarried mothers, and women heads of family.[3]

Among the legal measures that she introduced were proposals to give women the right to sign a declaration of income, to open all university competition to both sexes, and to raise the maximum age for civil service examinations to 45, so that women who had interrupted their studies or careers to raise children would not be excluded from government careers. She also proposed a maternal indemnity to permit one parent to remain at home until a child was old enough to attend nursery school.

On 27 August 1976 Giroud was transferred from the post of Secretary of State for the Status of Women to the post of Secretary of State for Culture by the new premier, Raymond Barre. At the same time Barre created a Delegation for the Status of Women, replacing the state secretariat established in 1974.[4] The present Delegate to the Premier for the Status of Women and Family Affairs is Monique Pelletier.

Simone Veil was appointed Minister of Health after serving as Secretary of the Higher Council of the Courts from 1970 to 1974. During her career as secretary general she drafted important legislation concerning the rights of prison inmates, mental patients, and adopted, retarded and illegitimate children. She has a degree in law and is a graduate of the *Institut d'Etudes Politiques*. The first woman to reach full ministerial rank in the Fifth Republic, Veil made her mark in the areas of birth control and abortion. In June 1974 the National Assembly gave overwhelming approval to a Bill, sponsored by the government and presented by Veil, that authorized the general distribution of contraceptives and provided that the social security system pay for the costs. The nearly unanimous approval given to the Bill – only one vote was against – demonstrated the reversal of previous attitudes towards birth control and replaced a 1967 law that permitted the distribution of contraceptives only on medical orders with a specific time limit. The new law also eliminated the restriction that women under 18 had to have the written permission of their parents as well as a doctor to obtain contraceptives. Veil promised a vigorous public information campaign on birth control to publicize the fact that birth control was now a matter of 'common right', freely available.

In addition to birth control reform Veil has also played a major role in the passage of new abortion legislation. The subject of abortion had been avoided in Catholic France. In 1974 the Pompidou government intended to introduce a Bill to liberalize abortion, but it dropped the Bill without debate when it ran into opposition from powerful sources.[5] The new law, drawn up and defended by

Veil with the support of the Giscard d'Estaing government, gave women the right to abortion within the first ten weeks of pregnancy. The Bill permitted any permanent resident 'distressed' by a pregnancy to have an abortion, provided it was performed by a doctor in an established hospital. Women under 18 had to have parents' permission. The law ended the prohibition of abortion in France; but it is still a matter of controversy, and many doctors are refusing to perform abortions. The public, however, strongly favours abortion. In a poll for the Ministry of Health, taken by the French Institute of Public Opinion, 73 per cent of those questioned favoured the right of abortion during the first ten weeks of pregnancy.[6]

Public opinion was indeed in favour of the programmes and measures adopted by the Giscard d'Estaing government regarding women's rights. In January 1975 a Figaro-Sofres poll indicated that a large majority of the French believed the status of women to be the most positive aspect of the president's programme. Moreover, they replied to the question 'To whom would you like to give greater responsibilities?' by placing Simone Veil first, ahead of the premier, followed by Françoise Giroud, ahead of the Ministers of State, Finance, and Foreign Affairs.[7]

Veil retained the post of Minister of Health until June 1979, when she was elected to the presidency of the first directly elected European Parliament. At the time of writing, there were four women in the Cabinet of Prime Minister Raymond Barre: Alice Saunier-Seïté, Minister for Universities; Monique Pelletier, Minister Delegate to the Prime Minister for the Status of Women and Family Affairs; Nicole Pasquier, Secretary of State to the Ministry of Work and Participation and, in particular, Women in the Labour Force; and Hélène Missoffe, Secretary of State to the Ministry of Health and Social Security. Thus, of the four women in the Barre government, one is a full-ranking minister, one a minister delegate, and two are state secretaries.[8]

Britain

In contrast to France's rather late acceptance of women in politics, the British government included a woman Cabinet minister as early as 1929. Margaret Bonfield was appointed Minister of Labour in the Labour government of 1929. Women were first allowed to stand for parliament in 1918, and one of the seventeen women standing, Lady Astor, was elected. Between 1918 and 1971 ninety-four women were elected to parliament and twenty-seven attained ministerial rank, eight as full ministers. The Life Peerage Act of 1958 admitted women to the House of Lords, and by 1975 twenty-six women had been created peeresses for life.[9]

The Labour Party has consistently placed more women in executive level positions than the Conservatives, who did not appoint a female minister until 1951, when Dame Florence Horsbrugh was named Minister of Education. Margaret Thatcher, former Secretary of State for Science and Education in the Conservative government of Edward Heath (June 1970 to March 1974), was only the second woman in the history of the Conservative Party to hold a full Cabinet position. Lady Tweedsmuir served as minister in the Scottish Office in Prime Minister Heath's government, but this was not a full Cabinet post. In addition, Peggy Fenner was Parliamentary Secretary of State in the Ministry of Agriculture, Fisheries and Food in 1973.

Included in the Labour government of Harold Wilson (March 1974 to March 1976) were two women in full Cabinet positions: Barbara Castle, Secretary of State for Social Services; and Shirley Williams, Secretary of State for Prices and Consumer Protection. Another woman, Judith Hart, was Minister for Overseas Development but not in the Cabinet. In the Labour government headed by James Callaghan (April 1976 to May 1979), Shirley Williams was the only woman to serve in a full Cabinet position: Secretary of State for Education and Science and Paymaster General. Judith Hart retained her position as Minister of State for Overseas Development under Callaghan.

There has been less dramatic progress in women's rights in Britain than in France during the mid 1970s, obviously because Britain made substantial progress many years earlier. Birth control is generally accepted as an integral part of family welfare. The National Health Services Act of 1967 provides for family-planning services under the authority of local health departments. Over 10,000 clinics exist for family planning, run by voluntary family-planning associations. The Abortion Act of 1967 permits abortion if the continuation of a woman's pregnancy involves a greater risk than its termination in view of the dangers to the mother's life, to the physical or mental health of her or her existing children, or to the physical or mental health of the unborn child. Two doctors must approve the operation, which must be performed within the first twenty-eight weeks of pregnancy.

In an effort to end discrimination in employment, Barbara Castle, then Secretary of State for Employment and Productivity, introduced and piloted through parliament the Equal Pay Act of 1970. This measure was designed to eliminate discrimination between men and women in both the terms and the conditions of employment by the end of 1975. According to the provisions of the Act:

Where men and women do the same or broadly similar work for the same or related employer, or where they do different jobs recognized by job evaluation schemes as equivalent, women will qualify for equal pay. The Act also removes the effects of any obvious discrimination there may have been in the actual process of job evaluation.[10]

The Equal Pay Act gave employers five years in which to implement its provisions. It came into full effect on 29 December 1975.

Barbara Castle was one of the Labour Party's 'regulars'. She was a member of the government throughout Wilson's two terms in office: 1964–70 and 1974–6. Castle's first position was Minister of Overseas Development from 1964 to 1965. She was then named Minister of Transport from 1965 to 1968, the first woman to hold this office. In this position she was responsible for the most comprehensive Transport Act ever enacted in Britain. Subsequently, she was appointed Secretary of State for Employment and Productivity in 1968, and she remained in this position until Labour's defeat in the March 1970 elections. It was in this position that she carried through parliament the Equal Pay Act of 1970. From April 1975 until April 1976 she held the Cabinet post of Secretary of State for Social Services. In this capacity Castle was concerned with a broad range of social welfare issues, including pensions, social security, and national insurance benefits. Castle lost her post as Secretary of State for Social Services in April 1976 when James Callaghan took over the Labour government after Wilson's resignation.

Shirley Williams, the only woman Cabinet Minister in the previous Labour government, rose rapidly in party politics, attaining ministerial rank (but not at Cabinet level) only two years after being elected to Parliament in 1964. She was a member of the Labour government from April 1966, first as Parliamentary Secretary of State in the Ministry of Labour, then as Minister of State in the

Department of Education and Science (1967–8) and subsequently as Minister of State in the Home Office (1969–70).

After the election of Wilson in 1974 Williams was appointed to the Cabinet as Secretary of State for Prices and Consumer Protection. In September 1976 she was transferred to another ministerial position, Secretary of State for Education and Science. She also held the Office of Paymaster General. In May 1979, Williams lost her Cabinet position as well as her seat in the House of Commons as a result of the Conservative victory in the British general election. Williams had been regarded as a possible successor to Prime Minister Callaghan.[11] A respected and competent politician, Williams [now President of the Social Democratic Party] remains an important political figure in Britain.

Margaret Thatcher is certainly the most prominent woman in British politics today. In the 1970–4 Conservative government Thatcher served as Minister of Education and Science for almost four years. The public image that she projected during this period was far from popular, exemplified by such epithets as the 'Iron Lady'. She supported the principle of meritocracy against the open-enrolment school policy of the Labour government. Moreover, in another unpopular move she raised the price of school lunches and eliminated the distribution of free milk to schoolchildren. In some ways Thatcher appears to be typical of the classic Conservative politician: middle class, Oxford educated, a member of the meritocracy, an upholder of traditional values. She stands for law and order, individual enterprise, and traditional moral values.

From February 1974 until her election as party leader she served in the Shadow Cabinet and was the spokesperson on Treasury and Economic Affairs. On 12 February 1975 Thatcher was elected head of the Conservative Party, becoming the first woman to lead a major British political party. Thatcher's emergence on the British political scene was surprising: she acknowledged that she did not think that the Conservatives would be ready for a woman leader in her lifetime.

On 3 May 1979 Margaret Thatcher and the Conservative Party won a decisive victory in Britain's general election. Thatcher thereby became the first woman prime minister in European history. The Conservatives won a comfortable majority of forty-three seats in the House of Commons, reflecting a shift to the right in the British electorate. The Conservative victory can be attributed in large part to Labour's failure to deal effectively with Britain's economic problems, including a series of strikes in the winter of 1978–9. Following her victory, Thatcher appointed an all-male Cabinet of twenty-two members. She did, however, appoint two women Ministers of State (without Cabinet rank): Sally Oppenheim, Minister of State for Consumer Affairs in the Department of Trade, and Baroness Young, Minister of State in the Department of Education and Science.

It is doubtful that Thatcher would do more to advance the cause of women in politics than would a male Labour prime minister. When asked her opinion of the women's liberation movement, she responded: 'What's it ever done for me?'[12] Historically, the Conservatives have placed fewer women in positions of influence and power. In fact Thatcher's voting record in the House of Commons over the past twenty years has been consistently right-wing conservative, especially on social reform issues. For example, she has voted in favour of restoring the death penalty and has opposed abortion reform laws.

The election of Thatcher as prime minister is a significant development in female executive leadership in Britain and Europe. Although there have been a few individual women of influence, British politics has never fully integrated women. Historically, of course, Britain has accepted female monarchs who came to the throne by succession, but it has not accepted them as actual contenders for political power. For this reason both Margaret Thatcher and Shirley Williams are important figures to watch in British politics. It is interesting that the two women contenders for political leadership are so different; neither stands for a feminist platform,[13] but each represents opposing political philosophies and programmes that will affect the basic direction and tenor of British society.

Two significant legal advances in the area of women's rights in Britain warrant special attention: the Equal Pay Act of 1970, and the Sex Discrimination Act of December 1975.

The Sex Discrimination Act of 1975 has been considered one of the most radical pieces of social legislation of modern times.[14] The Act made it unlawful to treat one person less favourably than another on grounds of sex in the following areas: employment; training and related matters; education; and the provision of housing and goods, services and facilities to the public. The Act also applied to discriminatory advertising in these areas.

The Equal Pay Act of 1970, as indicated previously, came into force in December 1975 after allowing employers five years to comply with its requirements. This Act complemented the Sex Discrimination Act by ending sexual discrimination in terms of employment. The Act covered basic pay as well as such other forms of additional payments as overtime pay, bonuses, holiday pay, and sick pay.

In order to ensure implementation of the equal rights legislation the Sex Discrimination Act also established and gave statutory powers to an Equal Opportunities Commission. The tasks of the commission are to work towards the elimination of discrimination, to promote equality of opportunity between men and women, and to monitor the implementation of the Sex Discrimination Act and the Equal Pay Act.

In November 1977 the Equal Opportunities Commission issued a report based on evidence to the Royal Commission on Income Distribution and Wealth, entitled *Women and Low Incomes*. The report discusses the status of women in Britain, with particular attention to sexual inequality in terms of income and state benefits. The commission found that, while the Equal Pay Act had to some degree reduced the relative gap between male and female basic wage rates, the gap remained significant.

The commission urged the distribution of women throughout all sectors of the economy. It recommended that women be guaranteed equal access to all fringe benefits and be provided with training facilities to enable them to acquire new skills. As regards social security and state benefits, the commission recommended a revision in social security laws and regulations, specifically the elimination of the dependency principle in favour of the principle that women are equal with men in terms of social security contributions and benefits. (Social security legislation presently treats the man as the automatic head of the household and the woman as the dependent party who is not in need of full social security benefits).

West Germany

The first woman Cabinet minister in the history of West German government, Elisabeth Schwarzhaupt of the Christian Democratic Union (CDU), was appointed by Adenauer to the newly created Ministry of Health in November 1961 in response to pressure by women members of the Bundestag (lower house). From 1967 to 1976 there were two women 'regulars' in the Cabinet: Kate Strobel and Katharina Focke, who were both Ministers of Health, a ritually female appointment. The social insurance system falls within the jurisdiction not of the Ministry of Health but of the Ministry of Labour, which is headed by a man.

Kate Strobel was in the Bonn government for almost six years (1967–72) as Minister of Health, first in the Kiesinger government and later in the Brandt government. She was replaced by Katharina Focke in 1972. Focke was elected to the Bundestag in 1969 and in the same year was appointed Parliamentary State Secretary in the Federal Chancellery. During this period she was responsible for European affairs, education and science, and co-operation between the federal government and the Länders (counties). She was named Minister for Health, Youth, and Family Affairs in 1972 and held this position until 1976. Dr Focke was also a Vice-President of the Bundestag.

As Minister of Health, Youth, and Family Affairs Focke was active in promoting women's rights, especially independent social security for women and recognition of women's work in the family and of their contribution to family maintenance. In addition, the improvement of educational and vocational training for women was given a high priority.

In an effort to facilitate reform in these areas the Bundestag appointed a commission to study the role of woman at all levels of society. In November 1976 the commission released a preliminary report on 'Women and Society'.[15] The report identified problems faced by women in areas of employment and education and concluded that West German women earned less and had fewer educational opportunities, fewer professional opportunities, and less chance for advancement than men.[16] The commission offered suggestions to correct these inequities and stressed the need for educational reforms, increased professional opportunities, increased job training, and an effective public relations campaign to make women more conscious of their rights. It was left up to the Bundestag to take specific measures to deal with the problems identified by the commission.

An important recent change in the legal status of women has been in the area of family law. A new marriage and family law, called the First Act for Reform of Marriage and Family Law, came into effect on 1 July 1977. Unlike previous family laws the new law does not give guidelines for marriage; for example, it does not state that a husband should work and a wife should take care of the home. Both husbands and wives are now jointly responsible for family income, education, and housework. Prior to this Act, if a wife wanted to work, she needed the permission of her husband. The new law provides for legal equality in marriage and family life.[17]

Another important aspect of the new law is the amended divorce law, which allows for divorce on grounds of irreparable marriage breakdown. The former 'guilt principle' has been replaced by a no-fault concept. After divorce all assets, including pensions, are divided between the partners, and each is responsible for his or her own maintenance. (Only the financially weaker partner who is unable to earn a living can be granted alimony.) Child support is awarded to the one who receives custody of children.

Perhaps the most prominent woman in the Bonn government is the former President and current Vice-President of the Bundestag, Anne-Marie Renger. The President of the Bundestag is accorded a formal position just below that of the President of the Republic. Renger, of the Social Democratic Party (SDP), was elected President in December 1972, becoming the first woman president of a West European parliament. She held this position until December 1976, when she lost her post to a Christian Democrat, Karl Carstens, following the Social Democrats' defeat in the October 1976 elections.[18]

Renger has directed her efforts towards equalizing employment opportunities for women. She has edited a book entitled *Equal Opportunities for Women*,[19] which consists of selected letters received from women employees describing instances of sexual discrimination at work. Although the principle of 'equal pay for equal work' has been recognized on paper in West Germany, it has not been consistently applied. A parliamentary commission on law reform found that on average women earned 30 per cent less than men. 'Nowhere is there such a wide divergence between men and women and day-to-day reality than in working life', said Renger.[20] Renger has also deplored the small number of women in politics and criticized the major parties for not placing more women on their electoral lists.[21] Yet, she is opposed to the more radical proposal of a constitutional amendment to assure women proportional representation in the Bundestag or in the Länder parliaments.

Despite Renger's prominent position in West German politics it is extremely unlikely that she will ever become chancellor. In fact, given traditional attitudes towards women, the likelihood of a woman chancellor, at least within the next generation, is remote.

The third woman Vice-President of the Bundestag, at the time of writing, was Lisolette Funcke of the Free Democratic Party (FDP). A member of the Bundestag for twenty years, she has been head of the Bundestag's financial committee and has been active in abortion reform legislation.

In June 1975 the Bundestag passed a law permitting abortion on demand during the first ten weeks of pregnancy. However, on 25 February 1975, the Federal Constitutional Court ruled that the law transgressed the Basic Law's principle that 'everyone shall have the right to life and inviolability of person'[22] and declared the law unconstitutional. Funcke said that West German women 'would not accept or abide by such a decision'.[23] Subsequently, on 12 February 1976 the Bundestag adopted a new Bill, which permits abortion on medical and emergency grounds. The new law does not permit abortion on demand but specifies conditions under which abortion is legal:[24] where there is a risk to the life or health of the pregnant woman or to the physical or mental health of the child; in cases of rape; or where there is the risk of other serious disadvantage to the pregnant woman.

Before an abortion can be obtained, a woman must receive medical and social advice from a doctor or recognized advisory service. She must also obtain a doctor's certificate indicating that the medical conditions have been fulfilled. The abortion must then be performed in a hospital by a doctor other than the one providing the certificate. Insurance companies and state assistance programmes cover all costs incurred in abortion. The Bundestag has also addressed the issue of birth control by providing free advice on contraception and free provision of contraceptive devices under social assistance schemes.

Another prominent woman in the government of Helmut Schmidt was Marie Schlei, the first woman to head the Ministry of Economic Co-operation. Prior to her appointment she served in the chancellor's office. In this role Schlei created a new department concerned with women's affairs, in particular with the advancement of women in developing countries.

This paper has discussed two separate yet closely related issues: women in politics, and women's rights. More specifically, it has discussed the role that women in politics have played in advancing women's rights. The final question to be answered is whether progress has been made in relation to both these issues. The question of 'progress' is a thorny one. The term is relative and must be viewed within the context of a particular society.

It could be argued that women have indeed made considerable progress in terms of increased numbers, greater representation, and greater influence. In France women have made inroads in the realm of government. In West Germany, at the time of writing, there were three women Vice-Presidents of the Bundestag and a woman minister. Most significantly, a woman has become prime minister in Britain. Given these facts, it can be concluded that women certainly have made gains in government during the past few years in all three countries. (See the summary in Table 20.)

On the other hand, in relation to the total population and to the composition of the government as a whole, women cannot be considered adequately represented or well integrated into politics. Given the fact that women represent over half of the total population of each country, they are seriously under-represented in the political processes in both the legislative and the executive branches of government. In the next generation, perhaps, women will become more fully integrated in politics. For the time being, however, women in government are the exception rather than the rule. The role that women in politics have played in improving the status of women is more impressive. Substantial progress has been made in recent years in all three countries in regard to women's legal rights to employment, to education, and in the family. These legal rights are in fact prerequisites for meaningful political integration.

Although the legal status of women has improved considerably, attitudinal changes have been slower, but they are evident nevertheless: '(T)hings are changing slowly. Already there are big differences in expectations and in education, in life styles, between men and women under 30 and those over 30.'[25] This observation was borne out by a poll conducted by the Commission of the European Communities in May 1975.[26] The poll, conducted in the nine member countries – Belgium, Denmark, France, West Germany, Ireland, Italy, Luxemburg, the Netherlands and Britain – was the most extensive international poll on sex roles and men's and women's attitudes towards social problems. One of the findings was that politics was still considered to be a 'masculine field' by both men and women *but much less so by young women and by well-educated individuals.* In fact the poll concluded that sex affected attitudes less than did age differences (i.e., 'the generation gap') and the effects of national culture and history.

Of the individuals questioned, 35 per cent thought that politics should be left to men, a view most pronounced in West Germany, Belgium and Luxemburg. Also, 38 per cent of those polled (42 per cent of the men and 33 per cent of the women) expressed a preference for a male representative in parliament. The most favourable attitude towards women's participation in politics was found in those countries where women have participated in the electoral and political process the longest, a prime example being Britain. Although the issue of women's participation in society was not considered a very great problem in Britain, it was in contrast considered particularly important in France.

Overall, the poll underscored the importance of age and education in the formation of attitudes, especially as they related to women in politics. The fact that younger and better educated individuals more readily accept women in positions of leadership is a sign that societal attitudes have in fact begun to change. It is realistic to expect that this trend will continue, especially as equal rights legislation is more fully implemented and more individuals receive better educational opportunities. Moreover, recent legislative reforms – marriage law, family law, abortion, social security provisions, etc. – will very much affect the lives of the younger generation. It is in both their immediate and their future impact that legal reforms are inextricably linked to changes in attitudes and, ultimately, to the status of women.

As women benefit from greater educational and professional opportunities, they will assume more – and more important and influential – positions in government. Despite national variations it is possible to generalize that the advances made in the sphere of women's rights have been to a considerable extent the result of the actions and influence of women in positions of political leadership. The continued expansion and implementation of women's rights can best be ensured by women themselves; and if past performance is an indication of future progress, women in roles of executive political leadership will undoubtedly be instrumental in the creation of a more equal society.

Table 20 *Number of political posts on executive level occupied by women/total number of posts (and percentage of women occupying executive level positions), 1965–79*

	1965		1966		1967		1968		1969		1970		1971		1972		1973		1974		1975		1976		1977		1978		1979	
	No.	Per cent	No.	Per cent	No.	Per cent	No.	Per cent	No.	Per cent	No.	Per cent	No.	Per cent	No.	Per cent	No.	Per cent	No.	Per cent	No.	Per cent	No.	Per cent	No.	Per cent	No.	Per cent	No.	Per cent
France																														
Ministers	0/22	0	0/21	0	0/21	0	0/22	0	0/20	0	0/19	0	0/18	0	0/21	0	0/22	0	0/22	0	1/14	7	1/16	6	1/15	7	2/20	10	2/20	10
Secretaries of state	0/4	0	0/5	0	0/10	0	0/6	0	1/10	10	1/13	8	0/13	0	1/15	7	1/14	7	1/13	8	3/22	14	3/23	13	3/25	12	2/25	8	2/20	10
Britain																														
Cabinet members	1/23	4	1/23	4	1/22	5	1/21	5	1/23	4	1/21	5	1/18	6	1/17	6	1/18	6	2/20	10	2/23	9	2/20	10	1/24	4	1/24	4	0/22	0
Ministers not in Cabinet	2/31	6	2/31	6	5/27	19	3/26	12	3/21	14	5/24	2	1/20	5	1/22	5	1/28	4	1/26	4	1/25	4	1/28	4	1/23	4	1/26	4	2/23	9

De Gaulle (RPF–UNR–UDT–Vᵉ République–UDR) is president from December 1958

Pompidou (UDR–Gaullist) assumes office in November 1970

Giscard d'Estaing (Republican Party) assumes office in May 1974

Wilson (Labour) is prime minister from October 1964

Heath (Conservative) assumes office in June 1970

Wilson (Labour) assumes office in March 1974

Callaghan (Labour) assumes office in April 1976

West Germany

Ministers	1/22 5	1/22 5	1/20 5	1/20 5	1/20 5	1/23 4	1/16 6	1/17 6	1/17 6	1/18 6	1/16 6	1/16 6	2/16 13	1/16 6	1/14 7
Parliamentary state Secretaries	0/19 0	0/19 0	0/19 0	0/19 0	0/23 0	2/23 9	2/15 13	1/15 7	1/18 6	1/20 5	1/20 5	0/20 0	1/20 5	1/16 6

Kiesinger is chancellor from December 1966

Brandt (SPD) assumes office in October 1969

Schmidt (SPD) assumes office in May 1974

Sources: International Yearbook and Statesmen's Who's Who, 1965–1977;
The Europa Yearbook, 1965–1977;
The Statesman's Yearbook, 1969/70–1978/79; and (for 1977) information also provided by embassies' information services.

17 Beyond leadership*

Hilary Wainwright

After a decade of intense socialist agitation, more working-class people than ever in post-war years voted Tory in the May 1979 election. At the same time, fewer people than at any election since 1931 voted for the Labour Party. It seems then that as far as the mass influence of socialist politics is concerned, not only have we a long way to go, but in one respect at least we have not been moving forwards.

Of course, the way people vote does not sum up their consciousness. Many of those who did not vote Labour will undoubtedly have been active in militant strikes and demonstrations during the months after the election. And a low vote for the Callaghan government was more indicative of the crisis facing the Labour Party than the failure of socialist agitation. But when the reactionary rhetoric of Tory 'freedom' can evoke such a groundswell of working-class support, socialists need to ask a few questions about our inability to translate the awareness of a vanguard of socialist activists into any lasting change in mass consciousness. The inability applies both to socialists organized through the Labour Party and, in a different way, to socialists organized in Leninist parties.

The flaw which they have in common is that they both are organized in ways more appropriate to seizing power – governmental power and state power respectively – than to the necessary preliminaries of raising and extending socialist consciousness and grass-roots organization among the majority of working people. In the former case the priorities of the electoral machine, the overriding imperative of retaining or gaining parliamentary/council power tends to suppress political debate and inhibit political involvement in industrial and social struggles. In the latter case, the pretensions and disciplines of democratic centralism tend to produce an arrogance and sectarianism which make the Leninist groups unable to

* This chapter is a selection of excerpts by Hilary Wainwright from S. Rowbotham, L. Segal and H. Wainwright, *Beyond the Fragments* (Merlin 1979), pp. 1–6, 249–53.

contribute to and encourage the *many* sources of socialist initiative and activity. The Communist Party too has its own version of organizing for power before organizing to change consciousness, in its desire for trade union positions often at the cost of challenging the apathy and conservatism still prevalent on the shop floor.

We feel that the women's movement has, at the very least, raised the consciousness, and encouraged the self-organization of thousands of women. In doing so it has also begun to challenge relations of power. If the left is to achieve the change in consciousness and the growth in self-organization which is a condition for resolving the problem of power, then there is much that socialists can learn from the women's movement's values and ways of organizing. For we cannot just put the problems down to 'objective conditions' in the way socialists tended to during the boom years of the 1950s and 1960s. In many ways objective conditions have never made socialism seem so necessary *and* so achievable. Capitalism's self-justification as the natural means of meeting human needs and expanding human possibilities seems more obviously groundless than ever, with every structure of the economy out of joint with human needs (not just the 'declining' sections of industry as in the 1930s). Health services are short of money while private corporations keep millions in 'deferred' – unpaid – tax; thousands are homeless with building workers on the dole; millions are spent on the technology of defence while cheap heating, nurseries, aids to the handicapped, preventive medicine, public transport systems, etc., still remain primitive; and so the list goes on, touching on everyone's day-to-day experiences. In such conditions the possibility of producing for need rather than profit, of planning production by working people rather than by the civil service or the corporations should seem more relevant than ever. Moreover, the means, or at least the groundwork, for achieving such a society, the organizations created by working people themselves, have grown in numbers and, with occasional setbacks, in strength, as the crisis has deepened. It's not like the 1930s when a socialist vision was there – whatever criticisms we may now make of it – but the strength was lacking. Not only have the traditional workers' organizations, so far, retained their grass-roots strength but also oppressed groups which were previously passive or angry in isolation, women, gays, blacks and youth, have become militant and organized.

Why go beyond the fragments?

Our concern in writing *Beyond the Fragments* is with the forms of organization necessary to develop socialist consciousness out of this grass-roots industrial and social strength. Perhaps this concern in itself needs some justification. 'Why go beyond the fragments?' radical feminists, syndicalists and others might ask. After all, they might say, socialist organizations have not been spectacularly successful in fighting against inequality, arbitrary power, exploitation, racial, sexual and other forms of oppression. A wider political organization, they might add, blunts the power of the autonomous movements. Their conclusion is that the best chance of success for each movement is through the direct exertion of their own power.

There might be some logic in this if all the inequalities and sources of exploitation and oppression, which the women's movement, the trade union movement, the black movement, etc., are up against were separate, unconnected to each other. If workers were simply up against bosses, women up against the sexual division of labour and sexist culture, blacks against racial repression and discrimination, with no significant connection between these forms of oppression, no state power linking and overseeing the institutions concerned, then strong independent movements would be enough. But it is precisely the connections between these sources of oppression, both through the state and through the organization of production and culture, which makes such a piecemeal solution impossible.

For example, consider all the connections which lie behind the demands of the women's movement. To win these demands there would have to be a massive shift from corporate profits to socially useful facilities (nurseries, abortion, day-care facilities, and so on) and from defence expenditure to expenditure on health and education; there would have to be a radical reorganization of work and control over work, to provide men and women with full opportunities for childcare and leisure, without jeopardizing job prospects; there would have to be a democratization of health and education and of the media, among other things, if women's needs were to be met. The list of all the wider ramifications of women's liberation could be extended, but from this list alone it is clear that our demands challenge all the priorities of the present, and previous, governments. Moreover they challenge the vested interests of the armed forces, the big corporations and hierarchy of the civil services. Changes of this sort affect and concern all the other movements of oppressed people, workers, blacks, youth, and so on. Unless women's demands are integrated with the needs of these other groups then it is unlikely that women's demands will ever get the support necessary to take on the powerful vested interests they are up against. For example, without incessant argument for an alternative which meets the needs of all oppressed and exploited groups, trade unionists in the private sector will see our demands for more social expenditure as a threat to their jobs; council house tenants will see our demands as competition for scarce resources, and so on.

So one problem is that of drawing up a common programme of political and social change, meeting the needs of all oppressed groups, and arguing for it among each group. The other problem is that of gathering together all the different sources of strength, uniting the social power of the community with the industrial power of those in production, and pitching this popular power against the existing state. This requires a strategy, based on the ideas and experiences of each movement, and drawing from the lessons of past struggles and from international experiences. The solution to these problems needs more than just *ad hoc* contact between the different movements. Neither is the merging of the movements any solution; there are good reasons for each movement preserving its autonomy, controlling its own organization. For women, blacks, trade unionists, gays, youth, and national minorities have specific interests which may sometimes be antagonistic to each other both now and probably in a socialist society. The solution lies in bringing together all those involved in the different movements and campaigns who agree on a wider programme of socialist change, based on the demands of the different movements in the context of organizing for social ownership and popular political power.

The relevance of the women's movement

All this concern with the Labour Party and with local socialist alliances must at first sight seem a long way from feminism. But women have a strong vested interest in the success of the socialist movement. And after organizing ourselves for some years we feel we have got things to say about all the wider organizing and agitating which needs to be done if we are to create a truly democratic and egalitarian society.

The movement that feminists and socialist feminists have

succeeded in organizing may not have achieved many effective legislative and industrial changes. But it has increased the strength and confidence of thousands of women, both those working in the home and those earning a wage, both in white-collar unions and in manual unions. It has drawn into political activity many of the millions of people who have always considered politics was not for them, it was for the politicians. In other words, the women's movement, in all its diverse ways, through all its different political tendencies, has helped to give women the power to organize ourselves to fight for control over the decisions by which our lives are shaped. And that surely is what socialist organization should most centrally be about, for all oppressed and exploited people.

Some might say that the objectives of the women's movement are very specific and limited; that, for example, it takes on the state in only marginal ways and over issues on which some concessions can and will be granted. Whereas, by contrast, a socialist organization has a far more fundamental, difficult task. The corollary of this is that the organizational forms of the women's movement may be appropriate for its specific tasks but organizing for socialism requires something very different. Not much can therefore be learnt from feminism. In a crude sense this contrast has some truth in it. A socialist organization will have to take on many issues and problems which do not now confront the women's movement. We are not holding out the organization of the women's movement as a complete model on which the left should base itself. But the women's movement has made an absolutely vital achievement – or at least the beginnings of it – which no socialist should ignore. It has effectively challenged, on a wide scale, the *self-subordination*, the acceptance of a secondary role, which underpins most forms of oppression and exploitation. This may not be confronting the state – though the women's movement does plenty of that – but unless such a self-subordination is rejected in the minds of men, of the unemployed, of blacks, gays, and all other groups to which socialists aim to give a lead, there will never be much chance of confronting the existing state with a democratic socialist alternative.

The ways in which the women's movement is achieving this then have a wider relevance. From the point of view of learning from the women's movement it is the *values* which underlie our organizations which are important. The particular organizational forms have relevance only to the specific purpose they were created to fulfil. The values underlying our ways of organizing have been ones which put emphasis on local control and autonomy; on small groups within wider co-ordinating structures; on local centres and social and cultural activities; on relating theory to practice; on discouraging forms of procedure and of leadership which make others feel inadequate or uninvolved; on recognizing that different views on strategy and tactics come from some real experience and are worth listening to and discussing.

These values have created a groundwork on which national and regional structures, co-ordination, theoretical debate and self-disciplined national action around an agreed programme of demands have been built. They have led to the creation of a movement with many focuses of initiative and leadership and a movement which combines unity with the existence of many different political tendencies. Such unity is not a matter of complacent tolerance. After periods of conflict and mistrust, the movement builds on the distinct contributions of different political views. For example, the movement gained a lot of its ability to influence the trade unions, to get trades councils to set up women's subcommittees, to involve union branches in actively campaigning for the demands of the movement from women in or close to the International Marxist Group (IMG) and the Communist Party (CP). Recently Women's Voice has been a strong influence in many areas in adopting a more aggressive, outward-going approach in many of our campaigns.

These ways of building a movement are not specific to women. They have been a necessary part of the women's movement because the subjective experience of political organizing, whether it is 'off-putting' or involving, whether it builds up your sense of your own power to change things or makes you feel powerless, is so vital to whether or not women become active. Distant national structures over which you feel little control, formal procedure which does not seem to achieve anything, rigid notions of the correct line which suppress hesitant disagreement and questions, theoretical debates which do not shed light on practice, solidarity based on abstractions with little commitment to each other – none of these could have moved women to cast off their passivity and self-subordination. And this probably applies to a lot of working-class men as well.

There are many lessons to be drawn from the women's movement which would help us as socialists to create structures, arrange meetings, debate with each other, plan tactics, take decisions in ways which draw new people into socialist activity, and which keep them involved far more effectively than in the past. Another shift which the lessons of the women's movement would produce would be a greater respect for initiatives which people are already taking in a socialist direction. I have tried to show in this piece how important this recognition is at the present stage of creating a more co-ordinated socialist movement out of the fragments. It has been the experience of the women's movement which has made us sensitive to these areas of growth. Finally, the women's movement, at its best, has taught us how to unite as a movement on the major practical issues of the day while debating and respecting each others political differences and frequently agreeing to differ and go our own ways without jeopardizing the single movement. If the left could achieve that, at least at a local level, we would be a long way towards showing people that there could be more than a choice between the 'bad and the very bad'; there could be real alternatives which they will have a hand in shaping.

Part Three

Women and the public sphere: conclusions

18 The politics of private woman and public man

Janet Siltanen and Michelle Stanworth

The fact that women's political capacity has been underestimated and undervalued in male-stream literature[1] is now well established. Various authors have taken issue with what Goot and Reid aptly term the 'mindless matron' profile of women in political science, and what Purcell terms the 'passive woman worker' thesis in industrial sociology. The affinity between the mindless matron and the passive woman worker often goes unacknowledged. In our view, both of these types are the result of conceptual errors and explanatory weaknesses common to political science and sociology. Our concern in this chapter is to explore these weaknesses and the ways in which they might be overcome.

The chapter is divided into three sections. The first section includes a summary of the major problems identified by critics of the male-stream portrait of women in politics. It offers a guide to trends in analysis that point towards a fuller understanding of women's political activity. Arguments are elaborated to the effect that gender differences in political experience have been exaggerated, and that, moreover, some of the political implications of women's distinctive experiences have been overlooked.

In the second section, we take issue with the theoretical terrain on which the engagement between the male-stream writers and feminist challengers takes place. Accounts of the relation of gender to electoral and work-based politics are founded, we shall argue, on the analytical separation of the public world of politics and employment from the private sphere of family and interpersonal relations. Such a separation is embedded in the notion of 'private woman' versus 'public man'. While feminist writers have challenged the apolitical characterization of 'private' women, many have to a large extent accepted the explanatory framework which seals women's experience in the private, and men's in the public. It is our contention that implicit or explicit reliance on the private woman–public man dichotomy has hindered an understanding of the political awareness and potential among women and men.

In the final section we consider the relationship between public and private, personal and political, in a more specific context. We focus on Elshtain's recent analysis *Public Man, Private Woman* which, in our view, crystallizes the deficiencies in an analysis of politics based on the public man–private woman dichotomy. We argue for a more adequate understanding of politics – one involving the recognition that the relation of public to private is itself a political issue.[2]

Challenges to the male-stream portrait of women's political activity

Male-stream politics and women's participation

As different as the objects and interests of political science, political sociology and industrial sociology may be, they have certain features in common. In particular, they present similar characterizations of, and explanations for, women's political involvement. Whether one is considering electoral behaviour and party-political activism or trade union support and industrial activism, accounts of the nature of the political involvement of women, relative to men, are similar. Women participate less than men. When women are politically active, their political orientation is argued to be less authentic than that of men, and based on a relatively unsophisticated political understanding. Women's concerns and demands in electoral politics are regarded as reflections of moral or familial commitment, rather than an authentically political stance; in workplace politics, women are seen as absorbed by humanistic concerns, in contrast to hard-headed male economism. Finally, the quality of women's political engagement is regarded in both spheres of politics as more conservative, and less radical, than that of men.

The empirical grounds for the apolitical or conservative portrait of women are, as many authors in this volume have testified, flimsy indeed. For example, Dowse and Hughes assert that the 'tendency of British women to vote Conservative is well documented', referring readers to a table that shows, in fact, the percentage of women voting for the Conservatives and for Labour to be equal.[3] In the male-stream literature the interest in establishing whether women are more conservative than men generally overshadows consideration of whether women are likely to support the Conservatives rather than Labour. As Goot and Reid remark, generally women are of interest 'only in so far as they resemble, or fail to resemble, men'.[4] A telling example can be found in Taylor[5] who is interested in identifying 'the reasons why women, compared with men, have tended to be disproportionately Conservative in their partisanship'. Arguing against Parkin, Taylor presents evidence to show that women's involvement in industry is likely to make them more sympathetic to Labour than previously thought. Both women and men in manual occupations were more favourable to Labour than were full-time housewives. Taylor fails to mention, however, that the more conservative characterization of full-time housewives is a relative statement for they too were more likely to support Labour than the Conservatives. Pulzer also refers to the 'overwhelming evidence' that women are more conservatively inclined than men.[6] In support, Pulzer cites Durant,[7] who analysed voter preference in the elections from 1945 to 1964, and concluded that while men show a consistent bias towards Labour and women towards Conservatives, 'the differences are so small proportionately that sex has little accuracy as a predictor of the vote of an individual'. Pulzer, it would appear, is 'fudging the footnotes', an extraordinary practice which underlies much subsequent exaggeration of the extent to which women differ from men in political potential and approach.[8] Indeed, generalizations about the conservatism of women often seem to rest on an unsupported identification of 'conservative' with 'feminine'. Nowhere is this more apparent than in the assertion sometimes encountered[9] that women's inherently conservative political orientations are revealed in the greater stability of their support for Labour![10]

Within the literature on work-based politics, several reviews have pointed to the similarity of women's and men's responses to similar employment circumstances.[11] Indeed, as Brown states,[12] 'the problem arises of accounting for the widely held conventional view of the woman industrial worker as a "sucker", easy to exploit, and with no capacity for collective action'. Part of the problem arises from the male-stream interpretation of issues and experience, including the tendency to assume that a militant or political stance is a masculine one. For example, looking at well-known works published between 1967 and 1979 we find that: women's complaints about monotonous and low-skilled jobs are labelled 'subjective and emotional';[13] that the question arises whether clerical workers have the 'necessary virility for a manly defence of their interests';[14] that female labour power represents 'an ontological state of being, not a teleological process of becoming';[15] that the working-class extended family is 'appropriately called a women's trade union';[16] that independence and dignity within work relations is an issue of manhood;[17] and that attitudes towards immigration or race relations are political, while attitudes towards equal pay for women are 'social'.[18]

Criticism of the male-stream portrayal of women's relation to politics has taken two major forms. First, critics have identified, and argued against, analytical procedures which unduly emphasize 'sex differences'. Second, critics challenge the criteria by which the political is defined and evaluated in male-stream analysis, and the degree to which these criteria underestimate women's political contributions. The result of both forms of criticism is a vigorous attack on those positions within male-stream literature that withhold from women the dignity of a political life.

Sex differences: feminist critiques and reassessments

Three practices can be identified which artificially inflate the degree of gender difference in relation to political experience. First, political characteristics are attributed to women and men as if they were homogeneous social groups, thus playing down the variations within each sex in order to highlight between-sex differences. As Purcell points out,[19] differences in performance between women and men, however slight, come to be reified as a 'sex difference'. The most thorough exploration of this problem appears in Feldberg and Glenn's discussion of the sociology of work.[20] It is an accepted practice when studying male workers to relate variations in, for example, job satisfaction, levels of alienation or forms of job control to differences in the work process, management practice or position in the labour market. However, the degrees of alienation or forms of job control which distinguish female workers from male workers are often explained by reference to women's relation to the family. Thus a 'job model' is applied to the analysis of male labour orientations, but a 'gender model' to the analysis of women in waged work. While Feldberg and Glenn develop their critique from within the sociology of industry, the assumption underlying the job and gender model of explanation – that the sexes are internally undifferentiated, and that the experience of one sex is by definition not that of the other – is equally characteristic of political science and political sociology.[21]

Critical responses to this form of analysis have varied. On the one hand, attempts have been made to turn away from an exploration based on 'sex difference' towards one based on other factors associated with being male or female. For example, higher rates of Conservative voting by women than by men in some British elections have been accounted for by the predominance of women in the older age groups.[22] The re-analysis by Feldberg and Glenn of Beynon and Blackburn's data emphasizes that differences between women and men with respect to the meaning of work, or sources of satisfaction are, in fact, differences between people on part-time and full-time employment contracts. Purcell identifies women's position in the labour market rather than 'sex or even gender *per se*'[23] as crucial in explaining their participation in industrial politics. Both Purcell and Brown discuss patterns of union support and industrial action that reflect factors which affect women and men equally when they are in similar employment situations. Jennings and Farah, in their examination of women's and men's involvement in both conventional and unconventional political activity, conclude that there are other political factors outweighing sex as a contributor to both types of participation.[24] The watchword, then, is the warning provided by Shabad and Andersen:[25]

to suggest that one should examine more systematically the impact of sex on political orientations and behaviour should not, at the same time, obscure the strong possibility that sex, in and of itself, is *not* the crucial explanatory variable.

As well as reinterpreting 'sex differences', greater attention must be focused on variations in the nature and extent of women's political participation. Childrearing is a major contributor to these variations, and it is no accident that women who are currently active in trade union and party politics tend not to have dependent children.[26] To this extent, obstacles to political engagement distinguish not women from men, but women who are responsible for dependent children from women and men who are not.

The second practice in the male-stream literature that lends itself to exaggerating gender differences in political life applies again to comparisons between women and men: when the sexes are being compared, a relation to, and relations within, the 'private' world are assumed to shape women's and only women's, 'public' participation. No one has suggested that the swing to the Conservatives by male skilled workers in the 1979 British election was due to the appeal of Margaret Thatcher's wifely qualities; yet, it is said that women choose male political candidates on the same basis as they choose a husband.[27] Shabad and Andersen demolish the idea that women personalize politics more than men. They show, for example, that both women and men pay attention to a personal dimension of leadership which is not trivial but politically relevant (such as, leadership capability, prior experience). The consequences of explaining gender differences in industrial sociology by invoking women's, but not men's, relation to the family and personal life are pursued by Feldberg and Glenn. Both discussions call for the incorporation of the full range of men's and women's experience into the analysis of their political interests and activity. Later in this article we will pursue the degree to which this call has been heeded in recent discussions of gender and politics.

Third, gender differences have been exaggerated as a result of the dubious assumption that 'political environments' (political parties, trade unions and the organizational and policy imperatives which shape their operation) are neutral as to sex, or gender-blind. Once this assumption is made different patterns of access or commitment of women and men appear as a property of the social group: while men forcefully and confidently manipulate political options, women's approach to politics is characterized as fearful, timid or *self*-effacing. Hence McCarthy argues that women in the Labour movement in Britain 'have been slow to seize what opportunity has been available to them',[28] while Le Lohe unblushingly asserts that 'the principal responsibility for the under-representation of women rests with women themselves'.[29] Such claims involve blaming the victims of political exclusion and neglect for their ambivalent relation to the machinery and objectives of politics. The error lies in not recognizing that the political environment is less responsive to women than to men; and that it is this, rather than a uniquely feminine ambivalence to politics, which underlies women's political profile.

In the area of electoral politics, the framing of party policy often bypasses issues central to women's experience. 'Definitions of practical politics', have been, as Jaquette argues, 'too restrictive to give women a real stake in the political process.'[30] Trade union activity also shows that political environments are not gender-blind. A considerable minority of women, who are committed to the principles of unionism, refuse to join a trade union or allow their membership to lapse. This may be regarded by some as a sign of inconsistency between belief and action. However, if women's accounts are taken seriously, the explanation is often to be found in disenchantment with trade union branches that are ineffectual and indifferent to the women's struggles.[31] In the few studies which explore women's relation to trade unions, women often complain not because the union is too radical, but because it is not stalwart enough in defence of jobs, or too much in the pocket of management.[32] Moreover, where the segregation of women into lesser-skilled, lower paid jobs ensures that the interests of male and female workers diverge, male workers often use union power to preserve the differentials that favour men rather than to erode such occupational divisions.[33]

In conclusion, the critics of the male-stream portrayal of women in politics have recovered aspects of women's relation to political life by challenging exaggerated claims of 'sex differences'. They have shown, first, that such 'sex differences' are not self-explanatory and that a focus on sex or gender may be misplaced. They have emphasized, moreover, that women's experience is internally differentiated as well as being different from men's. Second, critics have alerted us to the excess weight given to the impact of 'private' relations upon women's political life. Third, the assumption that women are uninterested in aspects of work-based or electoral politics has been qualified by the recognition that 'politics' presents a less open face to women than to men.

Revaluating women's political potential

If the feminist engagement with the male-stream literature ended there, it would risk succumbing to the threat which Evans has warned about[34] – replacing 'the old orthodoxy of women's lesser achievements by a new dogma that the sexes are politically identical'. However, this is not the only thrust of the feminist contribution. By questioning the taken-for-granted boundary of the political which operates so that women's expertise and concerns are often excluded, feminists offer an alternative interpretation of women's relation to political life. They suggest that the priorities and orientations evident in women's activity (including perhaps a forbearance with respect to political organizations) reflect a political sophistication that has been to date unacknowledged.

There are four trends emerging in the new interpretation. First is an *exposé* of the extent to which the 'male-as-norm' principle operates in political and sociological analysis. Political (or if not strictly political then politically progressive or sophisticated) attitudes and actions are assumed to be those expressed by men.[35] When, for example, American girls have displayed a degree of realism in making a higher assessment than boys of the influence of rich people and trade unions on legislation, they have been accused of 'personalising the governmental process', and of adopting a frivolous and sub-political approach.[36] In some instances it is argued that the same approach to politics is evidence of women's lower political sophistication and men's higher political enthusiasm. For example, Almond and Verba[37] argue, on the one hand, that women are more sensitive to emotional aspects of politics than men and, on the other hand, that women are more politically apathetic – because men report greater enjoyment, anger or contempt during elections.[38]

Second, linked to the male-as-norm principle is the tendency to demarcate in a sex-linked but otherwise arbitrary way the 'political' from the 'social' or the 'moral'. So, for example, when Greenstein finds that girls score higher than boys on measures of citizen duty and political efficacy he does not revise his assertions about apolitical females; but instead re-labels these attitudes as 'moral' rather than 'political'.[39] In a similar manoeuvre, Dowse and Hughes dismiss the similarities in the attitudes of women and men towards capital punishment and birth control as a 'moral' rather than a 'political' overlap,[40] while Lane differentiates men's approach to voting from women's 'moral route to the polls'.[41] These analyses appear to have no critical perspective on the separation between the moral and the political, nor on the assessment of what constitutes mature, sophisticated and worldly-wise political activity. The rejection of war, the appraisal of candidate qualities and the insistence on political integrity and honesty – qualities more often attributed to women than to men – have been dismissed by political scientists as part of a 'moral' rather than a 'political' stance. The tendency to regard the concern of women workers with working conditions or the length of the working day as 'social', while men's focus on the wage packet is readily accepted as evidence of political awareness and class consciousness, follows the same mysterious logic. Bourque and Grossholtz, and Goot and Reid are among those who forcefully challenge the male-stream claim that moral and political issues are qualitatively and politically distinct. They acknowledge that contemporary political practice may often favour expedience over moral integrity, but ask by what criteria political scientists decide to adopt these standards as the yardstick for mature political style.[42]

The third strand to the revaluation of women's political life involves attributing new meaning to variations in their participation in traditional areas of political activity. Where women refrain from voting, for example, we cannot dismiss the possibility that this involves an accurate assessment of the low efficacy of voting. Furthermore, women's supposed greater attention to candidates in elections may be a realistic, rather than an apolitical, response to the lack of choice presented by political parties on substantive issues.[43] In trade union activity, Purcell[44] argues that women's lower union membership and refusal to join trade unions may be a more politically conscious and rational decision than has been previously granted (for example, by Beynon and Blackburn). To assume that women are 'conditioned out' of political activity by male dominance, as some feminist analyses do, may be to miss the significance of their political restraint.[45]

Fourth, there have been a number of attempts at a revaluation of women's contribution as 'private' persons to political life. In the writings of Hunt,[46] and Wise,[47] the priorities, skills and resources that women bring with them to work from the private sphere are argued to be valuable, indeed indispensable, additions to the political repertoire. Hunt, for example, suggests that women's isolation as housewives and their relative lack of trade union experience is potentially, if only temporarily, advantageous. She says, 'As productive workers in the home women have been less subjected to the full force of the calculative relations characteristic of capitalism. . . .when women work in industry they put up a struggle to stay human.'[48] Thus women's 'humanistic' demands in work-based politics are cast in a more radical light. Purcell argues that for 'privatized' women, anti-strike activism may in fact have a 'militant' dimension.[49] Both Bourque and Grossholtz[50] and Elshtain[51] argue that the supposedly moral orientations of women to political affairs may evidence more promising political styles than those based on expedience or pragmatism.

In conclusion, far from erasing differences in the political response of women and men, feminists have insisted instead upon acknowledging and revealing women's distinctive political contribution. This project involves: a refusal to permit the privileging of a 'masculine' political stance; the rejection of arbitrary divisions between 'moral' or 'social' and 'political', and the broadening of definitions of 'the political' so they less often exclude anti-war programmes, attempts to improve working conditions, or demands for political integrity; an insistence that rational political assessments may be reflected in certain forms of political abstention or distancing; and finally, the recognition that political programmes and principles of organization are challenged and enriched by the recovery of concerns previously dismissed as apolitical. Not only is the characterization of women in relation to political life presented in a new light; our understanding of political analysis and practical politics is potentially revitalized from this new vantage point.[52]

The politics of private woman and public man: a failure in explanation

In the previous section we summarized the ways in which the portrait of women as apolitical and conservative has been constructed, and highlighted a number of empirical critiques that undermine this male-stream portrait. By challenging the analytical practices that inflate differences in women's and men's political engagement, and the male-stream definitions and evaluations of political activity, the feminist critiques have provided a corrective to the image of women as 'mindless matrons' and 'passive workers'. But, in our view, they do not go far enough. Although speaking against practices that misrepresent women's political involvement, those who challenge the male-stream literature sometimes speak its language.[53] They seldom take issue with the underlying premise that links 'politics' to 'public life' and counterposes 'private woman' to 'public man'.[54] Thus, in this section of our chapter we intend to reconsider the very terms of reference in which the debate about gender and politics has been conducted. We shall argue that underlying many of the explanations of the relation between gender and politics there is an illegitimate superimposition of three dichotomies: political–apolitical, public–private, and male–female.

The myth that politics is a man's realm has been sustained, we believe, partly through the types of explanation employed to account for the differences in the political life of women and men. Whether in political science, political sociology, or industrial sociology, explanations for gender patterns of political involvement highlight the effects of a separation between the public sphere of wage-work and formal politics, and the private sphere of domesticity and personal relations. Male-stream writers argue that the assignment of women to domestic roles, their primary commitment to home and family, their affective relations, and their indirect relation – through the family – to public life restrict the options for political engagement and limit the development of the political understanding and commitment that would encourage political involvement. By assuming the private is apolitical and that women are private beings, these writers consistently place women in a marginal relation to the public and the political. The force (and, we shall argue, the failing) of this position lies in its combination of three elements. On to the fundamental dichotomy of public and private is mapped the generic split[55] (man–woman) and the political–apolitical dimension, in such a way as to imply two appealing equations:

Man = Public   Public = Political   Therefore, Man = Political
Woman = Private   Private = Apolitical   Therefore, Woman = Apolitical

If politics is assumed to be the prerogative of the public sphere, and women are taken to be firmly located within the private domain, then the access of women to politics would appear to be understandably problematic.

However, we do not accept that politics is the prerogative of the public sphere, nor that women are firmly located in the private domain and men in the public. We intend to argue that the private woman–public man conception misleads as to the relationship of the political to both private and public, and that it fosters misunderstandings of the character and genesis of the political potential of both women and men. There are several stages to this argument. We explore first the private and public dimensions of politics, emphasizing on the one hand, the extent to which the private domain is implicated in political process and, on the other, the lack of fit between the public domain and the boundaries of the political. Our view is that the public–private split, while certainly having its uses in the analysis of gender, is a particularly clumsy vehicle for exploring *political* life. Second, we argue against equating woman with the private domain and man with the public domain. The private woman–public man dichotomy, in our view, detracts from the extent to which the political character of women is publicly generated, and from the ways in which the public profile of men is shaped by their relation to the private. Finally, we argue that the conceptualization of women as private and men as public contributes to a tendency, even among otherwise radical writers, to treat the political programmes and forms of political understanding generated by men as if they represented a universal position – a position to which women might, however, aspire or which might be supplemented with 'women's concerns'.

The private and public dimension of politics

The assumption that private = apolitical is clearly open to question. The private world – the world of personal relations and marriage, of friendships and family, of domestic routine and childcare – is, as feminists have persuasively demonstrated time and again, political as well as personal.[56] We will pursue this issue in detail later in the chapter. For the moment, it must be emphasized that both individual and collective forms of political practice are generated within, and are relevant to, the private domain as well as the public.[57] The individual politics of men asserting dominance within their households, or women struggling to assert their sexuality in autonomous ways have their collective counterparts in industrial bargaining predicted on a 'family wage', Conservative proposals to strengthen 'the family' and the subordinate position of women within it, or the campaigns of the Women's Liberation Movement. Indeed, not only is the private sphere addressed by both individual and collective political practice, but the commonsensical separation between private and public is itself influenced by particular political struggles. Witness the efforts of the Moral Majority in America to establish aspects of family relations – including wife assault – as private and, therefore, outside the province of legitimate political intervention.[58]

If the private = apolitical assumption is open to question, the notion that public = political is equally problematic. To treat *political* as coincident with *public* is to detract from crucial aspects of political process. First, in its most radical interpretation, the insistence within feminist analysis that the 'personal is political' strikes at the heart of a cordoned off public domain of politics, challenging not only the apolitical characterization of the private domain but also any claim that the political nature of the public arena can be constituted without reference to the quality of personal relations. Styles of interaction at trade union and other political meetings that efface and discomfit women are, for example, as 'political' as struggles that assert the interests of full-time workers at the expense of part-time ones.[59]

Second, to equate the political with the public is to ignore the question of why matters that occur in public space are sometimes regarded as political and sometimes not. It provides no framework to address the processes involved in the emergence of political issues, such as sexual harassment, or the ways in which the operations of the 'free market' are considered at some historical moments, but not at others, to be 'above politics'.

Third, the stubborn equation of 'public' with 'political' obscures the extent to which public life in liberal democracies is de-politicized. The routine exclusion of ordinary women and men from the assumption of responsibility for the definition and articulation of political affairs results in apathy and pragmatic acquiescence becoming the foundations of governmental stability. Political affairs may, according to O'Brien:

appear to the men and women on assembly lines as just as unreal and insignificant as they were for the medieval serf and his family. The impact of the public realm on the lives of the working classes was, for centuries, a reality only when they were called upon to fight and die in the power struggles of their paternalist masters. In the age of democracy, the experienced sense of ordinary people of shaping and forming public affairs is very problematic indeed.[60]

An important objection, then, to the notion that public equals the political is that it encourages silence on the degree to which public women and men are not politically-minded.

If political–apolitical cannot be mapped on to public–private in any straightforward way, so too the relationship of the sexes to a public–private separation is more complex than a simply dichotomy allows. It obscures the extent to which the public sphere is constituent of women's political consciousness, and the private sphere of men's. It implies that women are defined exclusively by the private sphere, and men not at all. These problems, we shall argue, pose serious obstacles to achieving an understanding of the political activity of both sexes.

The private and public lives of women

The continued use of the public man–private woman dichotomy, suggesting as it does that men and women are constituted as political beings by completely different realms, encourages forms of analysis which trivialize the impact of women's public activity on their political views and give undue weight to family or domestic experience. Blauner, for example, uses women's domestic responsibilities to explain why more women than men complain about their job conditions, ignoring the fact that the women were working, by his own account, in more stressful and pressurized jobs.[61] And, in Watt's view, women's industrial militancy is an extension of their family orientation.[62] In both cases, the political context and the importance of women's waged work is ignored. Women's views are persistently interpreted through the private sphere to the extent that even when engaged in matters which for men would have an undeniably public and political character, women are argued to be operating according to 'private' interests.

In fact, the private women–public man dichotomy cannot accommodate comfortably the undeniable presence of women in the public realm. Again, this is particularly noticeable in discussions of women workers in the public domain. In Parkin's classic formulation,[63] women are especially vulnerable to conservative ideology, even when in waged work, because their (assumed) overriding identification with the private sphere cuts them off from the radicalizing effects of the workplace.[64] It is not only Parkin who insists on the superficial impact of women's paid employment. Among industrial sociologists, Watson[65] follows a well-worn path in insisting that women's employment is culturally deviant, however commonplace it may be. His work finds echoes in Porter, who accords women a precarious status in work:

when a woman goes into the labour market, it is not as a primary role. She goes as a visitor to another world – almost as a migrant worker. . . .[66]

Pollert also suggests that women's consciousness of paid work 'is overshadowed by the family'.[67] The private location of women, when impervious to evidence about their public involvements, takes on the form of an essential characteristic. There *must* be a point at which women cease to be exclusively determined by the private.

Feminist writers have challenged the view that women are politically naïve, stressing the political and radical import of women's 'private' identity. Women's closer relation to caring and nurturing, it is suggested, enables them to retain and re-introduce to public life a commitment to the cultivation of peace and integrity in political affairs.[68] Similarly, in the area of work-based politics, socialist feminists such as Campbell and Charlton[69] and Hunt[70] contend that women are more responsive than men to issues concerning shorter working days, effective childcare provision and better working conditions.[71] Some insist, moreover, that these demands have a radical edge equal to that of the economistic concerns to which men are more wedded, and by which industrial militancy has been traditionally judged.[72] They base their case strongly on the reasoning that women's domestic relations, and their insulation from the chilling effects of the cash nexus, allow them to be in closer touch with personal relations and less resigned to frustration, individualism and dissatisfaction in the world of wage work.

Such revaluations serve an important purpose and we do not deny their value as a corrective to the assumption that women's relation to the private world is of no political importance. However, we have two major reservations about the direction of these arguments. First, in stressing the worthiness of 'women's concerns', the overlap between women's and men's demands may be overlooked. It may be the case, for example, that women value flexible working hours and rigorous health and safety arrangements more than men, but it need not follow that women value wages and job protection any less. Second, to state that women learn political lessons in 'their' private world, even to argue that those lessons are crucial correctives to a 'masculine' political ethos, is problematic. It implies that women have a unique responsibility for bringing the humanistic principles derived from the experience of nurturing and caring in the private world of personal relationships and family to bear on the public sphere. This skirts perilously close to recommending that women shoulder responsibility for humanizing a public arena brutalized by men's neglect. It ignores the potential for transformation of men's consciousness, and, far from exploding artificial divisions between public (male) and private (female), it threatens to institutionalize those divisions within the heart of the public sphere itself.

The public man–private woman division constitutes less an explanation than a misleading tautology. By assuming women are defined by their exclusion from the public sphere, or their marginalization within it, we fail to investigate the public sources of their political involvement.[73] By assigning virtues, or rationality, or radicalism to the actions of 'privatized' women the explanatory paradigm that defines women's experiences as privatized is not challenged.

The private and public lives of men

By polarizing women and men into opposite and exclusive spheres the public man–private woman division obscures the extent to which the private sphere is constituent of men's relation to work and to political life. All too often, family commitments and home-based concerns are acknowledged to be significant for men except where comparisons with women are made or implied. The evidence of Porter, of Beynon, of Goldthorpe, Lockwood, Bechofer and Platt, of Nichols and Armstrong, or Rubin, all testify to the extent to which home and family provide for men the motivation to seek particular jobs, to remain at one place of work, to endure degrading conditions.[74] It was a *male* assembly line worker at Ford's who said: 'I just close my eyes and stick it out. I think about the kids.'[75] The demands of home and family enter into men's decisions about shift work and overtime, outweigh the calls of trade union activism and underpin instrumental attitudes to workplace militancy.[76]

Why then, faced with the fact that the impetus for the unioniza-tion of the Brompton workers came from the men on the night shift, do Beynon and Blackburn offer an explanation in terms of 'the greater centrality given to work in the lives of the men'?[77] If *masculine* orientations were the crucial feature, why were the day-shift men not equally ready to unionize? Would it not make as much sense to point out the centrality of *family* for the mainly married night-shift men which made them more anxious for the job protection and regulation that the union could provide?

Or, why does Watt insist, on the basis of his study of female factory workers, that the '*peculiar* forms of female industrial militancy'[78] are extensions of motherhood? What is *peculiar* about the radicalism of the women he studied: their insistence upon union solidarity, their recognition of labour–management opposition, their ideological and instrumental reasons for trade unionism? The failure to enthusiastically endorse the erosion of 'breadwinner privileges' is certainly not peculiar to women, any more than is working or claiming to work primarily to support the family. Watt's analysis involves, alongside a matri-centred perspective on women, an oddly blinkered view of men.

We are by no means suggesting that men share equally with women the burdens of domestic responsibility or the rewards of employment. We are simply insisting that we will never produce an accurate account of the relations between women and men in the public world, until we recognize that in part men are already defined and define themselves in relation to their 'private' commitments.

If the public man–private woman formulation detracts from the importance of men's private commitments, it also lends itself to treating men's consciousness as unproblematic, as if men had already arrived at a less partial, more sophisticated form of political understanding than women. Discussions dealing with women's and men's relationship to political phenomena sometimes take the paradoxical position that while there is a public–private split coincident with gender, the division directly affects only women's political consciousness: women's relation to the public–private separation locks them into a partial form of understanding. For example, Porter:

Women's 'class consciousness' is therefore imprisoned in their 'women's consciousness' to the detriment of the development of class consciousness or class action by either men or women.[79]

Thus, for Porter, 'women's consciousness' works to the detriment of men, but not vice versa.[80] The 'problem' – for both women and men – is *women's* relationship to consciousness and class action.

An insistence on the curious genesis of 'women's consciousness' or 'their separate consciousness'[81] detracts from awareness of the deficiencies in, and partiality of, the forms of political understanding and political engagement which are characteristic of men – as if the programmes generated by men were, except for their lack of a 'feminine perspective' satisfactory, and as if there were no conflicting interests at stake. As Coote and Campbell argue:

When it comes to formulating policy, it is not enough simply to add on a shopping list of feminist demands to objectives which already exist on the left. We need a new starting point, a new set of criteria, a new order of priorities. Patriarchal politics – whether on the left, centre or right – has a distorted perspective.[82]

In other words, 'women's concerns' cannot simply be appended to trade union demands or to the politics of labour movements and political parties. Instead, the conception both of political struggle and of political objectives must be transformed.[83] The provision of greater economic security and independence for women, and for children, for example, may involve diverting industrial muscle and political clout away from the defence of a (male) 'family wage' and towards equal pay and realistic levels of child benefit.[84] And while the struggle for security and equality of conditions for part-time workers and those on job sharing schemes may benefit all workers in the long run by tightening up the labour market, it means in the short term the elimination of the privileges men have traditionally defended from the vantage point of their stronger bargaining position.

It is not enough that men complacently acknowledge, and agree to make space in the public sphere for, the re-invigorating political principles or concern with working conditions and purposes of production that women are said to be offering. The simple arithmetic of complementarity (men instrumental + women expressive = harmonious whole) does not work in public settings any more than it does in marriage. Nor is it conceivable that space can be created for women to assume their rightful place in public life, without men's consciousness and men's political programmes being drastically restructured in the process.

The politics of public and private life

We have argued that the continued use of a public–private separation equated with a generic division perpetuates the distortion of the political activities and capacities of both men and women. In both the male-stream literature and in some feminist analyses there is a persistent misconception about the ways in which the separation of social life into a private sphere of home, family and interpersonal relations and a public sphere of work and politics is reflected in the political consciousness and activity of women and men. However, to reject a one to one relation between public–private, political–apolitical and male–female raises a further series of questions. In this section, through an engagement with the controversial stance endorsed by Jean Bethke Elshtain's *Public Man, Private Woman*, we propose to explore further the issue of how the political is constituted, and of its relation to the public–private division and to personal and private life.

In opposition to the feminist claim that the personal is political, Elshtain insists that the personal and private must be preserved as areas distinct from the political and the public. To collapse the personal and political is to jeopardize the autonomy of private relations, and the very existence of politics.

Minimally, a *political* perspective requires that some activity called 'politics' be differentiated from other activities, relationships, and patterns of action. If all conceptual boundaries are blurred and all distinctions between public and private are eliminated, no politics can exist by definition.[85]

To assert that the personal is political is, in Elshtain's view, to succumb to a 'relentless power definition of social reality'.[86]

What is asserted is an identity, a collapse of the one into the other. Nothing 'personal' is exempt, then, from political definition, direction and manipulation – neither sexual intimacy, nor love, nor parenting. There is a total collapse of public and private as central categories of explanation and description. The private sphere falls under a thoroughgoing politicized definition. If there are no distinctions between public and private, personal and political, it follows that no differentiated activity or set of institutions that are genuinely political, that are, in fact, the bases of order and of purpose in a political community, exist. What does exist . . . is pervasive force, coercion and manipulation: power suffusing the entire social landscape, from its lowest to its loftiest points.[87]

Moreover, it is, according to Elshtain, only by the preservation of a non-political private sphere that we can provide a refuge from 'the force of the public',[88] and ensure the intimate relations which are essential for the formation of morally and socially responsible adults.

Elshtain advocates redeeming the private and re-politicizing the public: transforming the relations within each and establishing for each a moral code. The public world Elshtain proposes is an 'ethical polity' characterized by a 'politics of compassion' and a commitment to moral and political ideals.

Such a world would require private spheres bearing their own intrinsic dignity and purpose tied to moral and aesthetic imperatives, all the textures, nuances, tones and touches of a life lived intimately among others. A richly complex private sphere requires, in order that it survive, freedom from some all-encompassing public imperative, but in order for it to flourish the public world itself must nurture and sustain a set of ethical imperatives, including a commitment to preserve, protect, and defend human beings in their capacities as private persons, and to allow men and women alike to partake in the good of the public sphere on an equal basis of participatory dignity and equality. Rather than an ideal of citizenship and civil virtue that features a citizenry grimly going about their collective duty, or an elite band of citizens in their 'public space' cut off from a world that includes most of the rest of us, within the ethical polity the active citizen would be one who had affirmed as part of what it meant to be fully human a devotion to public, moral responsibilities and ends.[89]

We would like to pose three fundamental questions concerning Elshtain's analysis. Must politics be considered a 'public activity' differentiated from other activities? Is politics, by definition, distanced from the private? Does the preservation of the personal imply or require the separation of public and private?

Politics – a public activity?

Elshtain's insistence upon differentiating the political from other activities is in line with aspects of current political practice and forms of analysis. Attempts to de-politicize property relations, for example, or many aspects of production and distribution, create a politics delimited to such an extent that it appears to many people to be an activity remote from and largely irrelevant to their lives. Political analysis, as we have taken pains to show, bypasses or fails to address many activities and concerns precisely because the political has so often been arbitrarily severed from 'moral', 'social', or 'economic' issues. To insist that politics as lived and defined should continue to be distinguished from other activities skirts around the urgent question of precisely where the boundaries of the political will be drawn – and of who will stand to benefit, and who to lose, by a particular demarcation. In short, the determination of the political, within the public sphere, is itself a fundamentally political issue.

We would argue for a redefinition of the political that takes account of this fluidity: for a definition that does not locate the political in specific institutions (for example, the House of Commons), genderically (i.e., what men do), or by reference to the conceptual category of the public sphere. We are to some extent sympathetic to Boals's formulation of the political. She describes the political as 'any human relationship, at any level from the intrapsychic to the international, provided it can be shaped and altered by human decision and action'.[90] Thus to politicize means to 'bring to conscious awareness the political (i.e., contingent rather than inevitable) nature of existing social arrangements'.[91] The political, on this view, is intimately tied to the social: it is about the possibilities for human and collective intervention.

Boals's formulation, like Elshtain's, allows for the preservation of public and private realms which are to an extent distinct. But, unlike Elshtain, Boals does not make either sphere the exclusive province of the political. Moreover, Boals's formulation leaves room for historical shifts in the determination of the political. These shifts are related, as Boals points out, to the changing 'frames of meaning' or forms of consciousness by which social relations are understood. They are also related, we would add, to changes in material conditions affecting the mutability of social relations.

Reproduction, and the relations of marriage and mothering to which it is historically linked, provides a succinct example of the way in which the content of the political alters through the continuing transformation of material and social conditions. O'Brien argues[92] that the social relations of reproduction based on the appropriation by men of women and children can 'be abolished, not merely because they are unjust, but because they are incompatible with the newly transformed material base of reproduction'.[93] In other words it is only within this century, with the capacity to control the process of reproduction itself, that the political nature of the relations of reproduction is fully revealed. Reproductive relations span the public and private spheres. In what sense, then, can the political be distanced from the private?

Politics – distanced from the private?

Elshtain's concern to preserve a private realm, free from political intervention, involves the elaboration of the private realm not only as the sanctuary of the individual and the essential arena of privacy, but as providing through the family the developmental foundation for the social relations of the public world. Indeed, the family becomes in her vision 'a moral imperative'. While claiming not to promote a particular family form, Elshtain describes the essential family as intimate, warm, loving and secure; unencumbered by 'the isolation and debasement of women';[94] and free from the damaging impact of unemployment and economic recession.[95] But unemployment and recession are not, as Elshtain suggests, the only elements of the public sphere which reverberate to the detriment of family life, and contribute to the debasement of women. Her call to preserve the private from public encroachment ignores many of the ways in which the public currently constitutes and narrows private options.

The state, for example, has an ambivalent relation to the public–private division. Under the guise of government non-intervention, social problems are all too often abandoned to individual solutions, while in policies concerning maternity benefits and welfare rights a particular family form is reinforced.[96] To argue against Elshtain that the personal is political is to acknowledge the contingent nature of personal, intimate and familial relations, and to fully confront the ways in which the private sphere is already shaped by the public sphere. At the very least, it is to demand that governments drop the rhetoric of non-intervention so that the direction and extent of intervention can be a matter for public determination.

Elshtain's aspirations for the family and the private realm are marred by a reluctance to acknowledge the extent to which patterns of personal life are socially constructed and the extent to which they have a political dimension. In fact, her equation of private life with family life is an illustration of familistic and heterosexist assumptions underlying contemporary constructions of the personal.[97] The question is not whether our private lives should be free from social and political process, but rather the extent to which we can determine the direction of that process. To insist that the public keep its distance from the private will not improve the conditions in which private lives are lived. Any meaningful call to safeguard personal life must engage systematically with the interpenetrations between public and private, and the ways they are being transformed.

Preserving the personal

Elshtain's call for the preservation of a particular public–private separation rests on the contrast between a hard, impersonal public world – the repository of coercion and social, as opposed to individual, determination – and the warm intimacy of the private world, where we as individuals must be given the chance to live our personal lives free from the contamination of political imperatives.

This contrast is profoundly misconceived in its characterization of both the private and public spheres. It highlights a form of politics within the public sphere that is authoritarian and coercive – an emphasis that rests uneasily with Elshtain's faith in the possibility of an ethical polity. It is wrong in opposing the social to the individual, for the social establishes the conditions within which individual lives (in their private and public facets) may be lived.

It is a mistake, moreover, to conflate the private with the personal, and personal relations with intimacy. We live our personal relations in the public world as well as in the private – for example, in the routine day-to-day encounters between a worker and her boss through which class relations are enacted, or in the more-or-less satisfactory relations we establish with people with whom we share political commitments. In addition, as Colman[98] has pointed out, our personal relations in public and private life are characterized by acquaintanceship, by comradeship, by civility and incivility as well as by intimacy: and it is these and other 'impersonal' or non-intimate relations (as much as the intimacy and trust that Elshtain emphasizes) which establish a basis for social bonds within collective life.[99] Thus, a private–public separation does not and need not correspond to divisions between the individual and social, the personal and the impersonal, or the intimate and the impersonal.

Finally, it must be said that two ideals which are central to Elshtain's platform – the freedom to pursue private lives, and the protection of the private from political intervention – are difficult to reconcile. How does the public sphere make good its commitment to 'preserve, protect, and defend human beings in their capacities as private persons'? And, how is this to be done while at the same time maintaining within the private sphere the 'freedom from some all-encompassing public imperative'?

Far from political intervention undermining the intimacy and warmth of private lives, the morally reconstructed private world that Elshtain recommends could be guaranteed only by upholding the obligation to intervene into private situations, to protect against abuses of freedom and dignity. Intimacy and privacy are neither licences for, nor protections against, inhuman conduct. There may be no violence in Elshtain's ideal family, but this offers no solace to battered women and children who suffer from the neglect of our political institutions in the name of personal freedom. Whose freedom is being protected? Whose freedom from physical abuse is being denied? Campaigns around such problems are bringing about a gradual transformation in public–private relations. To hold up a vision of an ideal, loving and caring, family is to avoid the issue of existing coercive relations. This is not to say that family life is solely defined by power relations. It is to emphasize the unlikely possibility that existing power relations will be transformed by moral claims alone, however compelling these claims may be.

The politics of public man and private woman: conclusion

Four themes run throughout this article.

First, the tendency within male-stream analyses of political activity to exaggerate the extent of difference between women and men, and the recovery through feminist analysis of an unacknowledged political dimension underlying distinctive elements of women's experience.

Second, the need to interrogate more rigorously the theoretical terrain on which the feminist engagement with male-stream writings has taken place, particularly the unreflected emphasis upon the opposition between private woman and public man. Mapping political–apolitical and male–female on to the public–private divide encourages silence on boundaries of the political within the public sphere. It fails to address the political nature of the private, and implies that women are defined exclusively by the private sphere and men not at all.

Third, the importance of re-examining men's political capacity, and the distorted concepts and criteria of the political developed without sensitivity to gender. Male-stream writings misrepresent male political capacity by failing to recognize the parameters of men's political response – its parochialism and partiality, as well as the extent to which it is, like women's, reflective of 'private' experience. Whether in political analysis or practical politics, it will not do to treat men's concerns, or policies formulated largely through traditionally male institutions as the stuff of which politics is made.

Fourth, the recognition that myopic visions of the political underlying misrepresentations of women's and men's political capacity are reproduced in many accounts of the relation between the private and the public, the personal and the political. Against such short-sighted views of politics, it is crucial to assert that the boundary between private and public arenas does not mark the limits of the political, and indeed is itself constructed through political process.

Notes and references

Notes referring to articles or excerpts of articles reprinted in this volume are indicated by 'text'.

Chapter 1   General introduction

1 The four features often appear in combination in a particular writer's work. Hence, many of the examples in the following footnotes, although cited in connection with one specific feature of the political portrait of women, evidence other aspects as well.

2 With regard to electoral politics see, for example, R. E. Dowse and J. A. Hughes, *Political Sociology* (John Wiley and Sons 1972), p. 192, who summarize the profile of women in studies of British politics as follows:

> One of the best researched findings in British politics is that women participate less and declare lower levels of interest in politics than do men. Fewer women occupy significant political positions at all levels than men. Women are less likely to vote than men. In general, women are more Conservative politically and are usually less politically interested than men. . . .

Also, D. Butler and D. Stokes, *Political Change in Britain*, 2nd edn, (Macmillan 1974), pp. 53–4 discuss the 'greater politicization of men in British society', citing as evidence differences in women's and men's declared interest in politics and the fact that respondents were likely to attribute 'their mother's party allegiance to the influence of her husband or someone else in the household'. In work-based politics, for example, J. E. T. Eldridge, *Sociology and Industrial Life* (Nelson 1973), pp. 54–5, attributes to women an individualistic stance and a tendency to accept management definitions of the work situation. P. Kellner, 'The working woman: her job, her politics and her union', in A. Coote and P. Kellner (eds.), *Hear This, Brother: Women Workers and Union Power, New Statesman Report 1* (1980), p. 33, argues that 'even allowing for variations in experience, union men are more likely than union women to volunteer for the sharp end of union activity'. Porter sees women's assertions that unions do more for men as evidence that, for the women, 'Unions, strikes and even meetings were a distraction from the simple business of going out, doing a job and getting money as quickly and as painlessly as possible'; M. Porter, 'Standing on the edge: working class housewives, and the world of work', in J. West (ed.), *Work, Women and the Labour Market* (Routledge & Kegan Paul 1982), p. 125. A more comprehensive statement of the profile of women in analyses of work-based politics in Britain is provided by C. Crouch, *Trade Unions: the Logic of Collective Action* (Fontana 1982), pp. 70–1:

> women workers are almost universally more difficult to organise than their male counterparts. In some cases this might be attributed to greater difficulty in securing success through organisation, where women are concentrated in such sectors as catering characterised by temporary and casual employment. But the differential also holds true between men and women within the same occupation and working conditions . . . there are grounds for arguing that women's dependence on unionism is less than men's because their general commitment to membership of the labour force is less. By commitment we do not here mean psychological attitude to work, but the extent to which the worker is dependent on paid employment for his or her long-term standard of living. . . . For many female workers, paid employment has been a temporary condition until marriage or after the birth of a child. Even for those not in that category, married women's wages have often been regarded as a second income in the family, after the husband's, to be used for less 'essential' purchases. Similar arguments concerning commitment to the labour force apply to migrant workers and immigrants. . . .

3 See for example, M. Currell, *Political Woman* (Croom Helm 1974), pp. 47–52, who claims women 'tend to be more candidate than issue oriented', 'vote on personalities' and 'evaluate political objects on a lower level of conceptualisation than do men'. G. Shabad and K. Andersen, text, Chapter 14, provide many examples, and an extensive critique of, the claim that women personalize politics. D. Butler and D. Stokes, *Political Change in Britain* (Pelican 1971), p. 504, assume the influence of husbands over wives in their assertion that such activities as trying to persuade someone how to vote may be 'largely self-cancelling – for every Labour husband who argues his wife into voting with him there may be an equally compelling Conservative'. Dowse and Hughes, *Political Sociology,* pp. 277–8, noting that men and women have similar views on the abolition of capital punishment, offer the reservation that as

> a moral issue, the question was one upon which expert advice was not as salient as it is on more technical questions and probably most people felt competent to hold 'firm' opinions even when their level of factual knowledge was extremely rudimentary.

In summarizing the data on deference studies, R. Jessop, *Traditionalism, Conservatism and British Political Culture* (George Allen & Unwin 1974), reiterates that women are more deferential than men, even though the original evidence regarding deferential voting in R. McKenzie and A. Silver, *Angels in Marble* (Heinemann 1968), does not appear to support such a claim (see McKenzie and Silver's chart 5.3, (ibid., p. 88) which shows women to be more deferential than men in only one of their four sub-groups). That women are less likely to take their work-based class position seriously is argued in K. Roberts,

The Working Class (Longman 1978), p. 101, who suggests women are more likely to see their position in society as consumers rather than producers. Women's supposed isolation from an industrial sub-culture and from workplace militancy has been asserted for some time; even as wage workers, women's relation to collective action is argued to be marginal or distant (F. Parkin, 'Working class conserva-tives: a theory of political deviance', *British Journal of Sociology,* **18** (1967), pp. 248–90; Porter, 'Standing on the edge', p. 125; Crouch, *Trade Unions,* pp. 70–1, in note 2). How women can connect with collective work struggles is obscured by, for example, J. H. Gold-thorpe *et al.*'s view, *The Affluent Worker: Political Attitudes and Behaviour* (Cambridge University Press 1971), p. 74, that industrial camaraderie develops from 'pride in doing men's work'. Even when they are connected with work struggles, women's motives are seen as familial, as in I. Watt, 'Linkages between industrial radicalism and the domestic role among working women', *Sociological Review,* **28** no. 1 (1980), pp. 55–74, who explains women's 'radical male attributes' in paid work as an extension of family commitments.

4 Women's moralistic orientation to electoral politics is asserted in Currell, *Political Woman*, pp. 47–52; Dowse and Hughes, *Political Sociology*, p. 172; F. Greenstein, *Children and Politics* (New Haven, Conn.: Yale University Press 1969); and R. E. Lane, *Political Life* (New York: The Free Press 1965). With regard to work-based politics, R. D. Barron and G. M. Norris, 'Sexual divisions and the dual labour market', in D. L. Barker and S. Allen (eds.), *Dependence and Ex-ploitation in Work and Marriage* (Longman 1976), p. 64, suggest that women's low level of interest in careerism or in high pay 'reduces the need, in the eyes of many women, for solidaristic activity'. S. Alexan-der, A. Davin and E. Hostettler, 'Labouring women: a reply to Eric Hobsbawm', *History Workshop*, no. 8 (Autumn 1979), pp. 174–82, make explicit the distinctiveness of women's concerns:

When women come out on strike they raise issues related to the quality of life. Working conditions, childcare, holidays, time-off are central to women's daily domestic and wage working lives, though these demands are seldom taken up by union officials, bargaining over the size of the wage packet. . . .

Even a concern with equal pay for women and men may be designated as 'social' rather than political by, for example, K. Roberts, F. G. Cook, S. C. Clark and E. Semeonoff, *The Fragmentary Class Structure* (Heinemann 1977) (compare Tables 6.5 and 6.6, pp. 117–18); or by Kellner, 'The working woman', p. 38, who states that:

Only one-third of women unionists think their union fights hard for equality between men and women [at work]; but this seems to reflect the fact that unions are not generally expected to get involved in wider social or family issues.

5 See M. Goot and E. Reid, *Women and Voting Studies: Mindless Matrons or Sexist Scientism?* (Sage Publications 1975); S. Bourque and J. Grossholtz, 'Politics an unnatural practice: political science looks at female participation', *Politics and Society,* **4** no. 2 (Winter 1974), pp. 225–66; J. Siltanen and M. Stanworth, text, Chapter 18; R. Brown, 'Women as employees: some comments on research in industrial sociology', in Barker and Allen, *Dependence and Exploitation in Work and Marriage*; and Purcell, text, Chapter 5, for a closer consideration of this aspect of women's profile in the male-stream literature.

6 Bourque and Grossholtz, text, Chapter 10.

7 Goot and Reid, text, Chapter 11.

8 Brown, text, Chapter 6.

Chapter 2   Male and female: job versus gender models in the sociology of work

1 S. Hesselbart, 'Some underemphasized issues about men, women and work', paper presented at the annual meeting of the American Sociological Association, San Francisco (1978).

2 J. Acker, 'Issues in the sociological study of women's work', in A. H. Stromberg and S. Harkess (eds.), *Women Working, Theories and Facts in Perspective* (Palo Alto: Mayfield Publishing Co. 1977), pp. 1134–61; J. Acker and D. R. Van Houten, 'Differential recruitment and control: the sex structuring of organizations', *Administrative Science Quarterly,* **19** (1974), pp. 152–63; R. Brown, 'Women as employees: comments on research in industrial sociology', in D. L. Barker and S. Allen (eds.), *Dependence and Exploitation in Work and Marriage* (New York: Longman 1976), pp. 21–46; R. M. Kanter, 'Women in the structure of organizations', in M. Millman and R. M. Kanter (eds.), *Another Voice* (New York: Anchor Books 1975); R. M. Kanter, 'Some effects of proportions on group life: skewed sex ratios and responses to token women', *American Journal of Sociology,* **82** (1977), pp. 965–99; R. M. Kanter, *Men and Women of the Corporation* (New York: Basic Books, 1977); A. Oakley, *The Sociology of Housework* (New York: Pantheon 1974).

3 This paper does not offer a quantitative analysis of the proportion of studies exhibiting the use of this dominant paradigm. The reason for not doing so is that the paradigm is so pervasive that it is difficult to identify any studies which do not reflect its influence. This influence has been lessened by the growth of criticisms of particular aspects of the paradigm. While we credit these attempts to correct particular aspects of the paradigm, we aim towards more basic restructuring.

4 The basic assumptions of the sex-segregated models have never been wholly appropriate to men's or women's employment. As more

women have become employees for longer periods of their lives, and as more questions are being raised concerning the division of labour by sex (in both paid and unpaid work) these models have become more of a barrier to understanding both men's and women's relationships to work.

5 This assumption exemplifies the tenacity of beliefs which are congruent with the prevailing ideology of gender differences (cf. J. Laws, 'Feminism and patriarchy: competing ways of doing social science', paper presented at the annual meetings of the American Sociological Association, San Francisco (1978). R. Dubin, 'Industrial workers' worlds', *Social Problems*, **3** (January 1956) pp. 131–42; and Orzack, 'Work as a "central life interest" of professionals', *Social Problems*, **7** (Fall 1959) pp. 125–32, showed that the degree of 'central life interest' in work varied by occupation for men and women. Dubin and his associates (R. Dubin, R. A. Hedley and C. Taveggia, 'Attachment to work', in R. Dubin (ed.), *Handbook of Work, Organization and Society* (Chicago: Rand-McNally 1976)), have continued research in this area for over twenty years, yet the assumption persists that gender role, rather than occupation, is the primary variable which determines the degree of 'central life interest' in work.

6 R. Blauner, *Alienation and Freedom* (Chicago: University of Chicago Press 1964).

7 H. Beynon and R. M. Blackburn, *Perceptions of Work* (Cambridge University Press 1972).

8 Blauner, *Alienation and Freedom*, pp. 71–2.

9 ibid., p. 71.

10 ibid., p. 87.

11 ibid., p. 87.

12 Beynon and Blackburn, *Perceptions of Work*, chapter 3.

13 ibid., p. 75.

14 ibid., p. 149.

15 Interestingly, the relationship between men's employment and their family roles has been studied primarily for unemployed or underemployed men. Apparently, the problematic aspects of this relationship become more visible when the expected pattern does not hold.

16 C. F. Epstein, *Women's Place: Options and Limits of Professional Careers* (Berkeley: University of California Press 1970); M. L. Walshok and M. G. Walshok, 'The personal and social benefits of paid employment for urban women in skilled and semi-skilled occupations', paper presented at the Ninth World Congress of Sociology, Uppsala, Sweden (1978).

17 J. G. Hunt and L. L. Hunt, 'Dilemmas and contradictions of status: the case of the dual-career family', *Social Problems*, **24** (April 1977), pp. 407–16; L. Lein *et al.*, 'Work and family life', report to National Institute of Education, Center for the Study of Public Policy,

Cambridge, Massachusetts (1975); J. Mortimer, 'Social class, work and the family: some implications of the father's occupation for familial relationships and sons' career decisions', *Journal of Marriage and the Family,* **38** (May 1976), pp. 241–56; R. Rapaport and R. N. Rapaport, 'Further considerations of the dual career family', *Human Relations,* **24** no. 6 (1971), pp. 519–33.

18 cf. L. Lamphere, 'Women's work, alienation and class consciousness', paper presented at the 72nd annual meetings of the American Anthropological Association, New Orleans (1973); Walshok and Walshok, 'The personal and social benefits of paid employment for urban women'.

19 A. Kessler-Harris, 'Notes on women in advanced capitalism', *Social Policy* (July–August 1973), pp. 16–22; H. Hartmann, 'Capitalism, patriarchy, and job segregation by sex', in M. Blaxall and B. Reagan (eds.), *Women and the Workplace* (Chicago: University of Chicago Press 1976), pp. 137–69; T. Caplow, *Sociology of Work* (Minneapolis, University of Minnesota Press 1954).

20 See especially Kanter, 'Some effects of proportions on group life', pp. 965–99; Kanter, *Men and Women of the Corporation.*

21 Acker and Van Houten, 'Differential recruitment and control', pp. 152–63.

22 For example, E. Langer, 'Inside the New York Telephone Company', in W. O'Neill (ed.), *Women at Work* (New York: Quadrangle Press 1972); E. N. Glenn and R. L. Feldberg, 'Degraded and deskilled: the proletarianization of clerical work', *Social Problems,* **25** (1977), pp. 52–64.

Chapter 3   Industrial radicalism and the domestic division of labour

1 S. Taylor, 'Parkin's theory of working class conservatism: two hypotheses investigated', *Sociological Review,* **26** no. 4 (November 1978), pp. 827–42, excerpted in this volume Chapter 13.

2 This construction of a manual category was arrived at as follows: 'The working class was, for the present purposes, taken to be manual workers and members of the families of manual workers who either were employed inside the home or were employed outside the home in manual occupations', ibid., p. 831.

3 ibid., p. 836.

4 F. Parkin, 'Working class Conservatives: a theory of political deviance', *British Journal of Sociology,* **18** (1967), pp. 278–90. It is of interest to note that women constitute around 43 per cent of the workforce at present, and in fact there is an obvious teleology in the claim.

5 Taylor, 'Parkin's theory of working class conservatism', p. 836.

6 ibid., pp. 836–7.

7 ibid., p. 837. This has to be qualified since in 1975 over 55 per cent of all women workers were in jobs in three major service industries – distributive trades, professional and scientific, and miscellaneous services (Department of Employment 1975).

8 To some extent this appears an 'ideal type' construction with all its attendant problems – the generation of a non-dynamic series of 'discrete snapshots which reflects the extent of the divergence between consciousness and the ideal type', W. Holmes, 'The theory of alienation as sociological explanation', *Sociology*, **10** (1976), pp. 207–24. This is partially explained by the data being culled from a larger research project, nevertheless the resources mentioned do provide a basis for approaching the home–work interaction as the thesis interprets it.

9 At the time of the fieldwork, the numbers employed on production were: men 898; women, 1671 (full-time), 90 (part-time). Also between November 1976 and October 1977, 401 women were interviewed for shop floor jobs with 209 being engaged.

10 The issues work commitment raises are of wide-ranging interest since much discussion about orientations to work among women revolves around the assumption of the low work commitment or the familiar 'pin money' argument. This partially, on the ideological plane, is seen as a basis for the 'suitability' of women for 'secondary' labour markets. The statistics offered go some way to providing a much needed corrective to this. The question then becomes one of when the women will return to work. This of course raises the problem of state provision of nurseries, lengths of permitted absence etc. to facilitate this, and, in practice, bisects the desire to return to work and having the resources to do so.

11 This problem is not exclusive to women since men also have a 'clash' of values between their work and domestic settings. Rather it indicates unchallenged beliefs about the domestic role being solely an ideological burden for women. For a fertile appraisal of this issue see H. Beynon, *Working for Fords* (Allen Lane 1973), where he notes the distinction between class solidarity expressed as 'factory consciousness' and its dilution outside the factory gates.

12 This connection between organization size and authority relations has been documented in considerable detail. See G. K. Ingham, *Size of Industrial Organization and Worker Behaviour* (Cambridge University Press 1970), especially chapter 2. P. Bowen, *Social Control in Industrial Organizations: Industrial Relations and Industrial Sociology* (Routledge & Kegan Paul 1976), provides a particularly useful theoretical *and* empirical study of the dimensions of the topic.

13 Percentages quoted, though offering a stable pattern, have to be considered alongside the fact that 57 per cent had never been involved

in any dispute. Nevertheless, I would suggest that the 'legitimacy' of industrial action has recently been exposed to strongly critical treatment by the media and indeed the dominant ethos eschews militancy. To that extent then it would have been easier for respondents to reject union solidarity and its potential results. On the question of the power of dominant ideas to influence verbal responses and de-contextualize key ideological issues, see C. Woolfson, 'The semiotics of working class speech', *Working Papers in Cultural Studies*, no. 9 (Centre for Contemporary Cultural Studies, University of Birmingham 1977); F. Parkin, *Class Inequality and Political Order* (Paladin 1971), especially chapter 3.

14 P. Hunt, 'Cash transactions and household tasks', *Sociological Review*, **26** no. 3 (1978), p. 560.

15 These percentages were arrived at by combining those replies as *no* which claimed – 'women were just as good', 'all workers should be treated the same', and 'it is against the law'. To say 'women are just as good' is itself an equivocal statement since it takes the *male comparison* as a defensive criterion.

16 Further confirmation is suggested by the high number who have been 'compelled' to marry hurriedly due to pregnancy thus compounding financial strains.

Chapter 4   Workers side by side: women and the trade union movement

1 J. Mitchell, *Women's Estate* (Penguin 1971), p. 139.
2 P. Hunt, 'The differential response of men and women to trade unionism', unpublished British Sociological Association paper (1974).
3 T. Nichols and P. Armstrong, *Workers Divided* (Fontana 1976), p. 49.
4 K. Marx and F. Engels, *Manifesto of the Communist Party* (Moscow: Progress Publishers 1965), p. 43.
5 A. Wise, *Women and the Struggle for Workers' Control*, Spokesman Pamphlet, no. 33.
6 *The Sunday Times* (27 February 1977).
7 Nichols and Armstrong, *Workers Divided*, p. 49.

Chapter 5   Militancy and acquiescence among women workers

1 C. N. Parkinson (ed.), *Industrial Disruption* (Leviathan House 1973), pp. 177–8.
2 J. S. King, 'Women and work: sex differences and society', *Manpower Paper No. 1* (HMSO 1970), p. 15.
3 C. Middleton, 'Sexual inequality and stratification theory', in F. Parkin (ed.), *The Social Analysis of Class Structure* (Tavistock 1974).
4 R. McNabb, 'The labour force participation of married women',

Manchester School of Economic and Social Studies, no. 3 (September 1977).

5 The Stockport research referred to throughout the text is an ongoing SSRC-sponsored project entitled 'Manual workers and the sexual division of labour', jointly directed by the author and David Bennett at Manchester Polytechnic.

6 Stockport Metropolitan Borough, *Digest for the North Area 1974.*

7 G. Spray, 'Women's labour in an underdeveloped region: a perspective on Hull', unpublished paper given at British Sociological Association Sexual Divisions and Society Study Group Seminar, Bradford University (February 1977).

8 R. M. Blackburn, *Union Character and Social Class* (Batsford 1967), p. 31.

9 V. L. Allen, *Militant Trade Unionism* (Merlin Press 1966).

10 ibid., p. 19.

11 ibid., p. 41.

12 D. Thompson, 'Women and nineteenth century radical politics: a lost dimension' in J. Mitchell and A. Oakley (eds.), *The Rights and Wrongs of Women* (Penguin 1976).

13 T. Lupton, *On the Shopfloor* (Pergamon Press 1963).

14 Department of Employment, *Gazette* (February 1977).

15 H. A. Turner, *Is Britain Really Strike Prone? A Review of the Incidence, Character and Cost of Industrial Conflict* (Cambridge University Press 1969), p. 46.

16 Department of Employment, *Gazette* (January 1978).

17 Blackburn, *Union Character,* p. 56.

18 G. Bain, D. Coates and V. Ellis, *Social Stratification and Trade Unionism* (Heinemann Educational Books 1973); Blackburn, *Union Character.*

19 E. G. A. Armstrong, J. F. B. Goodman and A. Wagner, 'Normative consensus, constitution and aspects of ideology in industrial relations: the case of the footwear industry', *Journal of Management Studies,* **15** no. 1 (February 1978), p. 30.

20 Bain *et al., Social Stratification,* p. 138.

21 R. Coates and R. Silburn, *Poverty: The Forgotten Englishmen* (Penguin 1973), p. 128.

22 K. Purcell, 'Working women, women's work and the occupation of being a woman', *Women's Studies International Quarterly,* **1** no. 2 (Summer 1978).

23 M. Mann, 'The social cohesion of liberal democracy', *American Sociological Review,* **35** no. 3 (June 1970).

24 M. Porter, 'Consciousness and secondhand experience: wives and husbands in industrial action', *Sociological Review,* **26** no. 2 (1978).

Chapter 6   Women as employees: social consciousness and collective action

1 This point has also been made recently by H. Beynon and R. M. Blackburn, *Perceptions of Work* (Cambridge University Press 1972).

2 See V. L. Allen, *The Sociology of Industrial Relations* (Longman 1971).

3 *Editors' note:* But see J. Acker and D. B. van Houten, 'Differential recruitment and control: the sex structuring of organisations', *Administrative Science Quarterly,* **19** (1974), pp. 152–63, who re-examine the Hawthorne experiments pointing out that the controls imposed on the women workers were more severe than those imposed on the male assemblers.

4 T. Lupton, *On the Shop Floor* (Pergamon Press 1963).

5 See T. Lupton, *Money for Effort* (HMSO 1961), pp. 30–3; Lupton, *On the Shop Floor,* p. 91.

6 Lupton, *On the Shop Floor,* p. 191.

7 S. Cunnison, *Wages and Work Allocation* (Tavistock 1966).

8 L. Klein, *'Multiproducts Ltd.',* (HMSO 1964).

9 *Editors' note:* There have been many more recent studies of women's regulation of output. See, for example A. Bridgewood, 'Women workers in contemporary Britain', unpublished M.Sc. thesis, University of Bradford (1978), chapter 3; R. Cavendish, *Women on the Line* (Routledge & Kegan Paul 1982); articles by Lamphere and Shapiro-Perl, in A. Zimbalist (ed.), *Case Studies on the Labor Process* (Monthly Review Press 1979).

10 Lupton, *On the Shop Floor,* p. 191.

11 Recent studies have also emphasized the importance of the labour market in influencing 'orientations to work'. Beynon and Blackburn, *Perceptions of Work,* p. 159, conclude their discussion of women's 'orientations to work': 'It was their position within the labour market in combination with their position within the family which produced their particular and distinctive orientation toward the workplace.' A paper on homeworkers by E. Hope, M. Kennedy and A. de Winter, 'Homeworkers in North London', in D. Barker and S. Allen (eds.), *Dependence and Exploitation in Work and Marriage* (Longman 1976), illustrates similarly for the case of workers employed at home how their expectations about work and a very weak labour market situation combine and interact to perpetuate conditions of extreme exploitation.

12 *Editors' note:* Throughout the 1970s, trade union membership grew particularly rapidly among women, to a peak density of 39.1 per cent in 1979 – an increase of 42 per cent on 1970 figures. With rapid rises in unemployment, the density of trade union membership for women fell to 38.6 per cent. The density for men was 67 per cent in 1979 (an

increase of 13 per cent over 1970 figures) and 64.2 per cent in 1980, Equal Opportunities Commission, *Sixth Annual Report 1981* (HMSO 1982), Table 3.8, p. 70.

13 G. S. Bain and R. Price, 'Union growth and employment trends in the United Kingdom, 1964–70', *British Journal of Industrial Relations,* **10** (1972), pp. 378–9.

14 H. A. Turner, *Trade Union Growth, Structure and Policy* (George Allen & Unwin 1962), pp. 24–5.

15 ibid., pp. 293–5.

16 H. A. Clegg, A. Fox and A. F. Thompson, *A History of British Trade Unions since 1889,* vol. 1 (Oxford University Press 1964), pp. 469–70.

17 R. M. Blackburn, *Union Character and Social Class* (Batsford 1967), pp. 122, 125, 196–7, 257–8.

18 D. Lockwood, *The Blackcoated Worker* (George Allen & Unwin 1958), p. 151.

19 G. S. Bain, *The Growth of White-collar Unionism* (Oxford University Press 1970), p. 41–3.

20 Beynon and Blackburn, *Perceptions of Work,* pp. 115–17.

21 C. Kerr and A. Siegel, 'The interindustry propensity to strike – an international comparison', in A. Kornhauser *et al.* (eds.), *Industrial Conflict,* (New York: McGraw-Hill 1954), p. 195.

22 I am not clear how many women's jobs Kerr and Siegel, 'The interindustry propensity to strike', consider have these characteristics!

23 K. G. J. C. Knowles, *Strikes* (Blackwell 1952), pp. 182–4.

24 R. Hyman, *Strikes* (Fontana 1972), pp. 54, 119.

25 H. A. Turner, G. Clack and G. Roberts, *Labour Relations in the Motor Industry* (George Allen & Unwin 1967), p. 32.

Chapter 7 Unions the men's affair?

1 D. F. Roy, 'The union-organising campaign as a problem of social distance', in H. S. Becker, B. Geer, D. Riesman and R. S. Weiss (eds.), *Institutions and the Person: Papers Presented to Everett C. Hughes* (Chicago: Aldine 1968).

2 This assumption is called into question by the data we have presented (in other parts of the volume *Perceptions of Work* (Cambridge University Press 1972), from which this extract is taken).

3 During this period the stewards on the night shift were continually telling stories of how the shift had restricted output in the past, and as a result successfully obtained concessions from management.

4 The wording of the question was designed to avoid forcing ideological responses, by referring to the event rather than to attitudes as in the usual question 'Why . . .'. It is interesting that when a similar question was asked of bank clerks very few gave ideological responses. See

R. M. Blackburn, *Union Character and Social Class* (Batsford 1967), pp. 208–9.

5 The tendency is not significant for members alone, but is for non-members, and when reasons for membership and non-membership are combined it is highly significant ($p < 0.001$).

6 This tendency for women to be more influenced by social factors has been noted in a different work situation, where unlike Brompton, previous union contact was not relevant since virtually no one had any previous employment. cf. Blackburn, *Union Character and Social Class*, pp. 209–10.

7 This doesn't mean that members will not leave a union under any circumstances. The knife seems to cut both ways, for six of the men 'ex-members' were members on arrival. All had left the union, at least in part, because it compared badly with branch organizations they had experienced in the past.

8 *Editors' note:* Elsewhere in *Perceptions of Work,* Beynon and Blackburn offer data attesting to the militancy of the women's work groups.

9 Because the proportion in both cases was fairly large, the difference was not significant.

10 Sami Dassa, 'L'analyse contextuelle appliquée aux comportements syndicaux', *Sociologie du Travail,* **10** no. 4 (October–December 1968), observes that contextual influences on orientations towards unionism operate mainly on union *members,* who tend to be pro-union. This may explain the pattern here; the highly unionized male context had no influence on non-members and the members tended to be more pro-union, but among the women who were predominantly non-members the contextual effect reduced members' pro-union orientations to the level of non-members. See also Table 12.

11 The relationship is not even significant for the two groups of women taken separately, though it is when they are taken together. In each case phi < 0.2. The lower association for the women is mainly due to lower commitment among women members, which is again consistent with the contextual effect noted by Dassa. (See note 10.)

Chapter 8   Unity is strength? feminism and the labour movement

1 *Editors' note:* See H. Land, 'The myth of the male breadwinner', *New Society* (9 October 1975), pp. 71–3; and H. Land, 'The family wage', *Feminist Review*, no. 6 (1980), pp. 55–78; as well as M. Barrett and M. McIntosh 'The family wage: some problems for socialists and feminists', *Capital and Class,* no. 11 (1980), pp. 51–72; and B. Campbell and V. Charleton 'Work to rule', *Red Rag,* no. 14 (1979), for a feminist analysis of the family wage.

2 London Women's Liberation Campaign for Legal and Financial Independence and Rights of Women, 'Disaggregation Now!', *Feminist*

Review, no. 2 (1979), pp. 19–31. *Editors' note:* See also Department of Health and Social Security, *Report of the Committee on One-parent Families,* Cmnd 5629 (HMSO 1974); and J. Coussins and A. Coote, *The Family in the Firing Line* (NCCL Rights of Women Publications 1981).

3   See the *Fourth Annual Report* of the Equal Opportunities Commission (HMSO 1980). *Editors' note:* On the extent of occupational sex segregation in Britain see C. Hakim, 'Sexual division within the labour force: occupational segregation', *Department of Employment Gazette* (November 1978); and for the effect of occupational segregation on the Equal Pay Act, see S. Robarts, with A. Coote and E. Ball, *Positive Action for Women* (NCCL Rights for Women Publications 1981).

4   *Editors' note:* For a discussion of skill as a 'socially constructed' and male constructed category, see A. Philips and B. Taylor, 'Sex and skill: notes toward a feminist economics', *Feminist Review,* no. 6 (1980), pp. 79–88.

5   *Editors' note:* See Campbell and Charleton 'Work to rule'; and J. Gardiner and S. Smith, 'Feminism and the alternative economic strategy', *Marxism Today* (October 1981), pp. 24–30, for an analysis of changes in trade union strategy and labour movement objectives necessary to alter the structure of both domestic and wage labour.

Chapter 10   Politics an unnatural practice: political science looks at female participation

1   B. Abzug in *Women's Role in Contemporary Society: The Report of the New York City Commission of Human Rights* (New York: Avon Books 1972), p. 639.

2   The discipline's justification of existing power holders has been challenged in the case of class and occupation, and that challenge is now taken seriously. There is a growing body of literature criticizing political science on this score. See, for example, C. Pateman, *Participation and Democratic Theory* (Cambridge University Press 1970); L. Lipsitz, 'The grievances of the poor', in P. Green and S. Levinson (eds.), *Power and Community: Dissenting Essays in Political Science* (New York: Vintage 1969); A. Wolfe, *The Seamy Side of Democracy: Repression in America* (New York: McKay 1973); etc. However, political scientists still dismiss as polemics the same criticism when it is made on the basis of sex or race. Why this should be the case is one of our major concerns.

3   This is similar to the findings in recent psychological studies that ideal, or healthy, personalities are made up of what are regarded as masculine characteristics. I. K. Broverman, D. M. Broverman, F. E. Carlson, P. S. Rosenkrantz, and S. R. Vogel, 'Sex-role stereotypes and

clinical judgements of mental health', in J. M. Bardwick (ed.), *Readings on the Psychology of Women* (New York: Harper and Row 1972), pp. 320–4.

4 A. Campbell *et al.*, *The American Voter* (New York: Wiley 1960).

5 ibid., p. 487.

6 ibid., p. 488.

7 ibid.

8 ibid., p. 490.

9 ibid.

10 ibid., Table 15.4, p. 260. These are figures for the non-South only. The differences in the South were of the same order.

11 R. E. Lane, *Political Life* (New York: The Free Press 1965), paperback edition, preface.

12 ibid., p. 208.

13 E. E. Maccoby, R. Mathews, and A. S. Morton, 'Youth and political change', *Public Opinion Quarterly*, **18** (1954), pp. 23–9.

14 ibid., p. 33.

15 M. Kent Jennings, and R. G. Niemi, 'The division of political labor between mothers and fathers', *American Political Science Review*, **65** (March 1971), pp. 69–82.

16 ibid., p. 69.

17 ibid., p. 70.

18 ibid., p. 73.

19 The study also found variation in this model was related to whether the wife worked and the level of education. Although they concede that there is still a built in edge for males 'even in those cases where the male ego is clearly dominant, there are abundant instances where the distaff side of the family is paramount or the male advantage seriously impaired'. ibid., p. 82.

20 D. Riesman, 'Orbits of tolerance, interviews, and elites', *Public Opinion Quarterly*, **20** (1956), pp. 49–73, p. 57. Cited in Lane, *Political Life*, p. 213.

21 S. Stouffer, *Communism, Conformity and Civil Liberties: A Cross Section of the Nation Speaks Its Mind* (New York: Doubleday 1955), pp. 131–55.

22 Riesman, 'Orbits of tolerance, interviews, and elites', p. 58.

23 A. Campbell, G. Gurin, and W. Miller, *The Voter Decides* (Evanston, Ill.: Row Peterson 1954), pp. 152–6.

24 Lane, *Political Life*, p. 213.

25 ibid., pp. 354, 355.

26 The sources cited on this statement are: Lane's *Political Life*; M. Duverger, *The Political Role of Women* (Paris: UNESCO 1955); F. Greenstein, 'Sex-related political differences in childhood', *Journal of Politics*, **23** (1961), pp. 353–71; M. Dogan, and J. Narbonne, 'Les Françaises Facent a la Politique' and G. Bremme, 'Die Politische

Rolle der Frau in Deutschland'; all in G. Almond, and S. Verba, *The Civic Culture* (Princeton: Princeton University Press 1963), p. 388.

27 ibid.

28 For this data consult the tables on pp. 390–5, 397 in Almond and Verba, *The Civic Culture*.

29 ibid., p. 398.

30 ibid.

31 ibid., pp. 398–9.

32 F. Greenstein, *Children and Politics* (New Haven, Conn.: Yale University Press 1965).

33 This information is displayed in Table 6.1, in Greenstein, *Children and Politics*, p. 117. The table is somewhat hard to read and the actual questions are not given. The table is divided into 'specifically political responses' which includes the political information score which shows significant difference although all other measures show no significant differences; and 'politically relevant responses'.

34 ibid., p. 97.

35 ibid., p. 96.

36 L. M. Terman and L. E. Tyler, 'Psychological sex differences', in L. Carmichael (ed.), *Manual of Child Psychology* (New York: Wiley 1954).

37 ibid., pp. 1097–8.

38 Greenstein, *Children and Politics*, p. 121.

39 ibid., p. 126, n. 51.

40 ibid., p. 127.

41 Stouffer, *Communism, Conformity and Civil Liberties*.

42 ibid., p. 131.

43 Lane, *Political Life*, p. 213.

44 Lane cites David Reisman, 'Orbits of tolerance, interviews and elites'.

45 H. A. Bone, and A. Ranney, *Politics and Voters* (New York: McGraw-Hill 1967).

46 ibid., p. 399.

47 The documented source for the low rates of turnout for women in Greenstein was based on women's belief that voting is for men as reported by R. Lane and C. E. Merriam and H. F. Gosnell, *Non-Voting: Causes and Methods of Control* (Chicago: University of Chicago Press 1924), which is in turn the source of the Lane statement. It is worth looking at Merriam and Gosnell since this study has become the basis for so much assertion. These authors, studying Chicago voters in April 1923, found that over half the adult citizens not voting were women (p. 27). One-third of these women were foreign born women who had acquired citizenship by marriage. Of the women in the sample some 11.4 per cent said they did not vote out of disbelief. This number included 414 who disbelieved *and 54 more* who did not vote because

their husbands objected. The authors conclude that the disbelief in women's voting was 'an important but vanishing factor in the civic life of the community' (pp. 115–16). It is worth noting that this study, completed only three years after the women's suffrage amendment was passed, was the source of statements regarding women's low rates of turnout and male dominance in voting choices. The authors made no such claims, even in 1923.

48 R. Presthus, *Men at the Top* (Oxford University Press 1964).
49 H. Cantril, and M. Strunk, *Public Opinion 1935–1946* (Princeton: Princeton University Press 1951).
50 Lipsitz, 'The grievances of the poor'.

Chapter 11 Women: if not apolitical, then conservative

1 G. A. Almond and S. Verba, *The Civic Culture* (Princeton: Princeton University Press 1963), p. 388: A. Campbell, P. E. Converse, W. E. Miller and D. E. Stokes, *The American Voter: An Abridgement* (New York: Wiley 1964), p. 261.
2 R. E. Lane, *Political Life* (Glencoe: The Free Press 1959), pp. 15–16.
3 P. G. J. Pulzer, *Political Representation and Elections in Britain* (George Allen & Unwin 1967), p. 107.
4 D. Riesman, 'Orbits of tolerance, interviewers, and elites', *Public Opinion Quarterly,* **20** no. 1 (1965), p. 58.
5 A. King, 'A sociological portrait: politics', *New Society,* **19** no. 485 (1972), pp. 58–9.
6 M. Dogan, 'Political cleavage and social stratification in France and Italy', in S. M. Lipset and S. Rokkan (eds.), *Party Systems and Vote Alignments* (New York: The Free Press 1967), p. 160.
7 A. F. Davies and S. Encel, 'Class and status', in A. F. Davies and S. Encel (eds.), *Australian Society* (Melbourne: F. W. Cheshire 1965), p. 26; D. A. Aitkin and M. Kahan 'Australia: class politics in the New World', in R. Rose (ed.), *Electoral Behavior: A Comparative Handbook* (New York: The Free Press 1974), p. 457.
8 P. E. Converse, 'Some priority variables in comparative electoral research', in Rose (ed.), *Electoral Behavior.*
9 K. Amundsen, *The Silenced Majority* (Englewood Cliffs, NJ: Prentice Hall 1971).
10 M. Duverger, *The Political Role of Women* (Paris: UNESCO 1955).
11 ibid., p. 8.
12 R. A. Dahl, *A Preface to Democratic Theory* (Chicago: University of Chicago Press 1956), p. 74.
13 G. Sartori, *Democratic Theory* (New York: Praeger 1956), pp. 18, 250–77.
14 L. Lipson, *The Democratic Civilization* (Oxford University Press 1964), p. 278.

15 E. A. Nordlinger, *The Working Class Tories* (MacGibbon & Kee 1967), pp. 64–7.

16 M. Abrams, 'Social trends and electoral behaviour', in R. Rose (ed.), *Studies in British Politics* (Macmillan 1966), p. 16.

17 Almond and Verba, *The Civic Culture,* p. 177.

18 For example, C. Burns, *Parties and People* (Melbourne: Melbourne University Press 1961), pp. 82–3; W. G. Runciman, *Relative Deprivation and Social Justice* (Routledge & Kegan Paul 1966), p. 237; and R. T. McKenzie and A. Silver, 'Conservatism, industrialism and the working class Tory in England', in Rose (ed.), *Studies in British Politics,* p. 30.

19 J. D. Barber, *Citizen Politics* (2nd edn) (Chicago: Markham 1972), p. 33.

20 R. E. Lane, *Political Ideology* (Glencoe: The Free Press 1962).

21 R. E. Lane, *Political Thinking and Consciousness* (Chicago: Markham 1969).

22 Also A. Inkeles 'Participant citizenship in six developing countries', *American Political Science Review,* **LXIII** no. 4 (1969), pp. 1120–41; L. Tiger, *Men in Groups* (Nelson 1969), XIV; and L. Lipsitz, 'On political belief: the grievances of the poor', in P. Green and S. Levinson (eds.), *Power and Community: Dissenting Essays in Political Science* (New York: Random House 1970), pp. 142–72. A volume of Lane's collected papers (New York: The Free Press 1972) is aptly titled *Political Man*.

23 Abrams, 'Social trends and electoral behaviour', p. 134.

24 A. F. Davies, *Australian Democracy* (2nd edn) (Melbourne: Longmans Green 1964), p. 137.

25 In addition the conclusion is technically flawed in a manner common to all attempts to build a composite picture of the 'typical' person by aggregating such qualities as dominate among the marginal totals. More concretely, it does not follow that because more men than women and more of the old than the young participate, more old men *or* more old men than old women participate. Davies' figures are marginals to a table with two degrees of freedom not one.

26 Joreen, 'The 51 percent minority group: a statistical essay', in R. Morgan (ed.), *Sisterhood is Powerful* (New York: Random House 1970), p. 44.

27 H. Daudt, *Floating Voters and the Floating Vote* (Leiden: Stenfert Kroese 1961), p. 126.

28 But not, apparently, for R. Axelrod, 'Where the votes come from: an analysis of electoral conditions, 1952–1968', *American Political Science Review,* **LXVI** no. 1 (1972), pp. 11–20; or G. N. Pomper, 'From confusion to clarity: issues and American voters, 1956–1968', *American Political Science Review,* **LXVI** no. 2 (1972), pp. 415–28.

29 L. Iglitzin, 'Political education and sexual liberation', *Politics and Society,* **2** no. 2 (1972), p. 244.

30 Amundsen, *The Silenced Majority,* pp. 18, 121, 147–9, 155.

31 ibid., 80–2; but compare Iglitzin, 'Political education and sexual liberation', p. 248; G. Steinem, 'Women voters can't be trusted', *MS,* **1** no. 1 (1972), pp. 48–51, 131.

32 Pulzer, *Political Representation,* p. 107.

33 M. Abrams, 'Social class and politics', in R. Mabey (ed.), *Class* (A. Blond 1967), p. 21.

34 Though such differences do not emerge in M. Miller, 'The Waukegan Study of voter turnout prediction', in D. Katz, D. Cartwright, S. Eldersveld and A. M. Lee (eds.), *Public Opinion and Propaganda* (New York: Holt, Rinehart and Winston 1954), p. 757; A. De Grazia, *The Western Public: 1952 and Beyond* (Berkeley, Calif.: Stanford University Press 1954), p. 141; A. H. Birch, *Small-Town Politics* (Oxford University Press 1959), p. 102; Abrams, 'Social trends and electoral behaviour', p. 130; L. T. Sharpe, *A Metropolis Votes* (London School of Economics: Greater London Papers no. 8 1962), p. 65; I. Budge and D. W. Urwin, *Scottish Political Behaviour* (Longmans Green 1966), p. 79; A. Rabushka, 'A note on overseas Chinese political participation in urban Malaya', *American Political Science Review,* **LXIV** no. 1 (1970), p. 77; R. Laskin and R. Baird, 'Factors in voter turnout and party preference in a Saskatchewan town', *Canadian Journal of Political Science,* **III** no. 3 (1970), p. 457; or uniformly – despite his own words to the contrary – J. Blondel, *Voters, Parties and Leaders* (rev. edn) (Penguin 1965), pp. 56, 59.

35 In Britain: M. Benney, A. P. Gray, and R. H. Pear, *How People Vote* (Routledge & Kegan Paul 1956), p. 178; J. Trenaman and D. McQuail, *Television and the Political Image* (Methuen 1961), pp. 168, 208; Blondel, *Voters, Parties and Leaders,* p. 56; for the USA: G. Gallup and S. R. Rae, *The Pulse of Democracy* (New York: Simon and Schuster 1940), p. 68; F. I. Greenstein, 'Sex-related political differences in childhood', in N. W. Polsby, R. A. Dentler and P. A. Smith (eds.), *Politics and Social Life,* (Boston: Houghton Mifflin 1963), p. 245; Campbell *et al., The American Voter,* p. 256; and more generally, Almond and Verba, *The Civic Culture,* p. 388; L. W. Milbrath, *Political Participation* (Chicago: Rand-McNally 1965), p. 135; H. A. Bone and A. Ranney, *Politics and Voters* (2nd edn) (New York: McGraw-Hill 1967), p. 26.

36 P. L. Reynolds, 'Religion and voting in Auckland', *Political Science,* **24** no. 1 (1972), p. 41.

37 For example, Benney *et al., How People Vote,* p. 107; H. J. Eysenck, *The Psychology of Politics* (Routledge & Kegan Paul 1954), p. 23.

38 H. Durant, 'Voting behaviour in Britain, 1954–64', in Rose (ed.),

Studies in British Politics, p. 125; Eysenck, *The Psychology of Politics,* p. 23.

39 Blondel, *Voters, Parties and Leaders,* p. 59; R. Rose, *Politics in England* (Faber & Faber 1965), p. 29.

40 I. Budge and C. O'Leary, *Belfast: Approach to Crisis* (Longmans Green 1973), p. 215.

41 Durant, 'Voting behavior in Britain, 1954–64', p. 125.

42 R. Rose, 'Britain: simple abstractions and complex realities', in Rose (ed.), *Electoral Behavior,* p. 522.

43 B. R. Berelson, P. F. Lazarsfeld and W. N. McPhee, *Voting* (Chicago: University of Chicago Press 1954), p. 320; Budge and Urwin, *Scottish Political Behaviour,* p. 57; Abrams, 'Social class and politics', p. 21; and, of children, R. E. Dowse and J. A. Hughes, 'Girls, boys and politics', in the *British Journal of Sociology,* **XXII** no. 1 (1971), pp. 62–3.

44 M. R. Just, 'Causal models of voter rationality, Great Britain 1959 and 1963', *Political Studies,* **XXI** no. 1 (1973), p. 53.

45 Bone and Ranney, *Politics and Voters,* p. 26.

46 Durant, 'Voting behaviour in Britain', p. 125, his denial notwithstanding.

47 D. E. Butler and A. King, *The British General Election of 1966* (Macmillan 1966), p. 265.

48 For example, Trenaman and McQuail, *Television and the Political Image,* pp. 139–40.

49 For example, Benney *et al., How People Vote,* p. 108; Sharpe, *A Metropolis Votes,* p. 85; R. T. McKenzie and A. Silver, *Angels in Marble* (Heinemann 1966), p. 82.

50 Steinem, 'Women voters can't be trusted', pp. 50–1; H. Mendelsohn and I. Crespi, *Polls, Television and the New Politics* (Scranton, Penn.: Chandler 1970), p. 79; Virginia Slims, *American Women's Opinion Poll in Politics and the Economy* (1972), p. 16.

51 K. Hill, 'Belgium: Political change in a segmented society', in Rose (ed.), *Electoral Behavior,* p. 93.

52 A. Campbell, G. Gurin and W. E. Miller, 'Political issues and the vote: November 1952', in D. Katz, D. Cartwright, S. Eldersveld and A. M. Lee (eds.), *Public Opinion and Propaganda* (New York: Wiley 1954), p. 641.

53 Steinem, 'Women voters can't be trusted', p. 51.

54 J. Bonham, *The Middle Class Vote* (Faber & Faber 1954), p. 134; but compare D. E. Butler, 'The study of political behaviour in Britain', in A. Ranney (ed.), *Essays on the Behavioral Study of Politics* (Champaign: University of Illinois Press 1962), pp. 212–13.

55 M. Wood, 'On the brink: the Denison Pre-Election Survey', in H. Mayer (ed.), *Labor to Power* (Sydney: Angus and Robertson 1973), p. 123.

56 M. Dawson, *Graduate and Married* (Sydney: Department of Adult Education, University of Sydney 1965), pp. 80–1; S. Encel, B. S. Buckley and J. S. Schreiber, *The Sydney Jewish Community* (Sydney: School of Sociology, University of NSW 1972), 12a.

57 King, 'A sociological portrait: politics', p. 59.

58 Blondel, *Voters, Parties and Leaders*, p. 59.

59 Aitkin and Kahan, 'Australia: class politics', p. 457.

60 Campbell *et al.*, *The American Voter*, p. 261.

61 R. S. Milne and H. C. MacKenzie, *Straight Fight* (The Hansard Society 1954), p. 39.

62 Lane, *Political Life*, pp. 120–1.

63 For example, B. R. Berelson and G. A. Steiner, *Human Behavior* (New York: Harcourt and Brace 1964), p. 573; D. E. Butler and D. Stokes, *Political Change in Britain* (Macmillan 1969), p. 129 n. 1; in Germany, D. W. Urwin, 'Germany: continuity and change in electoral politics', in Rose (ed.), *Electoral Behavior*, pp. 156–7; and in the Netherlands, A. Lijphart, 'The Netherlands: continuity and change in voting behavior', in Rose (ed.), *Electoral Behaviour*, p. 255.

64 Pulzer, *Political Representation and Elections in Britain*, p. 107; A. R. Ball, *Modern Politics and Government* (Macmillan 1971), p. 132.

65 For example, Lane, *Political Life*, pp. 341–2; S. M. Lipset, *Political Man* (Heinemann 1960), p. 260.

66 Dogan, 'Political cleavage and social stratification', pp. 159–67; but compare Hill, 'Belgium', pp. 92–4.

67 But compare H. Mol, *Religion in Australia* (Melbourne: Nelson 1971), p. 298; and most importantly, Budge and O'Leary, *Scottish Political Behaviour*, p. 216, who uncover a whopping 24 per cent difference between male and female support for the Unionist Party unrelated to denominational differences.

68 Aitkin and Kahan, 'Australia: class politics', p. 457.

69 The Chase Manhattan Bank estimated a women's overall work week at 99.6 hours. M. Benston, 'The political economy of women's liberation', in L. B. Tanner (ed.), *Voices from Women's Liberation* (New York: The New American Library 1970), pp. 282, 290.

70 M. Stacey, *Tradition and Change* (Oxford University Press 1960), p. 136.

71 Amundsen, *The Silenced Majority*, p. 8.

72 H. Eulau, *Class and Party in the Eisenhower Years* (New York: The Free Press 1962), p. 45.

73 Dogan, 'Political cleavage and social stratification', p. 162.

74 L. Broom, L. F. Jones and J. Zubrizycki, 'Social stratification in Australia', in J. A. Jackson (ed.), *Social Stratification* (Cambridge University Press 1968), pp. 215–16; also J. Zubrizycki, *Settlers of the Latrobe Valley* (Canberra: ANU Press 1964); C. A. Price, 'Migrants in Australian society', in HRH The Duke of Edinburgh's Third Com-

monwealth Study Conference, *Anatomy of Australia* (Melbourne 1968), pp. 102–3.

75 For example, R. Centers, *The Psychology of Social Classes* (Princeton: Princeton University Press), p. 35.

76 Blondel, *Voters, Parties and Leaders,* p. 60.

77 This tripartite distinction follows D. Lockwood, *The Blackcoated Worker* (George Allen & Unwin 1958), especially pp. 201–13.

78 R. Rose, 'How the Party System Works', in M. Abrams, R. Rose and R. Hinden, *Must Labour Lose?* (Penguin 1960), p. 66; also Riesman, 'Orbits of tolerance', p. 61; and Birch, *Small-Town Politics,* p. 103.

79 R. Rose, *Class and Party Divisions: Britain as a Test Case* (University of Strathclyde, Survey Research Centre, *Occasional Paper no. 1* (1968)), p. 19; also L. Brooke and K. Richmond, 'Working wives and housewives', *Melbourne Journal of Politics*, no. 6 (1973), p. 78.

80 Aitkin and Kahan, 'Australia: class politics', p. 457.

81 Benney *et al., How People Vote*, pp. 109–10.

82 Trenaman and McQuail, *Television and the Political Image,* p. 40.

83 Rose, 'How the party system works', p. 66.

84 Burns, *Parties and People,* pp. 84, 127.

85 D. O. Sears, 'Political behavior', in G. Lindzey and E. Aronson (eds.), *The Handbook of Social Psychology* (2nd edn) (Reading, Mass.: Addison-Wesley 1969), p. 397.

86 For example, Burns, *Parties and People,* p. 84; P. Y. Medding, *From Assimilation to Group Survival* (Melbourne: F. W. Cheshire 1968), p. 239.

87 In Duverger, *The Political Role of Women,* p. 143.

88 Tiger, *Men in Groups,* p. 197.

89 However, note that he has since argued that what is at stake here is a central tendency and not an absolute condition, because 'no one community displays the modal pattern of the species' (L. Tiger, 'Comment on sex and social participation', *American Sociological Review,* **37** no. 5 (1972), p. 635).

90 Rose, 'How the party system works', p. 91.

91 For example, Burns, *Parties and People,* p. 79; N. Blewett and D. Jaensch, *Playford to Dunstan* (Melbourne: F. W. Cheshire 1971), pp. 164–5.

92 Benney *et al., How People Vote,* p. 178; Milne and MacKenzie, *Marginal Seat, 1955* (The Hansard Society 1958), p. 86.

93 For example, re party identification, De Grazia, *The Western Public,* p. 134.

94 Duverger, *The Political Role of Women,* p. 68.

95 Campbell *et al., The American Voter,* p. 259; A. Campbell and H. Valen, 'Party identification in Norway and the United States', in Campbell *et al.,* ibid., pp. 250, 254–5.

96 Riesman, 'Orbits of tolerance', p. 60.

97   B. R. Berelson *et al.*, *Voting* (Chicago: University of Chicago Press).

98   Berelson and Steiner, *Human Behavior*, p. 424.

99   Lane, *Political Life*, p. 216.

100 Riesman, 'Orbits of tolerance', pp. 58–9.

101 Lane, *Political Life*, pp. 212–13.

102 S. M. Lipset, P. F. Lazarsfeld, A. H. Barton and J. Linz, 'The psychology of voting: an analysis of political behavior', in Lindzey and Aronson (eds.), *Handbook of Social Psychology*, p. 1133.

103 Lane, *Political Life*, p. 160.

104 This, however, is no licence for the kind of logic that informs the following: '. . . in Finland the women's voting rate in 1908–50 was only about 10 per cent, in Norway about 20 per cent lower than the men's. The small difference is mainly due to the men's laziness in voting.' E. Haavio-Mannila, 'Sex roles in politics', in S. Safilios-Rothschild (ed.), *Towards a Sociology of Women* (Lexington, Mass.: Xerox College 1972), p. 156.
     For example, Milbrath, *Political Participation*; G. Di Palma, *Apathy and Participation* (Glencoe: The Free Press 1970).

105 For example, Dogan, 'Political cleavage and social stratification', p. 162.

106 Bone and Ranney, *Politics and Voters*, p. 26.

107 Lipset *et al.*, 'The psychology of voting', p. 1132; Campbell *et al.*, *The American Voter*, p. 258; Milne and Mackenzie, *Marginal Seat, 1955*, p. 69; Di Palma, *Apathy and Participation*, p. 128.

108 R. Rose, *Politics in England Today* (Faber & Faber 1974), pp. 148–9.

109 E. E. Schattscheider, *The Semi-Sovereign People* (New York: Holt, Rinehart and Winston 1960), pp. 104–5.

110 Trenaman and McQuail, *Television and the Political Image*, p. 170.

111 Almond and Verba, *The Civic Culture*, p. 397.

112 ibid., p. 398; Barber, *Citizen Politics*, p. 35.

113 A. F. Davies, 'Political socialisation', in F. J. Hunt (ed.), *Socialisation in Australia* (Sydney: Angus and Robertson 1972), p. 228.

114 Nordlinger, *The Working Class Tories*, p. 58.

115 For example, Amundsen, *The Silenced Majority*; Iglitzin, 'Political education and sexual liberation'.

116 Compare the view that newspaper reading is 'a more or less passive consumption of information', V. S. Heiskanen, 'Sex roles, social class and political consciousness', *Acta Sociologica*, **14** nos. 1–2 (1971), p. 90.

117 Trenaman and McQuail, *Television and the Political Image*, p. 170.

118 De Grazia, *The Western Public*, p. 141; Lane, *Political Life*, pp. 83, 209.

119 Burns, *Parties and People*, pp. 131–5.

120 'But if political science were surprised to learn that this was true for the

majority of men, there should have been no surprise at all that it was true for almost all women.' Iglitzin, 'Political education and sexual liberation', p. 244.

Chapter 12   Women and voting in Britain

1 I. Crewe, 'The voting surveyed', *The Times Guide to the House of Commons* (Times Books 1979), p. 52
2 A. King, 'A sociological portrait: politics', *New Society*, **19** (1972), pp. 57–60; J. Blondel, *Voters, Parties and Leaders* (Penguin 1963), p. 60; D. McKie, 'The hand that rocks the cradle', *Guardian* (5 May 1978), p. 11.
3 I. Crewe, T. Fox and J. Alt, 'Non-voting in British General Elections 1966–74', in C. Crouch (ed.) *British Political Sociology Yearbook*, **3** (1976), p. 59.
4 M. Lansing, 'Comparison of the voting turnout and party choice of British and American women', paper presented to the European Joint Sessions, Berlin (1977), pp. 6–12.
5 King, 'A sociological portrait: politics'; McKie, 'The hand that rocks the cradle'.
6 R. Rose, 'Social structure and party differences', in R. Rose (ed.), *Studies in British Politics* (Macmillan 1976), pp. 223–4.
7 Lansing, 'Comparison of the voting turnout and party choice of British and American women', pp. 19–20.
8 H. Durant, 'Voting behaviour in Britain 1945–1964', in Rose (ed.), *Studies in British Politics*.
9 I. Crewe, 'Who swung Tory?', *The Economist* **271** (12 May 1979), p. 26.

Chapter 13   The party identifications of women: Parkin put to the test

1 F. Parkin, 'Working class Conservatives: a theory of political deviance', *British Journal of Sociology*, **18** (1967), pp. 278–90.
2 'The commanding institutions of British capitalist society were the Established Church, the public schools and ancient universities, the elites of the military establishment, the press and the mass media . . . and most importantly, the institutional complex of private property and capitalist enterprise which dominates the economic sector.' ibid., p. 280.
3 R. Jessop, *Traditionalism, Conservatism and British Political Culture* (George Allen & Unwin 1974).
4 'Proxy' variables in the sense that there is not necessarily a direct relationship between them and partisanships. A manual worker may vote or identify with the Labour Party on the grounds that Labour is

perceived as the party that manual workers, as a group, vote for. Women do not vote for the Conservatives simply because their group does so: the old are not more Conservative than the young because the vast majority of the old are Conservatives. These variables stand 'proxy' for other experiences and social processes.

5 Parkin, 'Working class Conservatives', p. 288.

6 ibid., p. 288.

7 The proportion of females at 47 per cent is well below that in the population as a whole. The reason for this is that females were disproportionately represented among the working-class 'non-manuals' who were excluded from the sample. Fully three-quarters of this group were women.

Chapter 14   Candidate evaluations by men and women

1 P. Converse, 'The nature of belief systems in mass publics', in D. E. Apter (ed.), *Ideology and Discontent* (New York: The Free Press 1964); J. O. Field and R. E. Anderson, 'Ideology in the public's conceptualization of the 1964 election', *Public Opinion Quarterly,* **33** (1969), pp. 380–98; N. H. Nie, S. Verba and J. R. Petrocik, *The Changing American Voter* (Cambridge, Mass.: Harvard University Press 1976).

2 J. Jacquette (ed.), *Women in Politics* (New York: Wiley 1974), p. xx.

3 F. Greenstein, 'Sex-related political differences in childhood', *Journal of Politics,* **23** (1961), pp. 353–71; R. R. Boyd, 'Women and politics in the United States and Canada', *Annals of the American Academy of Political and Social Science,* **375** (1968), pp. 53–7; M. Guberg, *Women in American Politics* (Oshkosh: Academia Press 1968); L. Milbrath, *Political Participation* (Chicago: Rand-McNally 1965); R. E. Lane, *Political Life* (Glencoe: The Free Press 1959).

4 A. Campbell, G. Gurin and W. Miller, *The Voter Decides* (Evanston, Ill.: Row Peterson 1954).

5 ibid., p. 138.

6 M. Duverger, *The Political Role of Women* (Paris: UNESCO 1955), p. 71.

7 See studies cited in M. Goot and E. Reid, *Women and Voting Studies: Mindless Matrons or Sexist Scientism?* (Beverly Hills: Sage Publications 1974), pp. 28–9.

8 D. O. Sears, 'Political behavior', in G. Lindzey and E. Aronson (eds.), *The Handbook of Social Psychology* (Reading, Mass.: Addison-Wesley 1969).

9 R. Hess and J. Torney, *The Development of Political Attitudes in Children* (Garden City, NY: Doubleday 1967).

10 ibid., p. 186.

11 ibid., p. 193.
12 P. K. Hastings, 'Hows and howevers of the woman voter', *New York Times Magazine* (12 June 1960).
13 L. Iglitzin, 'The making of apolitical women: femininity and sex-stereotyping in girls', in Jacquette, *Women and Politics*; M. K. Jennings and R. Niemi, *Political Character in Adolescence* (Princeton: Princeton University Press 1974); A. Orum, R. Cohen, S. Grasmuck and A. W. Orum, 'Sex socialization and politics', *American Sociological Review,* **39** (1974), pp. 197–209.
14 J. B. Elshtain, 'Moral woman and immoral man – a consideration of the public–private split and its political ramifications', *Politics and Society,* **4** (1974), pp. 453–72.
15 S. Bourque and J. Grossholtz, 'Politics an unnatural practice: Political science looks at female participation', *Politics and Society,* **4** (1974), pp. 255–66.
16 Goot and Reid, *Women and Voting Studies.*
17 Lane (*Political Life*) is perhaps the most serious offender in this regard.
18 For example, in 1960 the percentage of the population giving 'don't know' or 'nothing' responses to the question of what they like about Kennedy was 42 per cent for the first response, 60 per cent for the second, 76 per cent for the third.
19 When the analysis is done using all responses (including don't know, refused to answer, and the like) in the denominator, the response profiles of men as a group and women as a group are very similar to those shown in Table 16. Thus, including 'missing' responses in the data analysis has little effect on the frequency with which women, compared with men, mention party, personality, and issue criteria. Of course, including missing responses does have the effect of depressing, for both men and women, the proportions of their responses which fall into these three categories.
20 K. Andersen, 'Working women and political participation, 1952–1972', *American Journal of Political Science,* **19** (1975), pp. 439–55.
21 A. H. Miller and W. E. Miller, 'Partisanship and performance: "Rational" choice in the 1976 presidential elections', Paper presented at 1977 American Political Science Association convention.
22 R. G. Niemi and H. F. Weisberg, *Controversies in American Voting Behavior* (San Francisco: Freeman 1976), pp. 161–74; E. Declercq, T. L. Hurley and N. R. Luttbeg, 'Voting in American presidential elections: 1956–1972', *American Politics Quarterly,* **3** (1975), pp. 222–46; Nie *et al., The Changing American Voter,* chapter 10.

Chapter 15   Gender, levels of political thinking and political action

1 Ideological thinking and conceptual sophistication refer to the degree
to which individuals understand and actively use symbols relating to
the left–right dimension of politics.
2 The survey was a collaborative study of political action in post-
industrial societies carried out in the early 1970s. Eight nations were
involved – this paper uses data from five of them.
3 A full account of the background, construction, and corollaries of the
participation variables used here is presented in chapter 3 of S. Barnes
and M. Kaase *et al.*, *Political Action: Mass Participation in Five Western
Democracies* (San Francisco: Sage 1979).
4 ibid., emphasis in the original.

**Chapter 16   Women in positions of political leadership in the United
Kingdom, France and Germany**

1 *L'Express* (30 December 1974–5 January 1975), p. 52.
2 *The New York Times* (26 August 1974).
3 French Embassy, Press and Information Division, *Giroud, Françoise*
(New York: 1975).
4 French Embassy, Press and Information Division, *Delegation for the
Condition of Women* (New York: 1976).
5 *The New York Times* (28 November 1974), p. 30. For an account of the
first victory in the abortion debate, see 'Pour la loi Simone Veil',
L'Express (25 November–1 December 1974), pp. 30–3.
6 *The New York Times* (28 November 1974).
7 *L'Express* (30 December 1974–5 January 1975), p. 59. The results
were: 55 per cent of the respondents chose Veil as first choice; 49 per
cent, Chirac; 45 per cent, Giroud; 41 per cent, Pontatowski, 30 per
cent, Lecamuet; and 28 per cent, Fourcade.
8 French Embassy, Press and Information Division, *The Third Barre
Cabinet* (New York: 1979).
9 British Information Services, *Women in Britain* (New York: 1971,
1975).
10 ibid.
11 Both *Punch* and *Time* have tipped Shirley Williams as a future prime
minister, and *L'Express* has made references to this possibility as well.
See, 'Madame le futur premier ministre', *L'Express* (17–23 February
1975), pp. 68–9. (This article is primarily about Margaret Thatcher.)
12 *New Statesman* (7 October 1977).
13 In contrast, there exists in Belgium a special women's party – the *Parti
Féministe Unifié* (PFU). In the election of March 1974 Belgian voters
were the first to have an option of a female candidate in all major cities.
The PFU was founded in September 1972; and its platform, which

accepts men but not for office or to stand for election, is for equal pay, opportunity, education, and social security.

14 *Sunday Times* (20 February 1977).

15 Deutsche Bundestag, *Zwischenbericht der Enquete-Kommission Frau und Gesellschaft gemass Beschluss des Deutschen Bundestages* (Bonn: 11 November 1967).

16 *The New York Times* (18 January 1977).

17 *Sozial Report* (July 1977).

18 *The New York Times* (18 January 1977).

19 A. Renger (ed.), *Equal Opportunities for Women* (Heidelberg 1977).

20 *Sozial Report* (June 1977).

21 *German International* (March 1974), p. 14. Half of the members of the Bundestag are drawn from lists made up by the parties; the other half are elected directly.

22 *German Tribune* (13 March 1975).

23 *Sozial Report* (July 1976).

24 ibid.

25 *The New York Times* (19 January 1977).

26 European Community Information Service, *European Community: Background Information* (New York: 5 March 1976).

Chapter 18   The politics of private woman and public man

Editors' note: a modified version of this article appears in *Theory and Society* (forthcoming).

1 'Male-stream' refers to traditions of thought that are, in both theoretical and empirical dimensions, rooted in masculine experience. See 'Introduction' in M. O'Brien, *The Politics of Reproduction* (Routledge & Kegan Paul 1981). For more detailed discussion of the male-stream portrait of women, and references to the literature, see General introduction in this volume.

2 The conception of politics we are working towards is presented in the General introduction (pp. 15–16).

3 R. E. Dowse and J. A. Hughes, *Political Sociology* (John Wiley & Sons 1972), refer the reader to Table 6 (p. 194) which shows an even 50/50 split between Conservatives and Labour for women, and a distribution for men of 56 per cent Labour and 44 per cent Conservative.

4 M. Goot and E. Reid, text, Chapter 11.

5 S. Taylor, text, Chapter 13.

6 P. Pulzer, *Political Representation and Elections in Britain* (George Allen & Unwin 1967), p. 107.

7 H. Durant, 'Voting behaviour in Britain 1945–64', in R. Rose (ed.), *Studies in British Politics* (Macmillan 1966), p. 125.

8 Fudging the footnotes is a practice named and identified in an extensively documented discussion by Bourque and Grossholtz

(Chapter 10). For a remarkable example of fudging the footnotes see Shabad and Andersen (text, p. 146). They examine the evidence for the assertion that women are more candidate oriented and less issue oriented than men. They show that while there *appears* to be a susbstantial body of congruent findings to this effect, all citations lead to one source, A. Campbell, G. Gurin and W. Miller, *The Voter Decides* (Evanston, Ill.: Row Peterson 1954).

9 Goot and Reid, text, p. 131.

10 Poorly-supported claims that women are Conservative or conservative are by no means confined to Pulzer, *Political Representation and Elections in Britain,* Dowse and Hughes, *Political Sociology,* or Taylor 'Parkin's theory of working-class conservatism'. See also: G. A. Almond and S. Verba *The Civic Culture* (Princeton: Princeton University Press 1963), p. 388. M. Currell, *Political Woman* (Croom Helm 1974) p. 52. S. M. Lipset, 'Voting behaviour', in A. Pizzorno (ed.), *Political Sociology* (Penguin 1971), p. 253; as well as examples cited by Bourque and Grossholtz, and Goot and Reid, in this volume. See also Hills, text, Chapter 12.

11 Brown, text, Chapter 6; Purcell, text, Chapter 5; G. S. Bain, *The Growth of White-collar Unionism* (Oxford University Press 1970), p. 43.

12 Text, pp. 69–70.

13 E. Mumford and O. Banks, *The Computer and the Clerk* (Routledge & Kegan Paul 1967), p. 14.

14 D. Lockwood, *The Blackcoated Worker* (George Allen & Unwin 1969), p. 156.

15 P. Willis, 'Shop floor culture, masculinity and the wage form', in J. Clarke, C. Critcher and R. Johnson (eds.) *Working Class Culture* (Hutchinson 1979), p. 197.

16 K. Roberts, *The Working Class* (Longman 1978), p. 74.

17 T. Nichols and P. Armstrong, *Workers Divided* (Fontana 1976), p. 62.

18 K. Roberts, F. G. Cook, S. C. Clark and E. Semeonoff, *The Fragmentary Class Structure* (Heinemann 1977), pp. 117–18.

19 Text, p. 56.

20 Text, Chapter 2.

21 For example, R. Lane, *Political Life* (rev. edn) (Glencoe: The Free Press 1965), pp. 47–8, shows in Table 4.1 that women are more likely to be non-voters than men in US elections from 1940–60, and higher rates of non-voting also for the 21–38 age group, for Protestants, Negroes, rural communities, lower income groups, those with lower education and people living in the South. He discusses these data with a careful warning that third factors may intervene – and then shows how this may be the case, in some detail, for every variable but sex.

22 Hills, text, Chapter 12.

23 Text, p. 67.

24 Text, Chapter 15, elaborated in the original article.

25 See original of Shabad and Andersen, text, Chapter 14.

26 M. Stacey and M. Price, *Women, Power and Politics* (Tavistock 1981); J. Stageman, 'A study of trade union branches in the Hull area', in A. Coote and P. Kellner, *Hear This, Brother: Women Workers and Union Power, New Statesman Report 1* (1980).

27 Shabad and Andersen, text, p. 147.

28 M. McCarthy, 'Women in trade unions', in L. Middleton (ed.), *Women in the Labour Movement* (Croom Helm 1977), pp. 169–70.

29 M. J. Le Lohe, 'Sex discrimination and under-representation of women in politics', *New Community: Journal of the Community Relations Commission,* 5 nos. 1–2 (1976), pp. 118–19.

30 J. Jaquette (ed.), *Women in Politics* (New York: Wiley 1974), p. xix.

31 Purcell, text, p. 66; Beynon and Blackburn, text, pp. 77–84.

32 Purcell, text, p. 66; Beynon and Blackburn, text, pp. 80–1; R. Cavendish *Women on the Line* (Routledge & Kegan Paul 1982), pp. 136–7. In P. Kellner, 'The working woman: her job, her politics, her union', in Coote and Kellner, *Hear This, Brother,* one of the few studies to offer a direct comparison of men's and women's views, women were considerably less likely than men to complain that their union was 'too involved in politics' or 'controlled by extremists and militants'. Women were also less convinced than men that their union 'would fight hard to protect my job' or that it 'tries to keep members in touch with what it is doing'.

33 See Nichols and Armstrong, *Workers Divided,* pp. 85–97, where male workers blocked a change of working hours which would have brought female workers a slight boost in wages; Stageman, 'A study of trade union branches in the Hull area'. As A. Coyle, 'Sex and skill in the organisation of the clothing industry', in J. West (ed.), *Women, Work and the Labour Market* (Routledge & Kegan Paul 1982), p. 10, points out:

although the actions of management and male workers derive from quite different imperatives, they can have a short-term coincidence of interest in keeping female labour segregated in certain jobs.

34 J. Evans, 'Women and Politics: a re-appraisal', *Political Studies,* 28 no. 2 (June 1980), pp. 210–21.

35 Watt unintentionally illustrates the 'male-as-norm' problem when he notes that his sample of women workers have 'what might be termed radical male attributes', text, p. 42. Bourque and Grossholtz discuss the 'male-as-norm' problem at length, as do Goot and Reid.

36 R. Hess and J. Torney, *The Development of Political Attitudes in Children* (Chicago: Aldine Publishing Co. 1967), p. 186. In the same chapter, in assessing children's views on whether it is ever acceptable for the American government to lie, Hess and Torney attribute girls' disagreement to their emphasis on *personal* morality, and boys'

agreement as acknowledgement of *political* expedience, ibid., p. 175.

37 Almond and Verba, *The Civic Culture,* pp. 396–7.

38 For an important critique of Almond and Verba, see C. Pateman, 'The civic culture: a philosophic critique', in G. Almond and S. Verba (eds.), *The Civic Culture Revised* (Boston: Little, Brown 1980).

39 F. Greenstein, *Children and Politics* (rev. edn) (New Haven, Conn.: Yale University Press 1969), p. 116.

40 Dowse and Hughes, *Political Sociology,* pp. 277–8.

41 Lane, *Political Life* (rev. edn), p. 160.

42 Jaquette, *Women in Politics,* p. xxiv explains:

A glance at the current critiques of pluralism with their emphasis on the unrepresentative nature of group conflict, the failure of pluralist politics to deal with important issues, and its encouragement of citizen apathy might put female political idealism into a very different perspective.

43 S. Bourque and J. Grossholtz, text, Chapter 10.

44 Text, Chapter 5.

45 Goot and Reid, text, p. 124.

46 Text, Chapter 4.

47 A. Wise, *Women and the Struggle for Workers' Control,* Spokesman Pamphlet, no. 33 (n.d.).

48 Text, p. 50.

49 Text, p. 67.

50 Text, Chapter 10.

51 J. B. Elshtain, *Public Man, Private Woman* (Princeton: Princeton University Press 1981), p. 335.

52 This claim is most persuasively advanced in a recent article by J. Lovenduski, 'Toward the emasculation of political science: the impact of feminism', in D. Spender (ed.), *Men's Studies Modified* (Pergamon Press 1981). She argues that feminist analysis points the way, not merely to new data about women within the old framework, but to a new feminist political science – less hedged about by positivist assumptions and methods, more committed to the kind of critical enterprise advocated in the work of C. Pateman, *Participation and Democratic Theory* (Cambridge University Press 1970).

53 In both feminist and male-stream accounts of gender differences in politics, there are three major types of explanation. We do not deny that each has some explanatory import, but we are concerned about the limitations produced by their reliance on the private woman–public man conception. The three types are:

1 Socialization and the development of sex role identities such that women achieve a self-identity which does not include an interest in things political nor an interest in developing capacities for political participation.

2 The separation of private family life from public work and political

life which, coincident with the traditional sexual division of labour assigning women to the private domain, isolates women from the public world of politics. Thus, as a structural feature of women's lives, they lack integration into the wider society. This is taken to account too, for women's lesser influence when they make public appearances since they voice concern for 'private' issues – issues which are marginal to the main public agenda.

3   Interests within the public sphere are such that women are systematically and actively excluded from it (or marginalized within it) through, for example, discriminatory practices and policies which protect male interests.

54 This is not to detract from the differences among feminist writers as to the centrality of private experience in explanations of women's public life. S. Rowbotham, for example, in her earlier writings (*Women's Consciousness, Man's World* (Penguin 1973)), argued that due to the traditionally feminine definition of the private world, women's integration into the public world is partial. She has, however, since changed her view, ('The trouble with "patriarchy"', *New Statesman* (28 December 1979)), to one that emphasizes the contradictory position of women in both public and private spheres. See also M. Coulson, B. Magas and H. Wainwright, 'The housewife and her labour under capitalism – a critique', *New Left Review*, **89** (1975), pp. 59–71. More recently, Stacey and Price, *Women, Power and Politics*, suggest there has been an erosion of women's position within the private domain without compensating increased access to the public sphere. There is, in addition, an argument from quite different feminist perspectives that men preserve and protect the public sphere as a male sphere in opposition to women and the private sphere. For this view, see O'Brien, *The Politics of Reproduction*; Elshtain, *Public Man, Private Woman*; and L. Imray and A. Middleton, 'Public and private: marking the boundaries', in E. Gamarnikow *et al.* (eds.), *The Public and the Private* (Heinemann 1983).

55 'Generic' means literally 'relating to gender'. We first came across this useful term in O'Brien, *The Politics of Reproduction*.

56 cf. C. A. MacKinnon, 'Feminism, marxism, method, and the state: an agenda for theory', *Signs*, **7** no. 3 (Spring 1982), pp. 515–44; Feminist Anthology Collective, *No Turning Back* (The Women's Press 1981).

57 We use the distinction between individual and collective forms of political practice in the sense that M. Colman, *Continuous Excursions: Politics and Personal Life* (Pluto Press 1982) uses 'personal' and 'social' politics.

58 S. Wexler, 'Battered women and public policy', in E. Boneparth (ed.), *Women, Power and Policy* (New York: Pergamon Press 1982); and M. David, 'Sexual morality, sex education and the New Right: a "policy of

restriction"?', presented to the British Sociological Association Annual Conference (1982).

59 J. Beale, *Getting It Together: Women as Trade Unionists* (Pluto Press 1982).

60 O'Brien, *The Politics of Reproduction*, p. 99.

61 R. Blauner, *Alienation and Freedom* (Chicago: University of Chicago Press 1964), pp. 71–2.

62 I. Watt, text, Chapter 3.

63 F. Parkin, 'Working class conservatives: a theory of political deviance', *British Journal of Sociology*, **18** (1967), pp. 278–90.

64 Parkin's argument is criticized and taken further in Taylor (text, Chapter 13) and Watt (text, Chapter 3).

65 T. Watson, *Sociology, Work and Industry* (Routledge & Kegan Paul 1980), pp. 105–9.

66 M. Porter, 'Worlds apart: the class consciousness of working class women', *Women's Studies International Quarterly*, **1** (1978), p. 181.

67 A. Pollert, *Girls, Wives, Factory Lives* (Macmillan 1981), p. 113.

68 Elshtain, *Public Man, Private Woman*; Bourque and Grossholtz (text, Chapter 10).

69 B. Campbell and V. Charlton, 'Work to rule', *Red Rag*, no. 14 (1978).

70 P. Hunt, text, Chapter 4.

71 See also Wise, *Women and the Struggle for Workers' Control*.

72 S. Alexander, A. Davin and E. Hostettler, 'Labouring women: a reply to Eric Hobsbawm', *History Workshop*, no. 8 (Autumn 1979), pp. 174–82, make this point in debate with Hobsbawm:

In their dual role of housewives and waged workers, women have at times come to the forefront of struggle or made decisive interventions. These have not taken the form of leading charges over the barricades with breasts exposed . . . but of raising issues which extend the boundaries of class struggle beyond the level of wages. . . . When women come out on strike they raise issues related to the quality of life. Working conditions, childcare, holidays, time-off are central to women's daily domestic and wage working lives, though these demands are seldom taken up by union officials, bargaining over the size of the wage packet. . . . Why are these issues seen as peripheral to 'real' class struggle?

That such points still need to be strongly expressed, in many forms, is evident, for example, in the continued opposition between the 'lifestyle politics' of the women's movement and 'real' working-class politics. The review of the *Spare Rib Reader* appearing in *Socialist Worker* accuses the women's movement of believing 'that government and council grants to help fund anything from rape crisis centres to local women's committees can substitute for real activity among women workers on the ground', *Socialist Worker* (14 August, 1982), p. 11. And, on the lighter (?) side, in the *New Socialist* quiz, attending your trade union branch wins you a left wing point, while choosing to attend a meeting of the *Spare Rib* editorial advisory board, or attending a self-defence class, win right wing points, *New Socialist*, no. 3 (January–February 1982).

73 A similar point is made by C. Hatch, 'Socialist-feminism and the workplace', *Socialist Review*, **9** no. 5 (September–October 1979), p. 128, in emphasizing the neglect by some socialist feminists of the importance of the workplace for women as workers:

> where is consciousness formed? Because we study the family as an institution and women's role in it, there is a tendency to assume that it determines how women's consciousness is formed as a worker. In fact, we don't *know* that to be true, and won't, until we study it.

74 M. Porter, 'Experience and consciousness: women at home, men at work', unpublished Ph.D. thesis, University of Bristol (1979); H. Beynon, *Working for Ford* (Penguin 1973); J. H. Goldthorpe, D. Lockwood, F. Bechofer and J. Platt, *The Affluent Worker: Industrial Attitudes and Behaviour* (Cambridge University Press 1968); Nichols and Armstrong, *Workers Divided*; L. Rubin, *Worlds of Pain: Life in the Working Class Family* (New York: Basic Books 1976).

75 Beynon, *Working for Ford*, p. 113.

76 cf. Porter, 'Experience and consciousness'; Goldthorpe *et al.*, *The Affluent Worker*; E. Chinoy, *Automobile Workers and the American Dream* (Boston: Beacon Press 1965).

77 Text, p. 75.

78 Text, p. 37.

79 M. Porter, *Home, Work and Class Consciousness* (Manchester University Press 1983) p. 174.

80 Porter usefully draws attention to *men's contribution* to the impoverished political capacity of their wives; central to her argument is men's reluctance to share insights and experiences gained from wage labour and industrial struggle with their home-based wives. However, to say that men contribute to women's 'backwardness', even to insist that men also suffer from that backwardness, is not at all the same as recognizing that the consciousness of men is sectional and limited.

81 R. Edwards, *Contested Terrain* (Heinemann 1979), p. 196.

82 A. Coote and B. Campbell, *Sweet Freedom* (Picador 1982), pp. 241–2.

83 Campbell and Charlton, 'Work to rule'; J. Gardiner and S. Smith, 'Feminism and the alternative economic strategy', *Marxism Today* (October 1981), pp. 24–30; M. Barrett, text, Chapter 8.

84 Beale, *Getting it Together*.

85 Elshtain, *Public Man, Private Woman*, p. 201.

86 ibid., p. 218.

87 ibid., pp. 217–18.

88 ibid., p. 335.

89 ibid., p. 351.

90 K. Boals, 'Political science', *Signs*, **1** no. 1 (Autumn 1975), p. 172.

91 ibid., p. 173.

92 O'Brien, *The Politics of Reproduction*, p. 193.

93 O'Brien's recent (ibid.) analysis of the politics of reproduction and the public–private separation is an exciting treatment of these issues.

94 Elshtain, *Public Man, Private Woman*, p. 333.
95 ibid., p. 337.
96 cf. M. McIntosh, 'The state and the oppression of women', in Kuhn and Wolpe (eds.), *Feminism and Materialism*; F. Bennett, R. Heys and R. Coward, 'The limits of financial and legal independence: a socialist feminist perspective on taxation and social security', in Editorial Boards (eds.), *Politics and Power One* (Routledge & Kegan Paul 1980).
97 M. Barrett and M. McIntosh, *The Anti-Social Family* (Verso Editions 1982).
98 Colman, *Continuous Excursions*.
99 See also R. Sennett, *The Fall of Public Man* (New York: Vintage Books 1978).

Index